Touch of
Evil

Rutgers Films in Print

Mirella Jona Affron, Robert Lyons,
and E. Rubinstein, editors

My Darling Clementine, John Ford, director
edited by Robert Lyons

The Last Metro, François Truffaut, director
edited by Mirella Jona Affron and
E. Rubinstein

Touch of Evil, Orson Welles, director
edited by Terry Comito

Touch of Evil

Orson Welles, director

Terry Comito, editor

Rutgers University Press

New Brunswick, New Jersey

Touch of Evil is volume 3 in the
Rutgers Films in Print Series.

Library of Congress Cataloging
in Publication Data
Main entry under title:

Touch of evil.

  (Rutgers films in print; v. 3)
  Filmography: p.
  Bibliography: p.
  1. Touch of evil (Motion picture)
2. Welles, Orson, 1915–   . I. Comito,
Terry, 1935–   . II. Touch of evil (Motion
picture) III. Series.
PN1997.T6353T6 1985   791.43'72
84–24918
ISBN 0–8135–1096–1
ISBN 0–8135–1097–X (pbk.)

New York Times review by Howard Thompson,
May 22 1958, © 1958 by The New York Times
Company. *Arts* review by François Truffaut,
translated by Leonard Mayhew, © 1975 by
Flammarion, translation © 1978 by Simon &
Schuster, Inc., reprinted by permission of Si-
mon & Schuster. "Orson Welles: Of Time and
Loss" by William Johnson © 1967 by The Re-
gents of the University of California, reprinted
from *Film Quarterly*, vol. 21, no. 1 (Fall
1967): 13–24, by permission of The Regents.
Screen review by Stephen Heath, © Society for
Education in Film and Television Limited. In-
terview with Orson Welles by André Bazin and
Charles Bitsch, no. 84 (June 1958) and Inter-
view with Orson Welles by André Bazin,
Charles Bitsch, and Jean Domarchi, no. 87
(September 1958), *Cahiers du Cinéma*. "The
Evolution of Orson Welles's *Touch of Evil* from
Novel to Film" by John Stubbs from *Cinema
Journal* 24, no. 2, reprinted by permission
of *Cinema Journal* of the Society for Cinema
Studies.

Acknowledgments

I want particularly to thank the staff
of the Motion Picture Division of The
Library of Congress; John Stubbs for
his kindness in permitting me to ex-
amine his rare copy of Welles's shooting script for *Touch of Evil*; Mirella
Affron and E. Rubinstein for advice
on the translations in this volume;
Charles Affron and Isabella Diaz for
assistance in making the frame en-
largements; and the editors of Films
in Print and of Rutgers University
Press for their unflagging patience
and helpfulness.

Contents

Introduction

Welles's Labyrinths

An Introduction to *Touch of Evil*

Terry Comito

N o single critical approach to so complex a work as *Touch of Evil* can hope to afford a complete and comprehensive view. There is always, as one says, another angle. What we see in such a work, what we are able to discover in it, depends to a large extent on our own starting point: the sort of context in which we choose to place the work, the specific questions we decide to ask about it. This edition provides materials for many different ways of inquiring about *Touch of Evil* and therefore many different ways of explaining or understanding it.

John Stubbs, for example, thinks of the film as an instance of narrative technique, and looks into the ways Welles uses, and transforms, his sources. The interview with Charlton Heston throws a good deal of light on the production history of *Touch of Evil*: the question he helps to answer is "how do films actually get made?" Stephen Heath considers *Touch of Evil* in the context of theoretical speculation about the nature of the film medium itself: his analysis of the signifying codes of Welles's film is less concerned with its meaning than with how that meaning is produced and communicated. William Johnson's essay puts *Touch of Evil* in the context of Welles's other films and traces the way it develops certain recurrent themes and images. Or we may want to place the film in the context of Welles's personal life, and ask how it reflects his political, moral, or aesthetic positions, his economic struggles with the Hollywood establishment, or his unconscious drives and obsessions. There are hints for such an inquiry in the biographical sketch of Welles and in his interview with André Bazin. Or we might want to relate *Touch of Evil* to the political or social or economic climate of America in the 1950s: what does it reveal about our attitudes toward race? toward women? toward the authority of the state?

And so on and on.

The essay that follows begins by putting *Touch of Evil* in contexts derived from film history—the history of crime films, a long running controversy about two fundamental kinds of cinematic style. But my primary interest is not in locating Welles's contribution to the "evolution" of crime films or to the "development" of cinematic style. On the contrary, I seek to isolate what is distinctive, even unique, about Welles's film. The question I most want to answer is, "What happens to us as we watch *Touch of Evil*?"

Crime and the Camera

In spite of what may appear an almost perverse abruptness, the explosive opening of *Touch of Evil* places it within a familiar narrative tradition. Crime thrillers of the thirties and forties, like the more sombre *films noirs* of the forties and fifties, characteristically begin with a sudden, spectacular outburst of violence, whose consequences the rest of the film seeks to untangle. This is a convention with implications quite different from (say) the usual strategies of a Hitchcock film, which accumulates menace gradually within a familiar and apparently stable environment. By transporting us immediately into the midst of an uproar, the crime thriller seems to conjure up a society, or a world, where violence is the norm rather than the exception: where the only context is disruption.

But this effect, reproduced again and again, would go stale. Within these general parameters, directors have been able to make the cinematic means at their disposal act upon their audiences in quite different ways. We have to suppose, in fact, that a conscientious director, beginning to work on a crime film, would be thinking at least as much of earlier movies as he would of the real world (if such a world exists) of mobs, machine guns, and exploding cars: wondering how he could go his predecessors one better, or give a surprising twist to familiar devices. This is why the important crime movies form a kind of sequence. Any given film may be seen not only as an attempt to document the existence of violence in the world around us but as a response to other violent films: a commentary, a critique, a rival.

One way a director may engage in this dialogue with his tradition is simply by upping the ante on the violence he represents. But this is a lazy and ultimately self-defeating procedure. More fruitful is his ability to vary the *way* in which violence is represented: to involve the spectator in violence in new ways and so to define in new ways the expressive significance of that violence, its meaning. He does not merely represent violence, he characterizes it. The history of crime movies is in part the history of the shifting definitions of violence made possible by different cinematic styles. In writing this history, it has been customary to distinguish broadly between the kinds of effect created by long uninterrupted shots in which the camera often moves about freely over a terrain, and those created by a succession of short, generally static shots—between what French critics in particular have called mise-en-scène and montage. The former is frequently associated with thrillers about the rise and fall of exuberant or fate-ridden gangster heroes; the latter, with the more constricted world of *film noir* with its petty thugs and hard-bitten private eyes.[1]

It is obvious from the start that neither the story of *Touch of Evil* nor its visual style falls neatly into either of these categories. But it is equally obvious that Welles's starting point was indeed the world of crummy pulp novels and film melodramas. It is just this that has alienated some of his critics, who expect a "major" artist to be more responsible in his choice of traditions. Like Uncle Joe Grandi, his trouble is supposed to be that he's been seeing too many gangster movies. I shall have more to say about Welles's relation to these somewhat seedy ancestors in a later section of this introduction. Here I want to focus on a single narrative strategy he inherits from them—the violent opening sequence. A few examples of the way this convention has been used before *Touch of Evil* may give us a context for thinking about what is strange in Welles's movie, what *remains* strange and disturbing even as we recognize its provenance.

Howard Hawks's *Scarface* (1932) begins with waiters sweeping up after a party. The camera tracks to a table where the mobster in whose honor the party was given says goodby to the last stragglers. He is left alone, and the camera tracks with him as he crosses the quiet, empty hall to make a phone call. But when he stops in the phone booth, the camera keeps going, penetrating a bare corridor at an oblique angle to the booth. Down the corridor we hear the approaching sound of someone whistling, and a shadow is cast on the window of

---

1. Some of these issues are discussed more fully in the essay by Collet included in this volume. For more on *film noir*, see essays by Place and Peterson and by Schrader in the Selected Bibliography. Cf., for "open" and "closed" form, Leo Braudy, *The World in a Frame* (Garden City, N.Y.: Doubleday, 1976): 20–103.

the phone booth. We hear, without seeing, someone say "Hello, Louie," then a shot, then silence again. It's a question of generating suspense. We understand that no good is in store for a gangster who proclaims himself on top of the world and then is left alone in the shadowy aftermath of his triumph. We only wonder when and where he will meet his fate. Hawks uses a long take with a constantly moving camera to heighten our anticipation of the inevitable: probing the space from which we know, somewhere, violence will erupt; waiting out the full duration of Louie's last moments that we know will, sometime, abruptly be terminated. The confetti-strewn hall doubtless owes something to Josef von Sternberg's silent melodrama, *Underworld* (1927).[2] But the camera work here has an objective briskness quite different in its implications from the soulful, dreamlike movement of the earlier film. Instead of expressing the giddy passion that leads von Sternberg's outlaw hero to a noble self-destruction, it announces precisely the gap between Louie's blindness and our knowledge of the fate that announces itself in the assassin's shadow and insouciant whistle. The corridor is not sinister to Louie, which is just his problem. But to us, the camera seems to move down it with the inexorability of the events themselves—an impression heightened by the Germanic chiaroscuro of the scene and the angular geometry of the passageway. If Hawks is thus questioning von Sternberg's sentimentalism, he also probably has in mind the moralism of Mervin LeRoy's *Little Caesar* (1931). Little Rico is a dogged, rather pathetic plugger, clearly out of his league. Tony Camonte, Hawks's version of Al Capone, has an engagingly boyish bravado and audacity. LeRoy's story is told in static set-ups, like neatly labeled tableaux in a morality play. Hawks's camera sweeps and glides through Tony's world, leaving a path of destruction behind it, with something of the brisk, mindless efficiency of the hood whose motto is "Do it fast, do it yourself, keep doing it."

The opening sequence of Raoul Walsh's *White Heat* (1949) defeats the expectations nurtured by such films as *Scarface* in a number of respects. The scene is outdoors, in the countryside, and it is brilliant daylight. Instead of mobsters in tuxedos that accommodate them visually to the geometry of the big city, the Cody gang turns out to be a drab, lower middle class, rural family, presided over

---

2. *Underworld* was based on a story by Hawks's script writer for *Scarface*, Ben Hecht, who had reportedly been unhappy with von Sternberg's treatment of his idea. (After seeing the film, he wired him: "You poor ham. Take my name off the film.") See Josef von Sternberg, *Fun in a Chinese Laundry* (New York: Macmillan, 1965): 215. And Hawks himself is said to have contributed to the script of the earlier gangster film: *Cinema: A Critical Dictionary*, ed. Richard Roud (London: Secker and Warburg, 1980): 476.

by an old lady in a dumpy hat. Walsh wants to suggest that violence is not an eruption of some sinister fatality but a part of these people's everyday business— more dangerous than most, perhaps—in a contingent world. We are engaged in the risk and excitement of their venture rather than feeling any particular suspense about their victims. In the opening sequence, the camera moves about obligingly to help us get our bearings as they plan to hijack a train. The film begins with a shot of the train emerging toward the camera from a tunnel. Then there is a leisurely 360-degree pan surveying the mountainous terrain, revealing Cody's car on the road far below, helpfully noting a sign marking the state line, and finally returning to the train, having made clear to us its situation. Once the circle is completed, the camera pans quickly to the right to inform us that the car, much closer now, is approaching its goal. The lucidity of this moving camera would appear to signify a kind of commonsensical "realism," Walsh's as well as the characters': a clear-eyed inquisitiveness about what lies beyond the edge of the frame, and a confidence that it is easy for someone truly enterprising to make his way from here to there.

This faith, traditional in the adventure movies with which Walsh was often associated, was never easily sustained for gangsters whose fall often seemed as inevitable as their rise had been irresistible. Coming near the end of the tradition, Cody can maintain his freedom of movement only by increasingly hysterical gestures of self-assertion. In the world of *film noir*, such gestures scarcely seem possible, and violence, accordingly, is given a quite different inflection. The mood is neither suspense nor excitement so much as a jumpy uncertainty, a numb sense of pervasive menace—feelings less oriented toward definable objects than the tensions or anxieties of earlier thrillers. In a world so claustrophobic, the camera cannot move with much fluidity or purposefulness. The *noir* director characteristically prefers to cut between static, tightly framed shots that rigidly define the limits of the spectator's awareness. In the opening of Billy Wilder's *Double Indemnity* (1944), the camera does not track with Neff's car as it careens through deserted, early morning streets. Instead, we get three discontinuous shots: two low angle shots of the car racing toward us, disappearing as it passes out of the frame, another shot as it moves away from us to park. When Neff emerges from the car, we see him from a high angle, his back to the camera, his privacy intact. We know something is wrong, but we're not sure what it is. We're uneasy, on edge, but we're not in suspense because we don't know what we're waiting for. The camera gives concrete form to our dilemma (and as it turns out, to that of the jittery amateur murderers as well): we can't "keep track" of the events, we can't "follow" them. We can only wait and hope our partial glimpses will reveal them as they come into the purview of our limited frame of reference, bit by bit, like gradually assembled pieces of a puzzle.

Sometimes they never do. Robert Aldrich's *Kiss Me Deadly* (1955) carries about as far as is feasible the epistemological violence implicit in *film noir*. Mike Hammer's world is less a puzzle to be solved than a chaos that threatens to engulf us along with him. The jaggedly edited opening sequence assaults us with images as randomly violent as the blows and kicks Hammer will soon suffer: a car speeding toward the camera, running feet, a woman's nude legs beneath a white raincoat, Hammer waking in a strange room and kicked to the floor. For us, the randomness of these images *is* their violence—their resistance to any attempt to force them into a coherent pattern, to make them add up to more than fragmented sensation. This is why the violence of *film noir* is not exhilarating as it often is in thrillers like *Scarface* or *White Heat*. It is an expression of powerlessness, debility, the breakdown of functions.

Orson Welles has always been difficult to place along the mise-en-scène/montage axis, just because he so clearly employs, with dazzling virtuosity, the resources of both.[3] And while it has generally been felt that *Touch of Evil* somehow places itself in the context of *film noir* (as well as of Welles's own earlier films), the nature of its relation to its predecessors has never been worked out with much care. To call it the "epitaph" of *film noir*, as Paul Schrader does, is suggestive but scarcely a definition. I am not sure we will arrive at a definition either, nor even that a rigorous definition is possible in such matters. But by setting *Touch of Evil*'s opening sequence against some of these earlier sequences, to which it can be seen as at least in part a response, we ought to be able to isolate some of Welles's defining differences.

To begin with: we know what is going on. We are waiting for a car to explode. The very first frame of the film thrusts into the camera a bomb's timing device, the instrument of a mechanical inexorability; and the blond victim's last words are a complaint about "this ticking noise." But the camera does not, as it does in *Scarface* or *White Heat*, move about in order to concentrate and guide our attention. Rather, it seems teasingly to withhold from us what we want to see, what we know—from what we've been permitted to see and also from other movies we've seen—must be coming. Welles's camera seems less concerned with monitoring the events on the screen than in disorienting the spectator. The use of a

3. See his interview with André Bazin reprinted in this volume.

twenty-two foot crane means that vision is constantly in motion, up and down as well as laterally; and the use of a wide angle lens gives it an exaggerated depth of space in which to play. And play is precisely what it seems to do, with no mimetic function—neither the point of view of a character nor the logic of events—to rationalize the camera's apparently independent life. Its long, graceful swooping, now speeding up in relation to the movement of the car, now slowing down, constantly changes both the angle and the distance from which we follow, or attempt to follow, the bomb's fatal progress. We lose sight of the car as it swings around behind a building; it reappears only to be half lost in a milling crowd; the camera tracks back slowly enough to let the car approach and then suddenly speeds up, leaving it far behind; Susan and Vargas pass in front of it and we turn to follow them, obviously the film's "stars," though the car, not quite forgotten, keeps crossing their tracks, as if (though we know better) it were only an accidental intrusion on the margins of the frame. We "lose track" not because our gaze is fragmented, as it is by Wilder or Aldrich, but because it is distracted, provided with too much information to pick and sort into stable hierarchies of attention.

We are not confused, as we are by the opening of *Kiss Me Deadly*. We are disoriented, dizzy. It is important that we insist upon this distinction. Near the end of the opening sequence, Susan and Vargas have crossed the border into America, and Susan realizes that "this is the first time we've been together in my country." But the camera is not allowed the easy access to their intimacy we might expect. However Susan may feel about her homecoming—this is a theme to which we will have to return—we see the lovers only through, and as a part of, a network of incommensurable movements—whirling, without stable center. This may seem a somewhat rhetorical way of speaking. French critics, especially, are fond of intoning "vertiginous" or "delirious" by way of evading any need really to explain Welles's "baroque" stylistics. But in fact I am trying to describe as literally as possible what goes on in these few frames. As Linnekar's car drives off from the customs booth in foreground, moving out of the left of the frame, we see: two MPs at the right of the frame striding purposefully toward the camera and eventually passing off in the right foreground; two civilian pedestrians passing from left to right in front of the MPs; and, in the far background, emerging from an arcade just as the MPs turn from the street to come forward, Vargas and Susan, walking from right to left. Meanwhile the camera, too, is in motion, but not along any of these paths. It moves toward Vargas and Susan, not directly, but diagonally, heading back and to the left as if hoping to intercept them. As it does so, Susan and Vargas continue to walk from right to left; in back

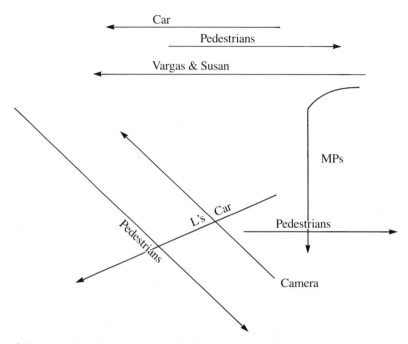

of them a pedestrian moves from left to right and a black car moves from right to left, overtaking and passing them. Still more disconcertingly, a stream of pedestrians passes in front of them in the foreground of the frame, blurred forms, half silhouetted, moving into the camera along a diagonal—off toward the right foreground—directly opposed to the camera's course. When Susan pauses long enough to speak her line about homecoming, the camera has got ahead of them; and the lovers, though now in medium range, are nearly out of the frame on the right. There is in all this no lack of distinctness. Each of the simultaneous movements I have been cataloguing is perfectly lucid, the interplay precisely choreographed. But it is a dance in which we lose our bearings. Our heads spin. With everything apparently in motion, there is no fixed point of reference by which to chart or rationalize any single trajectory. Welles's world is not a chaos but, as Welles himself repeatedly tells us, a whirling labyrinth[4]—one without a center, however, without a key that will unlock its mystery.

4. E.g.: "I believe, thinking about my films, that they are based not so much on pursuit as on a search. If we are looking for something, the labyrinth is the most favorable location for the search." Andrew Sarris, ed., *Interviews with Film Directors* (New York: Avon, 1969): 532.

The uncentered labyrinth is of course a familiar iconographic or thematic motif in many of Welles's films: the hall of mirrors in *Citizen Kane* and in *The Lady from Shanghai*; the fruitless search for Rosebud (it vanishes in smoke before our eyes, and leaves in place, in the film's last shot, the No Trespassing sign at Xanadu); the search for Arkadin by which the secret of the past, the truth of origins, is not pieced together but expunged. But I have been implying that the labyrinths that express most fundamentally Welles's sense of the world and his artistic intentions are not those he represents but those he creates. *Touch of Evil* invites us into a world that seems to resemble the one with which we are all familiar—but cut loose from its moorings, from the frames of reference by which we habitually seek to stabilize our situation in it. It has a share, I suppose, of the *angst* we associate with *film noir*, but without the glum claustrophobia: our anxiety is born not of powerlessness or confinement but of too much freedom. And there is, too, in Welles's films generally and in *Touch of Evil* in particular, something of the desperate exhilaration we find in the best of the crime thrillers. But it is an exhilaration associated less with theme and character, which may seem sombre enough, than with Welles himself, the prestidigitator on heights more dizzying than Tony Camonte ever dreamed of.

Crossing the Border: Space and Meaning

In Whit Masterson's *Badge of Evil*, the assassin's bomb is an intrusion into the comfortable precincts of the wealthy victim's San Diego beach house. The task assigned the protagonist of this routine thriller is to restore the equilibrium upset by an outsider's violence. It is a matter of keeping the peace. In transferring the story's action to the Mexican border, Welles suggests a more subversive vision. Los Robles is the sinister foreign place we discover on the margins of our own world, just over the border from the comfortingly familiar. As the film's critics have not failed to notice, Welles's most fundamental theme, from the opening sequence on, is the crossing of boundaries; or rather, the impossibility of sustaining an effective boundary between a world we recognize as normal and a realm of violence at once uncanny and, as in a dream, disquietingly familiar. To our discomfort, Welles engineers our complicity in violent fantasies, sexual and racial, of the most devious sort, at the same time he appeases the liberal in us with safe homilies on the evils of prejudice. But the crucial border, in spite of the swarthy rapists with whom Welles teases us, is not the one between Mexico and the

United States. It is just Janet Leigh's error to suppose that it is a simple matter to go home again, that she will be safe in the reassuring banality of an American motel, that the half-heard whispers behind its surprisingly flimsy walls have nothing to do with her. The most precarious boundary is one overseen by no friendly customs man. It is the boundary between the apparent solidity of our rational daylight world and the dark labyrinth in which, if we yield to its solicitations, we will lose our way. Welles's "Mexico" is a place of the soul, a nightmare from which a lost Hollywood sweater girl begs, mostly in vain, to be awakened.

Which is simply to reiterate what has already been implied in the first section of this introduction. Mexico is not a geographical place Welles represents so much as it is a visual space he creates—a reorganization of the data of perception in order to betray the spectator, as Susan is betrayed, into a new and disturbing way of experiencing the world. I know of few films whose expressive content is so indistinguishable from its visual style, so wholly illegible in the dialogue alone.[5] A good many episodes in the script, in fact—the acid throwing scene (nothing comes of it) or, more especially, the hysterical scene in which Uncle Joe chases Risto and loses his hair piece—seem no more than pretexts for the kind of vertigo we have already defined as a characteristic effect of Welles's cinematic technique. In choosing to tell a story about crossing boundaries, he has been able to thematize, to take as his subject matter, just that characteristic visual experience. What *Touch of Evil* is most immediately "about"—certainly more than it is about race relations or police corruption—is the confrontation with the labyrinth or vortex that opens before us once we transgress the boundaries of a world in which we are pleased to suppose ourselves to be at home. Or to put it differently: it is about a nice couple from Hollywood movies who stumble into a film by Orson Welles. We need to consider in more detail the dimensions of that deviousness, and then look at the effect it has on our misplaced star and starlet.

The French critic André Bazin has indicated why the eye-level medium shot (what is called in France the *plan-Américain*) gives classical Hollywood cinema the appearance of a kind of spontaneous and unselfconscious "realism." However fanciful or fraudulent the director's subject matter may be, his camera ap-

---

5. Compare Bazin's remarks: " . . . the world of Ford and Capra can be defined on the basis of their scripts, their themes, the dramatic effects they have sought, the choice of scenes. It is not to be found in the *découpage* as such. With Orson Welles, on the contrary, the *découpage* in depth becomes a technique which constitutes the meaning of the story. It wasn't merely a way of placing the camera, sets and actors . . . ; it places the very nature of the story in question." André Bazin, *Orson Welles*, trans. Jonathan Rosenbaum (New York: Harper & Row, 1978): 81.

peals to "the natural point of balance of [the spectator's] mental judgment."[6] It is just this natural balance that Welles is continually, with every means at his disposal (the angle of the camera, its distance, its movement) seeking to subvert; and with it our sense that we can take for granted the stability of the "real." The *plan-Américain* almost never appears. Quinlan looms up in extreme low angle or is dwarfed in empty space or in networks of light, shadow, and architectural detritus. He seems not so much to enter a frame or occupy a fixed position as to shape the space around him in accord with his own megalomania or despair. The optics of Welles's wide angle lens means not only that deep space is present to us in a hallucinatory sharpness of detail but also that figures move toward us out of that space, or disappear into it, with a preternatural swiftness, imposing themselves upon us or slipping away before we have had a chance to get our bearings. A favorite framing device is the torso swollen so large that it no longer fits within our field of vision but nevertheless looms over and dominates what we *can* see. (Susan's first trip across the border is framed in this way by Pancho's leather-jacketed form; Quinlan's dazed emergence from Tanya's, near the end of his rope, is framed by Menzies' brooding profile.) These are only a few of the effects that contribute to our sense of the radical, dreamlike subjectivity of space in *Touch of Evil*. Space is no longer a neutral and measurable vacancy between stable objects. It seems almost palpable, plastic, even viscous—shaping and being given shape by, in ways wholly unpredictable, the action that transpires within it. Welles's space is in this respect less baroque than manneristic. One thinks of the tempestuous plaza of Tintoretto's *St. Mark*. Even Sartre's overheated characterization of the delirious triumph of perspectivism in Tintoretto is not wholly inappropriate to our sense of the peculiar centerless mobility of Welles's world:

. . . reality slipped away, and the relationship of the finite to the infinite was reversed. Once an immense plenitude had supported the torments and fragility of the body. Now fragility was the only plenitude. . . . Infinity was emptiness and darkness   the Absolute was absence.[7]

Doubtless we should be cautious about claims so portentous. Nevertheless, it may not be wholly absurd to say that the world of *Touch of Evil* is without that "absolute" (in something like Sartre's sense) whose cinematic expression would

6. André Bazin, *What Is Cinema?*, trans. Hugh Gray (Berkeley: University of California Press, 1967): 32.
7. Jean-Paul Sartre, *Situations*, trans. Benita Eisler (Greenwich, Conn.: Fawcett, 1966): 39.

be the confident realism of the *plan-Américain*. Just because its explosions and contractions are not measured against anything fixed, the space of Welles's film is radically contingent as well as subjective. The habitual use of deep space, and the violent motion Welles sets plunging through it, means that any place a character may for a moment inhabit is only the edge of a depth that opens dizzily behind him. "Foreground and background no longer serve as static frames for a comfortable middle distance. . . . Instead, all three are points in a single [constantly shifting] system, through which, just beyond the circle closed around a given moment's awareness, the assassin pursues his prey, and through whose sinuous passages the investigator must seek out an unknown evil."[8] And since "foreground" and "background" are not only optical terms but measures as well of significance or importance, our bafflement is not merely visual. Welles's world is not one where it is ever simple to relegate anything to "the background." Just beyond your field of vision, but ready at any moment to make itself felt, is something that undermines the certainties you suppose you possess—that undercuts your "position." When Vargas talks on the phone to Susan at the motel (shots 261–271), Welles crosscuts with shots of Janet Leigh reclining in her nightie, hair unbound, dreamy eyed, looking like the pinup girl we know her to be. It is an image whose deliberate parodic banality signifies the limits of Vargas's imagination and understanding. But his spatial situation at the drug store makes abundantly obvious to us the fragility of this day dream and the complacency of his delusion. Behind him, visible to us out the window, Menzies arrives with Uncle Joe Grandi, the owner of the motel where Vargas thinks Susan will be safe and the source of her coming torments. (Grandi himself, in turn, keeps wondering "What am I doing here?": placement is never self-explanatory in Welles's world.) In the foreground, a blind woman, the proprietor of the shop, squints just past the camera. In part, she is merely an ironic commentary on Vargas's own blindness; but the odd hieratic stolidity of her skewed gaze also suggests she is the bearer of some knowledge we are unlikely ever to share.

It is because these spatial depths so brutally unmask the contingency of our situations that they are felt in *Touch of Evil* to be so menacing. Welles uses the arcades of Venice (California) to calibrate the depths from which violence emerges or into which victims are lured. Space is constricted, narrowed down

8. Terry Comito, *"Touch of Evil,"* in *Focus on Orson Welles*, ed. Ronald Gottesman (Englewood Cliffs, N.J.: Prentice-Hall, 1976): 158.

into corridors in which the eye can no longer range at will but is led inexorably toward infinity. The form of these arcades is echoed or alluded to again and again in *Touch of Evil*: in the vortex of buildings pulling away behind Vargas and Schwartz as they drive through narrow streets; in the bar down whose length Vargas assaults the Grandi gang; in the corridor of the jail where the camera tracks with Vargas to discover Susan, drugged and violated, in her cell. The depths of perspective become, in fact, something like a conventional signifier of the onset of violence. Crossing the border alone, Susan is engulfed in space: Pancho, leather-jacketed, leering, in the foreground; the street and arcades receding behind her. Vargas steps out of the brightly lit hotel lobby and all at once is swallowed up in distance, a tiny figure pursued through arcades and empty squares by a hoodlum with a bottle of acid. As Grandi's gang plots its blackmail scheme, we can barely make out Vargas and Susan, in the extreme distance, in front of their hotel, ignorant of the menace that rushes toward them through the empty foreground. Even in the confines of Marcia Linnekar's apartment, Welles punctuates the jumpy disequilibrium of the interrogation with a series of small eruptions from the background. When Menzies produces the dynamite Quinlan has planted, Grandi springs forward, exclaiming inconsequentially ("Dynamite?"): the momentary spatial dislocation gives visual form to Vargas's suspicion, his sense that something is awry. As all these instances suggest, the fundamental violence in Welles's world is the assault not on our bodies but on our certainties.

Nor is it just Welles's manipulation of deep focus that assaults us in this way. His editing creates its own sort of spatial labyrinth. The function of "classical" editing is logical and analytic. It breaks an event down into its essential components, so that, undistracted by irrelevancies, we can attend to fundamental relationships. This is how the Russian director Lev Kuleshov describes the "American" way of dealing with (for example) a suicide:

. . . when it was necessary to show . . . a person suffering they showed only his face. If he opened the drawer of a desk and took a pistol from it, they showed the desk drawer and the hand taking the pistol. When it came to pressing the trigger, they filmed the finger pressing on the trigger, because other objects and the surroundings in which the actor worked were irrelevant at the particular instant. This method of filming only that moment of movement essential to a given sequence and omitting the rest was labeled by us the "Ameri-

can method," and it was thus placed in the foundations of the new cinematography which we were beginning to form.[9]

Welles's editing, on the other hand, tends always to explode the event—shatter it
into bright shards like the fun house mirrors in *The Lady from Shanghai*. The
explosion of Linnekar's car coincides with an eruption in the style of the film
itself.[10] With the kind of self-referentiality that is prevalent in *Touch of Evil*—as
if bemused with its own outrageousness—Welles uses the moment to mark a
transition from the sinuous continuities of the opening shot to a jagged montage
sequence. Instead of the graceful movement of the crane, we get a tilted, handheld camera; instead of a labyrinthine density of space, we get a sense of discon-
nected fragments—flame, wreckage, shouting men, looming headlights, abrupt
closeups—that we find difficult to assemble into a single spatial field. In one case
as much as the other, we lose our grip on such centering concepts as "essential"
or "irrelevant." Rather than being spectators of a world in whose important features the director patiently instructs us, we are drawn into the vortex of the event
itself, an event whose peculiar violence is precisely the shattering of the world's
familiar outlines.

This disintegration is most extreme in the sequence of Grandi's murder. Welles
fragments the event into some seventy-eight different shots (412–490), many of
them, as the hysteria mounts, of only an instant's duration. And the blinking
light—during much of the sequence, the only illumination comes from a neon
sign outside the window—introduces a further source of discontinuity, almost as
if a second layer of montage, a light montage, had been superimposed on the
primary one. The principle of Welles's cutting is always a constant shifting of
spatial relations, not only in the alternation of high and low angle shots, long
shots and closeups, but also (and especially) in the unpredictable realignments of
figures within the shot. For example, when Susan is first apprehended by the
Grandi gang, Welles alternates between shots where we see Grandi on the left of
the frame and Susan reflected in a mirror on the right and shots where we see
Susan (in the flesh) on the left and Grandi on the right. Even in the relatively rare
scenes of quiet dialogue where Welles approximates the traditional shot/reverse
shot alternation, he usually introduces some such variation to throw the rhythm

9. Lev Kuleshov, *Kuleshov on Film*, trans. Ronald Levaco (Berkeley: University of California Press,
1974): 49.
10. James Naremore, *The Magic World of Orson Welles* (New York: Oxford University Press, 1978):
191.

off balance. In the murder sequence, these relatively minor disturbances become an absolute frenzy. The climax alternates shots of Susan as she wakes up, seen from above and upside down, with shots of Grandi's grotesquely contorted head, seen from below and also upside down, as he dangles over her bedpost. What is shocking is not so much the violence of the deed (by now, certainly, we are used to mutilations far more spectacular) as the violence of our own dislocation. In traditional montage, each shot represents a distinct act of attention. A cut from one character to another, or from a mid shot to a closeup, indicates that something of particular importance demands our scrutiny. But Welles gives us no fixed point of vantage from which to attend to events, no place to stand in the midst of the dizzying whirl of images. The succession of shots seems not to focus or concentrate our attention so much as to disperse or defeat it. We are helplessly caught up in an uproar that is—like the cacophony that greets the hysterical Susan as she stumbles out onto her fire escape—more than we can ever hope to take in.

As this analogy suggests, the sound track is equally unhelpful. Welles's habit of dubbing in the sound after the shooting of a film is complete no doubt grew out of economic considerations. It's cheaper than using live sound. But the practice allows Welles to shape and control the audio dimension of his films with the same disregard for ordinary modes of perception as he exercises in the case of the visuals. The sound is not dead, precisely, but it has lost its spontaneous life and become raw material for Welles's own devious projects. So it is not surprising that what we hear in *Touch of Evil*, or don't *quite* hear, has the same perplexing density as what we see. Welles as an actor—notoriously—grunts, hisses, or drawls out his lines rather than speaking them. All the characters habitually speak at cross purposes, or all at once. Welles's fondness for improvisation is evident in the stream of muttered asides and nonsensical byplay that forms a sort of counterpoint to what we would like to suppose are the dialogue's serious concerns—Quinlan's complaint about sweet rolls, for example, or the whole distracting business with Grandi's wig. It is as if the aural and dramatic surface, like the visual, were continually fracturing, splitting into incommensurable pieces.

Furthermore, much of the time the aural pieces and the visual ones don't fit one another.[11] A remarkable percentage of the film's dialogue is conducted off camera. Sometimes it is simply a matter of looking at one character while listening to another, or of being situated in one place while straining to hear what is going on

11. Cf. Phyllis Goldfarb, "Orson Welles' Use of Sound," in *Focus on Orson Welles*: 85–95.

somewhere else. In the interrogation sequence, we hear bits of the third degree Quinlan is conducting off camera only in the interstices of an apparently trivial conversation in the bathroom. Elsewhere, the trick of overlapping dialogue Welles had been developing since his Mercury Theater days is carried a step farther—given a cinematic equivalent—by letting lines from one shot spill over into the next one. This may serve to link shots together, but in a subtly disorienting—labyrinthine—way. We don't see a speaker finish his line; instead, we hear it in a new shot where it distracts us from what we do see. The two dimensions of our experience of the film, seeing and hearing, are out of phase, never *quite* cohering. This effect may seem a minor one, but, even where we are not fully aware of it, it conditions in a pervasive way our experience of the film's texture.

Its most flamboyant development comes in the last sequence. Not accidentally, one supposes, *Touch of Evil* ends with a bravura display of montage that parallels the display of Welles's mastery of mise-en-scène with which the film opens. Space is fragmented and reassembled to present us with a landscape wholly of the mind. The transitions between closeup and long shot are abrupt and managed in such a way that we cannot rationalize them in terms of the point of view of any of the characters. The transitions, that is, have no mimetic explanation. They occur according to the logic of dreams rather than the logic of realistic narrative. As a consequence, we cannot visualize the shifting spatial relations between the characters, nor map out in our imaginations the terrain through which they prowl and scramble. Bridges, derricks, scaffoldings, and echoing distances are elements in the expressionistic architecture of the frames of the film, rather than a representation of any conceivable place outside. The tape recorder in which Vargas captures the disjointed tale of Quinlan's life—in the end Quinlan slumps listening to it as if that life were no longer his own—becomes an emblem of the similarly denaturing and objectifying work of Welles's own soundtrack. There are three distinct kinds of sound in the sequence: "live" voices, recorded voices, and voices that are live but heard from a great distance, often doubled by echoes. A given sequence, or even line of dialogue, will characteristically pass through at least two of these registers and often all three. In this kind of sound montage, words become as fragmented as the images, literally disembodied, sundered from their presumed origin. It is as if the centerless labyrinth, which has been implicit all along just below the still marginally realistic surface of the film's story, now manifested itself, both visually and aurally, in its pure form; and manifested itself as the terrain in which Quinlan's life has in fact been played out.

People seeing *Touch of Evil* for the first time invariably notice that Janet Leigh and (perhaps to a lesser extent) Charlton Heston seem out of place in such a terrain. They don't fit. It is not only that the characters are uncomfortable on so treacherous a border, which is after all explicit enough in the script. It is as if the actors themselves shared the characters' anxieties and their determination to assert the reality, in spite of what they take to be an accidental or temporary transgression, of the border between Welles's nightmarish labyrinth and the world in which they believe themselves at home. The deliberate antinomies of the script— the good cop and the bad cop, the young bride and the aging whore—emphasize rather than smooth over the disparities between the actors, disparities in their bearing, their styles of physical presence. If what Leigh and Heston offer, a kind of well-scrubbed clarity of demeanor, speech, and bearing, is not precisely realistic, it is at least familiar: normal in the sense that Hollywood versions of reality have become normal, corresponding to our habitual expectations. In contrast, Welles and Dietrich, not to mention the outrageous Akim Tamiroff and Dennis Weaver, seem bizarre, exaggerated, close to parody or self-parody. Even visually, Heston and Leigh seem to inhabit a world that reminds us of the "rationality" of their Hollywood past. In the scene at the hotel where Susan is menaced by the Grandi gang, we see Pancho and Uncle Joe in progressively more portentous low angles, distorted in mirrors or by the lens through which we regard them, lit from below and thrown into garish shadow. Only Susan is seen in eye level shots, her white sweater, like her angry eyes, ablaze with light. "You've been seeing too many gangster movies," seems like an indictment not only of Uncle Joe's extravagant manner but also of the overheated visual atmosphere of the sequence itself. (A similar contrast appears in *Citizen Kane*, where "The March of Time" purports to return us to "reality" after the gothic excesses—we might suppose we are in for a James Whale thriller—of the film's mysterious opening.) Later, when Susan and Vargas are reunited in the lobby of their hotel, their space is shallow and evenly lit (a nondescript wall in the background, a phone booth to one side); they are seen in a medium two shot, the *plan-Américain* of our waking lives. Even the slight staginess of the scene, its banality, is reassuring in its intimation that we have returned to a mode of seeing with which we are familiar.[12]

But just outside the hotel are those depths where Risto waits for Vargas with his bottle of acid—just as the confusions of an unwonted perspective entangle Susan the moment she makes her way alone across the border. As Vargas and

---

12. If in fact the scene was directed by Harry Keller (see Naremore, p. 179), then the solicitude was his, not Welles's.

Susan are increasingly drawn into the foreign place, it becomes increasingly difficult for them to maintain the boundaries of their normalcy. The clean well-lighted places where they seek security turn out to be singularly porous, riddled with gaps and subject to alien incursions. The windows of Susan's hotel room have no shades: she is transfixed in the flashlight beam that penetrates them. The "safe" American motel turns out to be a cube perched on the edge of nothingness. Inside, a low angle shot exaggerates the geometrical bareness of the looming bed, the low ceiling, the stark walls. It is a parody motel, a parody of the flimsiness of the shelters by which Yankee reasonableness seeks to shut out the void. Raucous music pours in through an implacable loudspeaker. The crazed Night Man bobs in and out windows and doors. (In shot 240, Susan stands caught between these two ruptures in the security she hoped to find, the window with the gurgling Night Man on the left, the blaring speaker on the right.) Later, there are yet more threatening intrusions: whispers from the next room of drugs and sexual violation. "What's that got to to with me?" Susan asks, though she's beginning to find out. The shots are lit in such a way that she seems to be interrogating her own shadow on the wall, her own sinister double beginning to emerge from behind inadequate barriers. The violence of the Grandi gang is dramatized less as a physical assault than as an invasion of Susan's space, its gradual but inevitable disintegration. Through windows and doors she anxiously observes a swarmlike gathering of hotrods. A window shade opens on Pancho's leering face. The final terror is the terror of a door opening, silently and without resistance. The repetition of this shot—each time the hoodlums are a bit further into the room—has an effect like slow motion, distending and prolonging the moment of violation.

The fixity whose disintegration is most traumatizing for the lovers is their intimacy with one another. The explosion that interrupts their kiss exiles them from the emotional center by which their world of chocolate sodas and straightforward expectations had been guaranteed. At first, it is only a series of irritations and misunderstandings that divide the lovers. But soon it is physical distance as well. Instead of embracing Susan, Vargas must address her fantasy image on the telephone. We know how unreliable such mediations can be, particularly when the switchboard is presided over by a leather-jacketed nemesis. The labyrinth in which Susan and Vargas lose their way, and eventually Quinlan as well, is a place whose winding corridors and unexpected gaps permit one to see or to be seen but not to communicate. The jumpy byplay of Susan and the

Night Man, popping in and out of doors and windows in a fruitless attempt at dialogue, is a comic version of her later ordeal after the murder of Grandi. Half naked on the fire escape, she can see her husband but her cries are lost in the cacaphony of street sounds as he disappears in the crowd and traffic of the narrow road. His blindness, oblivious beneath a "Jesus Saves" sign, is complemented by the jeering voyeuristic awareness of the crowd, pointing and laughing at the spectacle just outside the range of Vargas's perception. "I want to watch" (shot 378) might be the slogan of the alien world through which Susan finds herself wandering. The final sequence of the movie engulfs Quinlan in a similar, though more complex, network of voyeurism, violated intimacy, and unreliable mediation. He supposes he is communing with himself, or with himself through Menzies; but in speaking to Menzies he is in fact opening himself to Vargas's scrutiny. He is speaking not to a person from whom he can expect an intimate response but to a "walking microphone" that steals from him his own language, objectifies it, sets it over against him. His words become a trap whose only outlet is the rubbish heap on which, as he dies, he listens to their mechanical iteration.

The difference between the dream of intimacy and the voyeuristic labyrinth in which the characters stray is marked by two contrasting gazes. As Tanya, Marlene Dietrich is almost invariably filmed in close-up, staring moodily into the camera. What she is looking for is the human being beneath the "mess" Quinlan has become, beneath the accretions of candy bars, booze, and despair. The gaze of the voyeur, however, the gaze of Uncle Joe licking his lips in the hotel, or of Pancho looming over Susan in a fish-eye lens, or of the sullen moll who wants to watch: such a gaze is one that denies the humanity of its victim, that turns the person on whom it is directed into an object. The shadow that crosses Susan's face in the course of her ordeal—several times and then, definitively, darkening her terrified eyes—signalizes this obliteration of the self. The last and most frightening dislocation suffered by those who lose their way in Welles's labyrinths is just this loss, this displacement from one's own vital center.

Story and Theme

I have been talking about the crossing of borders in a rather general way, with reference mostly to cinematic style and to a few fundamental visual motifs. Now it is time to attend more closely to the plot and characters Welles derived from

Whit Masterson's novel. In emphasizing the expressive primacy of our visual experience of the film, I do not mean to imply that the story doesn't count. It is a question, rather, of establishing a hierarchy of the elements of the film. What the plot does is specify the kinds of experience which are likely to carry us beyond the boundaries of the everyday: to suggest where, within the whole terrain of experience, we are most apt to find ourselves swallowed up in a nightmarish labyrinth. We should perhaps state the relationships in a summary way. The annihilating depths of space are associated first, mostly but not exclusively in connection with Susan's story, with sexual experience; and then, mostly but not exclusively in connection with Quinlan's story, with the passing of time. The link between these two associations would appear to be the loss of innocence to which Welles's title refers us.[13] By the end of the film, we see Susan's (apparent) violation not only as the result and therefore the measure of Quinlan's corruption, but also as an emblem of that corruption, a parallel instance played out in a different register and at a different pace. We come to see the sudden violent loss of sexual innocence as only a special case of the slower, unnoticed perhaps, but more inevitable privations that finally leave Quinlan (like Kane) dying in a rubbish heap.

The film's opening shot allows us to suppose there is no connection between the Hollywood honeymooners and the pleasure seekers introduced by raucous laughter in deep focus. Susan seems to be looking forward chiefly to a chocolate soda, while Linnekar's date is Zita, the sizzling stripper (as critics have noted, she literally sizzles—for the second time, in fact—when Risto's acid hits her poster). But the paths of the two pairs of lovers keep crossing in an odd way, and Welles contrives the shot so that it is Susan's and Vargas's kiss that appears to ignite the explosion. Certainly the explosion means, as Vargas says, that Susan will have to defer her soda. Instead, she is sent almost at once across the border toward drugs, rape, and murder. The Hollywood sweater girl was always an image founded on a precarious balance of sexuality and wholesomeness. Engineered during World War II chiefly for the benefit of our "boys" overseas, her provocations expected no real response. Ensconced safely on the "home front," she could flaunt her sexuality and still maintain her perky, not to say juvenile, innocence. The antithesis of all this in *Touch of Evil* (and in the popular repertory of images on which it draws) is of course Dietrich's weary cynicism. For Tanya,

13. In his Brussels press conference, however, he denied knowing where it came from or what it meant. *Cahiers du Cinema* (September 1958): 31–32.

sex is a paying proposition. Susan's trials seem to represent the unravelling of the sweater girl's image once she strays from familiar territory; and an unravelling that happens from within, the result of some looseness in the original weave. Susan's whispered dialogue with her own shadow ("What's that got to do with me?") suggests that the most fearful antagonist stirring within the depths of Los Robles is the alien or uncontrollable side of her own sexuality. The stylized hysteria of the rape itself makes the same suggestion. It is as if Uncle Joe's boys were obligingly acting out Susan's own fantasies about swarthy rapists (with a leather-jacketed lesbian thrown in for good measure). "I understand very well what he wants," she had announced in her first encounter with Pancho. But then Susan Vargas scarcely seems a "round" enough character for us to find much profit in speculation about her subconscious. We should probably say that the gang enacts the fantasy implicit in the Hollywood stereotype itself, its dark underside and complement. Grandi's gang stands in as much for our own dream life as for Susan's. Having enticed us with the sweater girl, Welles implicates us in her violation. It's the dark side of our own voyeurism that throws us off balance.

Voyeurism, we have said, results from the break down of intimacy. The violence in *Touch of Evil* is continuously associated with the deflection of desire into labyrinthine bypaths, and not only in the case of Susan. Welles has described the Night Man as the inevitable product, a sort of precipitate, of the world around him; and his hysteria—shuddering as he contemplates Susan's bed, wildly sniffing a marijuana butt, speechlessly gurgling as he seeks to recall the "wild party"—is explicitly a sexual panic.[14] Sanchez complains excitedly that it is a woman's sexual advances that have embroiled him in violence (his job as a shoe clerk—"I've been at her feet ever since"—gives a certain kinkiness, though unstated, to his relations with the energetic Marcia). In the episode in which Vargas, furious at the loss of Susan—and also, one might note in passing, at the disappearance of his gun: another Freudian detail?—arrives at Grandi's Rancho Grande to beat the truth from Pancho and his gang, we first see the deep space of the bar framed by the spread legs of a stripper. It is as if for Vargas, too, the entrance into violence is through sexuality; as if it were sexuality itself Vargas hopes to batter into submission. Quinlan's obsessions spring from the loss of his wife, and Tanya's premonition that her chili will be too hot for him evidently suggests some doubt about his potency (a good deal has been made, too, of his

---

14. Dennis Weaver describes the character as being "tremendously attracted to women but at the same time totally scared of them." *American Cinematographer* 56 (April, 1975): 469–470.

lost or variously misplaced cane). In any case, as Stephen Heath in particular has noticed, in strangling Grandi he takes the role of his wife's murderer.[15] By cutting in the climactic moments between the killing and Susan writhing in her bed, Welles manages to suggest that sexual passion has for Quinlan been transformed into a murderous violence; or that the two, in this foreign place, have become identical. The same equivalence may be suggested earlier, when Welles cross cuts between Susan's "rape" and Quinlan's melancholy visit to Tanya's brothel, the site of his former erotic triumphs ("What would you do in a place like this?" she now cooly wants to know).

But the relation between Quinlan and Tanya opens out from the question of impotence to questions of more comprehensive kinds of loss, and indeed to the question of loss in general. Tanya, literally enough, is a figure from Quinlan's past. And her "place" is presented less as part of his present world than as the place of memory. "Still open for business," he discovers wonderingly, as if, though it remains so close (just across the border), he had somehow forgotten it, and now was surprised by the power of the claim it appears to have on him still. The pianola theme (announced in a tilted inset that situates the instrument not in physical space but in Quinlan's head) is a summons from the past, its simple and repetitious theme cutting with a quiet insistence through the jagged brass and bongos of the rest of the film's score. The space through which Quinlan is summoned is empty, indeterminate, away from the rigor of the arcades, but no longer subject to his domination. We see him as a tiny figure, alone with his musing, in an open square through which litter blows at random. The arched porch of the brothel is a kind of shadowy portal marking the boundary of two worlds: Quinlan is framed by it as he hesitates, turned to silhouette. Inside, in contrast to the deep perspective characteristic of the rest of the film—and especially, as Heath has seen, of the strip joint from which Quinlan has just come—the room is crowded with objects: bric-a-brac, mirrors, pictures, a timeless jumble of old and new (a TV on the pianola). Instead of the glare of bare bulbs or blinking neon, the light is shaded, diffused. This is essentially furnished space, a familiar, welcoming sort of space because its contours are shaped by a clutter dense with memory and association. It is not a vacancy but the space created by the objects themselves. For once, Quinlan permits himself to subside into the decor. When Tanya appears through a haze of smoke, framed in the doorway, she hovers in the center of the

15. Stephen Heath, "Film and System: Terms of Analysis," *Screen* 16 (Spring 1975): 76. His entire discussion of the film's sexuality, barely touched upon in the excerpt included in this volume, should be consulted.

frame, gazing steadfastly into the camera. This is the way we almost invariably see her. She is more like an obsessive image than a person encountered in the physical world. When she speaks with Quinlan, their dialogue is visually a still center in the vortex all around these scenes. Without the compulsive need for variation he elsewhere displays, Welles cuts quietly back and forth between the same close-ups of Quinlan and Tanya—each alone in his or her own frame, each rapt in his or her own musing. This oneiric stillness is as different from the hopeful medium shots of Vargas and Susan (e.g., their colloquy in the hotel lobby) as it is from the disorienting virtuosity of the rest of the film. Quinlan and Tanya are never seen in a classical two shot because the place they share is not a physical one.

It is, indeed, only in nostalgia that Quinlan can inhabit the refuge he seeks in Tanya's intimacy. The warm embrace of her "place" defines for us precisely what he can no longer return to, what he has irretrievably lost. Tanya's first words to him are "We're closed," and nearly her last ones indicate that his future too is "all used up." Even physically, it is clear that Quinlan is no longer at home at Tanya's—and not just because of worries about his ability to handle her chili. His monstrously bulky figure, so commanding in the empty distances of Los Robles, seems hemmed in by the clutter in Tanya's parlor, slumping inertly or moving about (one might say) like a bull in a china shop. Of course it is not by accident that he most frequently comes to rest beneath the stuffed head of a bull, complete with banderillas. Welles is at pains to remind us in the final episode that Vargas is waiting outdoors to administer the coup de grace (shots 535–539). But the cruelest fatality by which Quinlan is pursued is visible right from the start, in the physical transformations that keep Tanya from recognizing him. It is the grossness of the creature he has become that makes him a stranger to his own past. As Tanya says, he's a mess. The man he might once have been is obliterated by too many candy bars; but if it hadn't been candy bars, it would have been hooch, for as Quinlan ruefully says, everybody is hooked on something. Quinlan eats candy bars so as not to drink and drinks so as not to think about his murdered wife. "What else is there to think about?" he asks Menzies, and the question is a rhetorical one. At the center of Quinlan's bulk is an aching awareness of loss. Or rather, the bulk has grown up, like a kind of carapace or monstrous scar tissue, to hide—from others but also from himself—an emptiness, an absence. As with Kane and Arkadin, physical corpulence is an index of spiritual disintegration. One becomes more and more a mere body. But the accumulating layers of flesh represent also the cost of a certain sort of knowledge unavailable to those who have not suffered Quinlan's fall into labyrinthine ways: knowledge of the impossibility of holding on to what one most cherishes, whether a wife or an ideal; of the inevitability of loss and contamination in a world where all, as Quinlan keeps insisting, are "guilty, guilty, guilty." The significance of the oil derrick that is so spectral a presence in several shots is at last, in the final sequence, made clear. Quinlan looks up and sees in its impersonal movement—the camera too is caught up for a few instants in its impervious rise and fall—an image for the inexorability that has shaped his life and led him to this tangled and rubbish-strewn landscape.

Quinlan's self-righteousness and maudlin self-pity are of course part of what has happened to him, and are often as palpably greasy as his flesh. They hardly serve to mitigate his ruthlessness and low cunning. But the nostalgia of Tanya's parlor gives a temporal dimension to our understanding of how one might happen to cross the border into such a labyrinth. One may be betrayed into those devious paths where one loses not only one's way but also one's very humanity not only by some sudden assault or violation, but also, and no doubt more frequently, simply by the processes of time and experience. And it is their painful consciousness of those processes—draining away the world's clarity with the imperviousness of the pumping derrick—that distinguishes the labyrinth's inhabitants, permanent residents of a sordid border town, from those who suppose they can remain mere tourists. Charlton Heston's actorish good looks and clipped diction are as clear-cut as the moral certainties by which Vargas orders his world, or seeks to. Welles's shapeless mass and slurred speech are a physical manifestation of the centerless ambiguity of Quinlan's moral universe—the whole grotesque zoo of Los Robles. In one shot (330), Welles juxtaposes Quinlan and Vargas in such a way as to enforce just this contrast. Vargas, on the right, in square-jawed profile, utters unexceptionable homilies about the sanctity of the law. Welles slumps on the left, his sagging unshaven face half-turned toward the camera, partly in annoyance and impatience, partly as if to seek our complicity. When Vargas has finished, Quinlan's muttered response, an aside, a throwaway, does not even attempt to respond to Vargas's high-minded arguments. "Where's your wife, Vargas?" For all Vargas's certainty, Quinlan knows something he has not even dreamed of: his virginal bride is in the clutches of perverted rapists. The contrasts of this shot help to explain a paradox critics of *Touch of Evil*, and Welles himself, have often described, a split between our intellectual condemnation of Quinlan (Welles has repeatedly insisted that Vargas expresses his own views) and our emotional complicity with him. His "famous intuition" is nothing but a long familiarity with corruption ("guilty, guilty, guilty, all of them guilty") that allows him to scent it out where others more respectful of abstract principle might suspect nothing. As he boasts in the shooting script (perhaps the line seemed too explicit to retain in the film), he has "a nose for guilt." He would appear to have been right about Sanchez, though hints about a third degree might throw the "confession" into some doubt. Certainly he is prescient in detecting Menzies' betrayal. Furthermore: Quinlan really has lost his wife, while Vargas only imagines he has. Quinlan recognizes the irrevocability of his loss, while Vargas continues to trust in happy endings, to believe that he will finally be able to take Susan "home" for good. Seen in this perspective, Vargas's certainties begin to look like a kind of innocence, the bright rational daydream of Hollywood "realism."

A similar, though not identical relation exists between Susan and Tanya. We have said that they are antithetical, just as Vargas and Quinlan are antithetical. Now we may define their relation in a more dialectical way. They are antithetical in the way that innocence and experience are antithetical: innocence that secures itself in its ignorance of experience, experience that founds itself in its awareness of the vulnerability of innocence. The peculiar magic of Dietrich's gaze, from the very beginning of her career in *The Blue Angel*, is its rueful awareness of the transcience of romance at the very moment ("Falling in love again . . .") she passionately launches herself on another adventure. Dietrich's "cynicism" or "experience" do not therefore negate Janet Leigh's version of romantic innocence in quite the same way that Quinlan's cynicism utterly negates Vargas's idealism. Rather, she superimposes upon the honeymooner's dream the knowledge that it can't last, that it is too good to be true. She provides an image for the beauty we know we have lost and perhaps never had—beauty apprehended (as we have said) from the perspective of nostalgia.

It is this principle of nostalgia, Quinlan's dream of what he has lost, that allows Welles to counterpoint his story with Susan's. As Susan is trapped by the Grandi gang, so Quinlan finds himself trapped by his own past. For Vargas, the twenty-four hour ordeal at Los Robles is a sudden violent assault on the ideal image on which the blind woman's telephone gave him so precarious a hold. For Quinlan, it is a gradual realization, through a kind of reenactment, of how far his whole life has carried him from the image whose irrevocable pastness is announced in Tanya's gaze. And as we might expect, each stage of this reenactment is visualized as Quinlan's diminishment in those same depths of space that engulf Vargas and Susan.

As the insidious Grandi offers Quinlan his service, the two men crossing the street, arm in arm, become dim images reflected in the window through which Menzies sadly looks on as a church bell tolls in the distance. The frame dissolves gradually into a long shot of the desolate landscape where Susan, too, is about to be defiled. Later, in the bar, Grandi scurries and gesticulates in the distance while Quinlan slumps in the foreground; but at the moment of his capitulation, the camera rises sharply to see the two men together, as if at the bottom of the same deep shaft. After Quinlan has been accused, it is as if his imposing daylight presence had lost its accustomed solidity. In the deserted ballroom of the hotel, he is a tiny figure in a spectral dance of silhouettes, shadows, and echoing spaces, his whole career seeming to dissolve into unsubstantiality. In the Hall of Records where Menzies encounters Vargas, however, Quinlan's past is embodied in the deep perspective of steel file cabinets holding the annals of his deceptions: hard-edged, without reprieve, under the glare of institutional light. And in the final sequence, it is not just Quinlan's crime but the whole of his life that is played out as a night journey through a labyrinth of sight and sound whose only exit, as we have indicated, is the rubbish heap where Quinlan dies. The past and future are both exhausted. Quinlan has killed (as Tanya observes) the man who really loved him and who was his last link to any spontaneous generosity of feeling. In the end, he listens inertly to the story of a life that no longer seems to be his own, and then, used up as the debris around him, topples into stagnant water.

Tone and Genre

Once Quinlan is disposed of, Susan and Vargas drive away, headed for home, as if the nightmare eruption of their honeymoon had never occurred. And, indeed, in a certain sense it has not. Susan, it turns out, has not "really" been drugged or violated. Although critics have not failed to notice Vargas's initiation into violence and deception, he seems remarkably unaffected by his experience, and even less concerned than the moderately rueful Schwartz about the sacrifice of Menzies' life (and of his conscience). Even the Grandi gang for all their elaborately orchestrated intimations of degeneracy, turn out to be little worse than high-spirited kids. They never touch dope themselves, we are assured, and have only—in spite of some very peculiar carryings-on—been "putting on a good show" to frighten Susan—which might appear to confirm her earlier complaint about gangster movies. We too have only been given a familiar kind of scare and now need to be assured that everything is fundamentally okay. At first viewing, I suppose, most of us are apt to feel cheated by this sudden apparent mitigation of the accumulated ferocity of the film. It may strike us as a lamentable, and perhaps cynical, capitulation to the demands of Hollywood morality, or of the box office. In spite of the teasing suggestiveness of some of the publicity stills ("Danger! Soft Curves!"), audiences in 1958 did not pay good money to see Janet Leigh assaulted, raped, and turned into a hopeless junkie. We might remind ourselves, though, that a year later, in *Psycho*, Hitchcock was able to defeat their expectations in a way still more bloodily surprising, though not perhaps so degrading, by killing Leigh off early in the film. Welles, I think, was just as cunning in exploiting the conventional expectations of Hollywood morality as Hitchcock was in violating them. The point to be made is that *Touch of Evil* does not really conclude, does not really come to rest, with its happy ending. It merely dismisses that "ending"—which ends nothing—as irrelevant. Vargas and Susan drive off with a perfunctory kiss, but the camera stays with Tanya and what remains of Quinlan ("Isn't someone going to come and . . . take him away?" she asks).

Schwartz, too, remains, perhaps as our stand-in, to demand of Tanya some last words to tell us what we are finally to think of Quinlan. This demand is traditional in tragedy, whose heroes—Hamlet, for example, or Othello—are anxious, even in death, that their stories be brought to a comprehensible resolution. It is like the demand for the "real" meaning of Rosebud, and Tanya's response is about as unhelpful as what we get in *Citizen Kane*. "He was some kind of a man. What does it matter what you say about people?" She is testifying, of course, to the ethical ambiguity to which Welles's crossing of borders has, in spite of his own protestations, led us. Welles's dismissal of Quinlan as an embodiment of everything he hates is a half-truth on the order of the characterization of Macbeth and his spouse as "this dead butcher and his fiend-like queen." More suggestive is his confession that in playing monsters he detests, all of them "bigger than life," he gives himself up to them in a quasi sexual way—putting at risk, one supposes, his own liberal certainties as well as the audience's. In any case, Tanya's question points us beyond the moral quandary to a still more comprehensive account of what I have been calling the uncentered quality of Welles's film. I think Tanya is speaking, on some level, for Welles himself when she calls into question the adequacy not merely of Hollywood definitions of character and morality but any definition whatever, any attempt at coherent representation. Is anything you can say ever enough? does it ever matter? The portentous emptiness of her line (much remains to be discovered about the effectiveness of such memorably "awful" lines) is part of the joke.

One critic of *Touch of Evil* has objected to the "frivolous exhibitionism" that has the effect, he says, of "wrecking the mood of realism" Welles creates elsewhere in the film.[16] He has in mind such episodes as those involving the Night Man or the wild spats between Uncle Joe and his "boys." But nothing could be further from Welles's true aim, or accomplishment, than a "realistic mood of squalor." On the contrary, *Touch of Evil* wobbles continually between melodrama and farce; or rather, it occupies that ambiguous border region where one spills over into the other, where "farce is born from the convulsions of melodrama." [17] What these two often debased and "popular" genres have in common is a blithe disregard for the mimetic responsibilities of more respectable forms like tragedy or comedy. They are extravagant, exaggerated forms, closer to the texture and logic of dreams than to the decorum of our waking lives, particularly vulnerable to incursions of unconscious impulse and subterranean fantasy.

In fact, where Welles feels the constraint of a Great Text, his style is apt to become rather stiffly monumental, as it notably does in *The Trial*. The sleazy world of the pulp thriller, on the other hand, seems to liberate his imagination, providing a space where the intricate deviousness of his style can assume its own proportions. *Mr. Arkadin*, the film he made just before *Touch of Evil* (with which it has important thematic links), is afflicted with an unbelievable plot and an unbelievably wooden hero and heroine. But it is brilliantly successful in sustaining its peculiar slippery mood, a jittery mix of real menace and nervous giggles. Like *Touch of Evil*, though with a less successfully articulated structure, it is a pinwheel of tics and crazy mannerisms—cinematic and histrionic—around a center of emptiness and loss. Of course the element of black comedy in *Touch of Evil* has been acknowledged. James Naremore, for example, has pointed out the intolerable running gag about feet: Sanchez is a shoe clerk, he worships the ground Marcia walks on, the dynamite is found in a shoe box, an old woman finds a shoe with a foot in it at the scene of the explosion. More fundamentally, it is just when the world threatens to come most completely unstuck for Welles's characters—as it does for Vargas, for example, when the gurgling Night Man

16. Charles Higham, *The Films of Orson Welles* (Berkeley: University of California Press, 1970): 155, 157.
17. Comito, *"Touch of Evil,"* p. 159.

reveals the real owners of the motel where Susan had gone for safety—that the melodramatically threatening is apt to give way to the grotesquely comic. The instability of tone in *Touch of Evil* is the equivalent of the visual instability of which I have already spoken at length, another aspect of our disorientation. To call such figures as Grandi or the Night Man grotesque is thus not merely to apply to them a disparaging epithet. It is to approach an exact definition of Welles's peculiar mixture of menace and absurdity. A grotesque world, the German literary critic Wolfgang Kayser has written, is an "estranged" world. The grotesque appears not through the agency of any supernatural intrusion but when our own world "ceases to be reliable," when "the categories which apply to our world . . . become inapplicable," so that we are "unable to orient ourselves" in a world become strange and alien. The grotesque is a "play with the absurd." It may begin exuberantly enough, even lightheartedly, but "it may also carry the player away, deprive him of his freedom, make him afraid of the ghosts he has so frivolously evoked." [18]

Kayser has in mind a mode of vision that originated in an odd sort of painted decoration, in which stone columns well up into vegetable forms, and luxuriant tendrils are apt to sprout mythological beasts: a fantastic improvisation subject to no laws but the inventiveness of its maker's imagination. In certain respects, *Touch of Evil* is a similar fantasia, a dreamlike collage of the flora and fauna of popular culture: gangster movies, erotic fantasies, Hollywood memorabilia, in-jokes about Welles's own career. It is less an attempt to fabricate an authentic representation of the world than to reassemble—in patterns that are surprising, strange, and ultimately disquieting—familiar fragments from earlier representations, kaleidoscopically askew, as in a dream. Seen in this perspective, *Touch of Evil* is an instance of what some French literary critics have called *bricolage*: the art work as an improvised assemblage of cultural fragments, the result not of some vision that gives the artist privileged access to reality, but of a sort of inspired tinkering with whatever materials he finds at hand. As Susan complains, Uncle Joe Grandi owes his preposterous mannerisms, cigar and all, to *Little Caesar*: his menace is a routine he never quite manages to bring off. We keep being reminded that Susan Vargas is really Janet Leigh—Mrs. Tony Curtis, as the production stills insisted for the benefit of the press: Hollywood's favorite pinup. We do not believe for a minute that Tanya is anyone but Marlene Dietrich,

18. Wolfgang Kayser, *The Grotesque in Art and Literature*, trans. Ulrich Weisstein (Bloomington, Ind.: Indiana University Press, 1963): 184–185.

improbably transported from a von Sternberg film to a Mexican brothel, her German accent intact. Her final "adios" is addressed at least as much to us—we wonder if her cameo is a farewell performance—as it is to Schwartz. Zsa Zsa Gabor becomes a madame and Mercedes McCambridge a leather-jacketed lesbian, and the whole joke depends upon our recognizing who they are, recognizing the coincidence of the "star" with her ideal archetype. All these are instances of what Higham, disapprovingly, calls a strain of "high camp" in *Touch of Evil*. He disapproves because all these jokes and references make us lose faith in the reality of what we are watching, fracture the coherence and autonomy of the world Welles's characters are supposed to be inhabiting, and undermine its mimetic respectability. The peculiarly insidious power of camp lies (as Susan Sontag has noted) in its tendency to put everything into quotation marks.[19] It calls attention to the artificiality of a gesture or an attitude at the very moment it most enthusiastically embraces it. Grandi is not a gangster; he is a "gangster"—with a vengeance! This is a dangerous "play with the absurd" because it is a kind of playfulness that risks severing the link between what we say ("What does it matter what you say about people?") and the way the world, or our feelings, "really" are. It undermines the possibility of sincerity.

Welles, to be sure, lays claim to a kind of sincerity, but of a characteristically devious sort. In a revealing interview conducted just after *Touch of Evil* appeared in France (reprinted in this volume), André Bazin keeps trying to pin Welles down to the sort of realism Bazin himself admired. But Welles insists that his choice of stylistic devices was motivated chiefly by a desire to avoid boredom.

> I'm not interested in works of art, you know, in posterity, in renown—only in the pleasure of experimentation itself. This is the only domain where I feel myself truly honest and sincere. I have no commitment to what I've made: it's really without value in my eyes. I'm profoundly cynical about my own work and about most of the works I see in the world. But I am not cynical about the act of working with a medium. . . . It's the act that interests me, not the result.

Looking back on his experience of making *Citizen Kane*, Welles had famously remarked that Hollywood offered "the biggest electric train set any boy ever had!" In the interview with Bazin, he says he is thinking about giving up film and theater altogether, though he was not to do so for another decade, at least. It is surely appropriate, even if it was not deliberate, that Welles's final project as a

19. Susan Sontag, *Against Interpretation* (New York: Dell, 1966): 280.

director (to date) should have been a film he, quite literally this time, put together from footage shot by someone else, a film that tells the story of a famous forger of old master paintings. Near the beginning of *F For Fake*, Welles, *in propria persona*, confides in the spectator yet more intimately than he had in Bazin. "I am a charlatan," he says. "Was I not a magician?" Welles is "truly honest and sincere" in the way a truly committed charalatan is, working his material with great dexterity and high spirits, like a juggler keeping the bright fragments spinning bravely in mid air. Welles has never been the sort of magician to be contented with producing rabbits from hats. His is the more dangerous trick of making the world disappear and leaving us, with no firm ground under our feet, confronting only the enigmatic smile of the prestidigitator.

Orson Welles

A Biographical Sketch

he main sources of information about Welles's life are *Orson Welles, A First Biography* by Roy Alexander Fowler (London: Pendulum Publications, 1946) and *The Fabulous Orson Welles* by Peter Noble (London: Hutchinson, 1956); a *New Yorker* profile by Alva Johnson and Fred Smith (October 5, 1938); a series of articles in *The Saturday* *Evening Post* (January 20, 27, February 3, 1940); and memoirs by John Houseman (1972) and Micháel Mac-Liammóir (1950). The Welles Archives at the Lilly Library of Indiana University cover principally the years 1936–1947 and include correspondence, memorabilia, radio, theater, and film scripts, tape recordings and photographs.

On May 6, 1915, Welles was born into an upper middle-class family in Kenosha, Wisconsin, a few miles outside of Chicago. His father was a hotel manager, inventor, manufacturer, and apparently something of a playboy; his mother was a concert pianist of considerable talent. His was not a typical midwestern childhood. Almost at once he was recognized as a prodigy—"Cartoonist, Actor, Poet—And Only 10!" a Madison newspaper proclaimed—and spent his early years in experimental schools under the watchful eyes of psychologists and in incessant travels through Europe, Asia, and the Caribbean. His parents divorced when he was six; his mother, with whom he lived for three years in Chicago, died when he was nine; his father, who retired in order to travel with his son, died in 1927, leaving him, at age twelve, in the care of a family friend,

Dr. Maurice Bernstein (to whom homage was paid in the devoted Bernstein of *Citizen Kane*). André Bazin, among others, has written of the importance in Welles's cinematic career of his "obsession with childhood," his nostalgia for lost innocence. Even more striking than the sense of loss, however, is the tenacity in Welles's career, and in his character, of the aptitude nurtured by the child's precosity, isolation, and mobility. Welles never lost the boy's prodigious capacity, in the absence of a compelling external order, to improvise worlds subject to no laws but their own. Three gifts Bernstein mentions giving the young boy have a peculiarly prophetic significance for the man he became: a conductor's baton, a set of magic tricks, and a puppet theater. From his earliest years, Welles seems to have found in the theater—in the theatrical, more broadly—not merely a mode of artistic expression but a way of life.

John Houseman has written that it was "always a shock to see Welles without the makeup and the false noses behind which he chose to hide himself" (*Run-Through*, p. 150). Bernstein mentions discovering him made up as a grotesque ten-year-old King Lear, and in subsequent years he was seldom without roles to play and disguises to assume. At twelve, at the Todd School in Woodstock Illinois, he directed a production of *Julius Caesar* in which he also played Marc Antony, the Soothsayer, *and* Cassius. At sixteen, a recent graduate of the school with five hundred dollars in his pocket, he descended upon the venerable Gate Theater in Dublin, presented himself as "the star of the New York Theater Guild," and won his first professional role, the sixty-year-old Duke Alexander in *Jew Süss*. In the next few years, Welles (as a foreigner) was refused permission to work in London; returned to Chicago and prepared acting editions of *Julius Caesar*, *Twelfth Night*, and *The Merchant of Venice* (later published as The Mercury Shakespeare); sketched and wrote pulp thrillers in Morocco; was a picador in Seville (his bullfighting memorabilia turns up in Tanya's parlor in *Touch of Evil*); returned penniless to Chicago, where he wrote two plays, one about the abolitionist John Brown, the other, *Bright Lucifer*, a melodrama about an orphaned child prodigy much like himself; met Thornton Wilder, Alexander Woollcott, and, through their intercession, Katherine Cornell, with whom he landed a job touring as Mercutio; organized a drama festival at the Todd School, featuring his mentor from Dublin, Micháel MacLiammóir; and in 1934 opened with Cornell on Broadway (demoted, to his chagrin, to Tybalt), where his performance—he was already, although not yet twenty, something of a legend—caught the eye of John Houseman, an aspiring theatrical producer, then thirty-two, and launched his theatrical career in earnest.

During the thirties, Welles and Houseman collaborated in the short-lived Phoenix Theater, the Federal Theater Project, and finally in their own Mercury Theater. Of their years together, Houseman has observed that Welles was "always, at heart, a magician" (*Run-Through*, p. 233; cf. Noble, 116–117), astounding audiences with audacious transformations and precariously balanced theatrical sleights of hand. His first production for the Federal Theater Project was a "voodoo" *Macbeth*, transposed to Haiti and enlivened with hints of savage ritual; his version of Marlowe's *Dr. Faustus* was literally a magic show, with floating objects and characters who materialized and disappeared without explanation. Welles's final project for the Federal Theater, one that severed his and Houseman's connection with the program, was a proscribed production of Marc Blitzstein's radical musical, *The Cradle Will Rock*: finding his company locked out of its theater, Welles led two thousand people through the streets of New York in search of a stage, "perched on a truck and mesmerizing the crowd like Marc Antony over the corpse of Caesar" (Bazin, *Orson Welles*, 40). Later, at the Mercury Theater, there were (among others) a much praised modern dress *Julius Caesar*, with Caesar and his cronies as black-shirted fascists; an embattled production of *Heartbreak House* ("If I've cut Shakespeare," Welles raged in response to Shaw's protectiveness about his text, "why can't I cut Shaw?"); and an abortive *Five Kings*, a grandiose conflation of five Shakespeare history plays that had its beginnings in a project at the Todd School.

What was always most striking about Welles as an actor was his peculiarly resonant voice. When Houseman first met him, he was supporting himself and his young wife, Virginia Nicholson, by working on the radio for *The March of Time*, whose characteristically omniscient tones (Welles himself did voices for Hindenburg, Hirohito, and Haile Selassie) were satirized in *Citizen Kane*. He also acquired considerable (though anonymous) popularity as *The Shadow*: playboy Lamont Cranston to his friends, but in reality an invisible and ubiquitous scourge of evildoers ("Who knows what evil lurks in the hearts of men?" he intoned at the start of each show. "The Shadow knows!"). In 1938, CBS radio engaged him for The Mercury Theater of the Air, a series of dramatizations of "classics," which Welles would narrate as well as direct and act in, beginning each episode by telling the story or reading from the original author and only gradually introducing sound effects and dramatic dialogue. The program was called *First Person Singular*. Its most notorious episode was "The War of the Worlds" (October 30, 1938), when a last minute decision to present H. G. Wells's story of a Martian invasion in documentary form caught up the whole nation in one of Welles's playful contrivances, setting off widespread panic, riots, and over a hundred lawsuits. ("It's Halloween," he had assured his by now hysterical audience at the end of the broadcast, hoping thereby to dispell the vision of "glowing, globular invaders.") But the first person singular remained a favored format for Welles. His first movie project was to have been a version of Conrad's *Heart of Darkness*, in which Welles would play both Kurtz, the tragic hero, and Marlowe, the invisible narrator in search of ultimate evil. At the end of *The Magnificent Ambersons* (Welles's second film and the only one in which he does not appear as an actor) he narrates the credits instead of using titles: as he speaks, we see members of the cast in their roles, then technicians busy fabricating the illusion in whose spell we have just been held, and finally a microphone on a boom, as he gravely tells us "I wrote the script and directed. My name is Orson Welles." Then the microphone turns away from us.

Welles came to Hollywood in 1939 with a carte-blanche six–film contract with RKO. The studio trumpeted its new "Genius at Work!," but in fact he was not permitted to work as much as might have been expected. (As he later remarked, "A genius in Hollywood's dictionary . . . is somebody who is either unavailable or dead" [Noble, 161].) The first three scripts he prepared were never produced: *The Heart of Darkness*; a version of a popular spy novel, *Smiler With a Knife*, that Welles intended to do as comedy; and a Hitchcock-style "Mexican Melodrama" about an amnesiac desperately searching for his own identity. Then, at the age of twenty-five, he directed his first feature, a movie that has done more than any other to revolutionize the art of the American film: *Citizen Kane* (1941). Gregg Toland's deep focus photography and fluid camera work, the elaborate use of flashbacks, the intricately sophisticated soundtrack based on the kind of overlapping dialogue Welles developed in the Mercury Theater (many of the company were featured in *Kane*): all these suggested cinematic possibilities that still were being worked out decades later, and *Kane* invariably is designated in international surveys as one of the "ten best" pictures ever made. The script, on which Welles worked along with Houseman and filmwriter Herman Mankiewicz (see Filmography), was transparently based on the career of newspaper magnate William Randolph Hearst, who attempted to have the film suppressed, boycotted RKO in his papers, set loose gossip columnist Louella Parsons in a public battle that was promptly joined on the other side by her arch rival Hedda Hopper, and decreed that Welles should henceforth never be mentioned for any reason in a Hearst paper.

In spite of (or partly because of) all the scandal, the film was an immense critical success. But it did not make money. Welles's next project was an apparently safe one, a film version of Booth Tarkington's classic exercise in nostalgia, *The Magnificent Ambersons*, which Welles had already produced for The Mercury Theater of the Air. The film contains some of Welles's most brilliant work, but the release version was badly mutilated by the studio and fitted out with an incongruously cheerful ending: "They let the studio janitor cut [it] in my absence," Welles complained. And in spite of these "improvements," it was not a financial success. Welles was on an even shorter leash for his third film, a more or less conventional Eric Ambler spy thriller, *Journey Into Fear* (1943), which Welles produced, acted in, and doubtless had a large hand in directing, though the official credit goes to Norman Foster. Then, while Welles was in South America shooting for a semidocumentary, *It's All True*, his mentor at RKO, George Schaefer, was displaced from the presidency. The studio, determined to cut its by now considerable losses, severed its connection with Welles and refused to proceed with the nearly completed South American film. Thirteen thousand feet of film, including some reportedly stunning color footage of the carnival at Rio, were printed but have never been shown.

Already—with what justice commentators still argue—Welles was saddled with the reputation for profligacy and commercial unreliability that was to make his career in film sporadic and difficult. In 1943, Houseman got him the part of Rochester in a staid Hollywood version of *Jane Eyre* that, ironically, promoted Welles for the first time to the status of a box office star, a feat he repeated in the 1945 melodrama, *Tomorrow is Forever*. Meanwhile, he launched his one-man circus and magic show for the entertainment of servicemen: The Mercury Wonder Show ("Mysterious, Thrilling, Sensational"), whose climactic act—Welles sawing Marlene Dietrich in two—was included in Universal's war-effort compilation, *Follow the Boys* (1944). In 1946, partly in order to demonstrate his ability to work within the studio system, he undertook for producer Sam Spiegel to direct and star in *The Stranger*, the story of a nazi war criminal hiding out in a small American town. Like *Journey Into Fear*, this is a relatively conventional and impersonal product, but it was finished on time and within budget. Welles considers it his worst film, but "I did it to prove I could put out a movie as well as anyone." Won over by this display of docility, Columbia agreed to let Welles direct a vehicle for one of the studio's most valuable properties, Rita Hayworth, who had in 1943 become Welles's second wife. Intended by the studio as a commercial thriller, *The Lady from Shanghai* (1946) turned out to be what André Bazin has called (with no derogatory intent) "the most demented work" of Welles's career. Dazzlingly tricky, and enigmatic at times to the point of incomprehensibility, it committed the further unpardonable sin of shearing off Hayworth's famous locks and casting her as a heartless villain. The result was a financial disaster that effectively ended Welles's Hollywood career and hastened the dissolution of his marriage. Only two more projects kept Welles in the United States: an extravagant musical stage version of *Around the World in 80 Days*, the basis of the film later made by the show's original backer, Mike Todd; and a "quickie" film version of *Macbeth* featuring a not very distinguished cast Welles had already worked with in a Salt Lake City production and filmed on a shoestring budget in an amazing twenty-one days on a Republic backlot.

For the next nine years, Welles was in exile in Europe, accepting roles in mostly mediocre films in order to finance his own intermittent and often aborted projects. The first of these roles was the mesmerist and adventurer Cagliostro in Gregory Ratoff's *Black Magic* (1947). The only one of any real distinction was Harry Lime, the sardonic villain of Carol Reed's *The Third Man* (1949), a picture for which Welles is said to have written many of his own lines and directed his own scenes. Two films of his own were completed during this period. *Othello* was improvised over a period of four years, in several different countries. At least three different Desdemonas were involved at different stages of the project. Roderigo is murdered in a Turkish bath because costumes failed to arrive on time. Nevertheless, upon its completion in 1952, it won first prize at the Cannes Film Festival. *Mr. Arkadin* (1955) is drawn from Welles's own novel, based on the life of Sir Basil Zaharoff, an international munitions speculator, whose voice, according to Houseman, Welles had supplied back in his *March of Time* days. Starring Paola Mori, an Italian countess who became Welles's third wife in 1956, it too was put together in bits and pieces, and features a half-dozen brilliant cameos by some of Europe's best known actors, who were always eager to work with Welles, however adverse the conditions. Dozens of other projects were announced and abandoned. It was during this period, around 1955, that Welles began shooting his most famous unfinished film, the frequently promised and endlessly deferred modern dress *Don Quixote*. Meanwhile he kept busy with stage productions: his own satirical play, *The Unthinking Lobster*, in Paris (1950); another version of the Faust legend, with the newly discovered Eartha Kitt as Helen of Troy (she reports that in one of the play's climactic moments Welles kissed her so fiercely that her mouth bled); a production of *Othello* in

London (1951); a stage version of *Moby Dick*, also in London (Welles had always wanted to do a film of Melville's classic, but had to content himself with playing Father Mapple in John Huston's 1956 film).

In 1953 Welles starred in Peter Brook's version of *King Lear* for American TV. In 1956 he returned to the United States to star in New York in his own production of *Lear*, which he did from a wheelchair thanks to an accident during rehearsal. Back in Hollywood for the first time in years, he sardonically flaunted his corpulence in two red-neck roles that might be seen as trial runs for the character of Hank Quinlan in *Touch of Evil*: in *Man in the Shadow* (1957) and in Martin Ritt's version of a Faulkner story, *The Long Hot Summer* (1957). As has often been recounted, his involvement in *Touch of Evil*, his first Hollywood film since the ill-fated *Lady from Shanghai*, was the result of a misunderstanding. Though Welles was slated only for an acting role, Charlton Heston, attracted to the project by the prospect of working with the great man, agreed to appear only if Welles were allowed to direct. Universal released the completed film as a cheap bottom-of-the-bill thriller, and declined to enter it officially in a competition at the 1958 Brussels World Fair, surprised that foreign critics should consider it an "art" film. Nevertheless, it took first prize and European critics hailed it as Welles's return to the standards set by *Kane* and *Ambersons*.

In the more than a quarter of a century since *Touch of Evil*, Welles's career has been singularly fragmented. Two more major features were produced in Europe: a version of Kafka's *The Trial* (1962) and *Chimes at Midnight* (1966), which in a way realizes the old *Five Kings* project, conflating several Shakespeare plays in order to focus elegiacally on the rise and fall of Falstaff, played by Welles himself. Between 1967 and 1969, Welles reportedly completed a thriller in Yugoslavia, starring himself, Laurence Harvey, and Jeanne Moreau, *The Deep*; but it has never been released. Increasingly, his last works have been self-reflective, preoccupied with the role of the artist, and often sceptical about its worth. In *The Immortal Story* (1968), an hour long adaptation for French television of an Isak Dinesen tale and Welles's first film in color, the protagonist is a rich merchant who bears a more than passing resemblance to such Wellesian manipulators as Kane and Arkadin. He becomes the center of an allegorical meditation on the equivocal triumphs and failures of the artist's attempt to juggle reality in pursuit of his own fantasies. In *F For Fake* (1973), Welles combines some new scenes and some footage shot for other projects with great chunks of an earlier documentary (by French director François Reichenbach) about the life of a forger of old masters. It is an odd collage that raises disturbing questions about the thin line between art and charlatanry. In the early seventies, Welles was said to be nearing completion of *The Other Side of the Wind*, a satirical film à clef— described by one of the participants as a kind of gigantic home movie—about an aging Hollywood director. But it too remains unseen.

The American Film Institute's 1975 Life Achievement Award might seem at last to have restored Welles to his rightful place in the Hollywood establishment. But it did not lead to any new film projects, nor to the release of old ones— neither the twenty-year-old *Quixote* nor the current *The Other Side of the Wind*, from which Welles showed two clips during the ceremonies. In the past decade, Welles's public appearances have been limited to TV talk shows ("I do it for exposure," he has said. "If you don't, you are forgotten") and to a series of commercials in which he bulkily denies releasing any wine "before its time." In 1982, however, a new project, *The Dreamers*, financed by the French Ministry of Culture, was announced. Perhaps it is too soon to give up hope that Welles's time will come again.

Touch of Evil

Touch of Evil

In 1958 Universal released a ninety-three-minute version of *Touch of Evil*. Virgil Vogel and Aaron Stell are credited as editors. Charles Higham, in his study of Welles, indicates that Welles declined to make a final cut; others, including Welles himself, have said he was denied the opportunity. In any case, the release version, while not outrageously scrambled, left out a number of key scenes and included some footage not shot by Welles. "The additions: four scenes between Vargas and his wife, particularly in the hotel lobby, but they only last about a minute of screen time" (Peter Bogdanovich, drawing on a press conference Welles gave after the screening of his film at the Brussels Festival). In 1975 a UCLA film archivist, Bob Epstein, discovered a 108-minute version of *Touch of Evil*, and it was at first supposed that this was Welles's own long lost version of the film. This proved to be not quite the case. It contains at least one long expository scene apparently shot after Welles had left the project by Harry Keller, a TV and movie director hitherto best known for *The Loretta Young Show*. And it continues to run the credits over the first shot, rather than at the end of the film as Welles intended. Nevertheless, the 108-minute version clearly is closer to Welles's intentions than what Universal originally released, and it is on this version we have based our script. Shots that appear only in the long version are designated with an asterisk. Other differences between the two versions are described in footnotes to the script. The fullest analysis of the differences between the two versions is John Belton's essay, which is cited in the bibliography.

The continuity script is intended as a guide for the study of Welles's film, not a substitute for it. Accordingly, only a bare minimum of novelistic or psychological description has been included. On the other hand, it seemed important to include, in a concise form, as much information about the visual and audio tracks of the film as was feasible—even at the risk of some loss of readability. The somewhat telegraphic style that has resulted is not meant to reproduce the effect of Welles's film. We hope that it will assist in uncovering some of the sources of that effect.

The overlapping and frequently inaudible dialogue has been untangled as completely as possible. A few particularly resistant uncertainties have been acknowledged.

Since there is no adequate way to articulate in words the very considerable contributions of Henry Mancini's score, it has been referred to only on those occasions when it seems particularly important.

As complete as possible an account has been given of the spatial rela-

tions, movement, and camera movement within each shot. These almost always have an expressive, in addition to a merely narrative, function, and they are important for a study of Welles's complex editing. Naturally this "completeness" is an ideal limit. It has not been thought plausible, or possible, to pin down *every* movement in Welles's peculiarly fluid visual style.

We have rarely been able to summarize sequences of shots. The movement from shot to shot almost always has expressive effect. Even in those rare instances when Welles seems to be alternating identical shots (as in the classical shot/reverse shot) the overlapping of dialogue between shots is a conscious element of his style.

The analytic language has been kept as untechnical as possible. It should be remembered that the classification of shots indicated by standard abbreviations listed below are—like such designations as "low angle" and "high angle"—approximations:

CU   close-up
MCU medium close-up
MS   medium shot
MLS medium long shot
LS   long shot

Credits and Cast

Director
Orson Welles

Producer
Albert Zugsmith

Production Company
Universal

Production Manager
F. D. Thompson

Screenplay
Orson Welles, from an earlier script
by Paul Monash, based on the novel
Badge of Evil by Whit Masterson

Director of Photography
Russell Metty

Camera Operator
John Russell

Art Directors
Alexander Golitzen, Robert
Clatworthy

Set Decorators
Russell Gausman, John P. Austin

Costumes
Bill Thomas

Music
Henry Mancini

Musical Supervisor
Joseph Gerhenson

Sound
Leslie I. Carey, Frank Wilkinson

Editors
Virgil Vogel, Aaron Stell, Edward
Curtiss

Assistant Directors
Phil Bowles, Terry Nelson

Location
Universal Studios in Hollywood,
Venice, California

Process
Black and White

Release Date
February 1958

Length
93 minutes, 108 minutes

The cast list is based chiefly on the
filmography in Naremore (see Bibliography), which was compiled from a
number of sources. It includes some
character names (Ginnie, Lackey,
Jackie, Bobbie) apparently not mentioned in the film. Conversely, some
named characters (Rudy Linnekar,
Eddie Farnham, Howard Frantz, Ed
Hansen) have not been identified.

Hank Quinlan
Orson Welles

Ramon Miguel "Mike" Vargas
Charlton Heston

Susan Vargas
Janet Leigh

Pete Menzies
Joseph Calleia

"Uncle Joe" Grandi
Akim Tamiroff

"Pancho"
Valentin De Vargas

District Attorney Adair
Ray Collins

Motel Clerk (the "Night Man")
Dennis Weaver

Marcia Linnekar
Joanna Moore

Schwartz
Mort Mills

Tanya
Marlene Dietrich

Manolo Sanchez
Victor Milan

Risto
Lalo Rios

Pretty Boy
Michael Sargent

Gang Leader (the "brunette")
Mercedes McCambridge

Coroner
Joseph Cotten

Madame of Strip Joint
Zsa Zsa Gabor

Blaine
Phil Harvey

Zita
Joi Lansing

Police Chief Gould
Harry Shannon

Casey
Rusty Wescoatt

Gang members
Wayne Taylor, Ken Miller, Raymond Rodriguez

Ginnie
Arlene McQuade

Lackey
Dominick Delgarde

Delinquent
Joe Basulto

Jackie
Jennie Dias

Bobbie
Yolanda Bojorquez

Lia
Eleanor Dorado

Plainclothes cop
John Dierkes

The Continuity Script

1. *An ominous chord introduces an extreme* CU *of an explosive device being turned toward us. It is evening, we hear street sounds. We see only the midsection of the man holding the bomb. His hand adjusts the timer and the bomb begins to tick. A woman's laughter is heard off camera, coming from some distance. The man whirls around abruptly to the left, in the direction of the sound. Almost at once the camera pans in this direction too, and we see a man and the laughing woman, tiny figures in deep focus, approaching along an arcade on the left. The back of the man with the bomb crosses the foreground of the frame, in* MS, *as he darts from right to left in order to observe the two figures turning and disappearing down a passage toward the right. On the soundtrack: insistent latin bongo rhythms. The man with the bomb again crosses the foreground, this time from left to right, still turned away so we cannot make out his identity. The camera follows, with increasing speed, as he races along a garishly lit wall, plastered with posters, followed at some distance by his exaggerated shadow. The camera moves in on him as he kneels behind a large convertible, plants the bomb in its trunk, and runs off to the right. Then the camera begins to swing upward as the man and the laughing woman approach from the left, so that by the time they enter the car we look down on them from a great distance. As they get in, sinister jazzy brass joins the percussion on the soundtrack. The car drives off to the left, disappearing behind a building. As it does so, the camera draws slightly back and moves left over the top of the building, then, when it reaches the street, begins to move down again as the car enters from the right and turns into the street, moving toward us. The street here is mostly empty, lined on both sides by illuminated arcades. The camera tracks back from the approaching car; but when the car stops for an intersection, the camera keeps moving, back and also up, leaving it behind. In the foreground are a traffic policeman, a few pedestrians, a large white car crossing the intersection from left to right. As the camera continues to move further away, a gaudily decorated white pushcart crosses the intersection from left to right, and then a second car. By now the convertible is far away. Finally it resumes its forward*

motion, but the camera, continuing to move back, doesn't allow it to catch up. When it stops for a second intersection, two pedestrians cross from right to left, a young blond American woman and a square-jawed Mexican man with a moustache: Susan and "Mike" Vargas. The camera moves to the left and downward, losing sight of the convertible for a moment, in order to follow them as they walk along the edge of the cross street, in front of an arcade. The convertible, having turned the corner, catches up, passes them in the foreground, and disappears off to the left, the camera keeping pace with Susan and Vargas as they make their way along the increasingly crowded street. They catch up with the convertible, stalled by some trouble on the road, the driver angrily trying to see ahead. He is middleaged and balding, she is a flashy blond: Rudy Linnekar, an American contractor, and Zita, a stripper in a joint on the Mexican side of the border. Vargas smiles and points: he and Susan pass the herd of goats that was causing the trouble. As they cross the street diagonally, we can again see the convertible, now some distance behind them. Increasing confusion of cars, pedestrians, a pushcart, crossing in front of and behind them. As they approach the border, the camera draws up and back so that, as Susan and Vargas pass to the right of the brightly lit Mexican customs booth, we can see, an instant later, the convertible passing it on the left. The camera stays with the convertible, momentarily losing sight of Susan and Vargas; but then they appear on the extreme right, walking alongside the convertible toward the customs booth on the American side of the border.

CUSTOMS OFFICER (*off camera in right foreground*): Uh, you folks American citizens?

As they approach the booth, the camera moves back down so they are in MS, *the convertible stopped on the left, Vargas and Susan on the right, with the customs officer at the extreme right edge of the frame. Two service men in* CU *briefly cross the frame, right to left, in the extreme foreground.*

SUSAN (*coming forward*): I am, yes.

CUSTOMS OFFICER: Where were you born, Miss?

SUSAN: Mrs.

CUSTOMS OFFICER: What?

SUSAN: Philadelphia.

VARGAS (*gesturing to his passport*): The name is Vargas.

CUSTOMS OFFICER (*calling to another officer standing behind the car with a clipboard*): Hey, Jim, see who's here?

JIM: Sure! Mr. Vargas. Hot on the trail of another dope ring?

VARGAS: Hot on the trail of a chocolate soda for my wife.

CUSTOMS OFFICER (*surprised, leaning forward over his desk*): Your wife?

SUSAN (*turning back as Vargas leads her off the left foreground*): Barely a bride, officer.

LINNEKAR (*he has been fuming impatiently in his car*): Hey, can I get through?

The camera pans to the left so that we see Susan and Vargas on the other side of the car: the customs officers continue to chat over the heads of Linnekar and Zita.

JIM: Lot of talk up here about how you cracked that Grandi business.

LINNEKAR (*over*): What?

CUSTOMS OFFICER: I heard you caught the big boss.

VARGAS: Only one of them. The Grandis are a big family. (*Moving off into the background with Susan.*) Good night.

JIM: Good night. (*Turning back to the car, with his clipboard.*) No purchases, Mr. Linnekar?

ZITA (*turning around anxiously to Linnekar*): Hey . . . hey, I've got this . . .

CUSTOMS OFFICER: You an American citizen, Miss?

ZITA (*ignoring the question*): No . . . I've got this ticking noise . . .

CUSTOMS OFFICER (*ignoring her, patting Linnekar's shoulder*): Yeah, okay.

ZITA: No, really, this . . .

CUSTOMS OFFICER: Good night.

ZITA: . . . ticking noise in my head!

The car drives off toward the left foreground. Through a disorienting maze of traffic and pedestrians, we see Susan and Vargas emerge from an arcade in the background, walking from right to left. The camera moves diagonally toward them until they are in MS at the right of the screen.

SUSAN: Mike, do you realize it's the very first time we've been together in my country?

The camera is stationary as they pause.

VARGAS (*embracing her*): Do you realize I haven't kissed you in over an hour?

As they kiss, the sound of an explosion off camera: they both look up, startled.

2. LS *of the explosion: brilliant flame in the night air. The camera zooms in slightly for emphasis.*

3. *Low angle* MLS: *Vargas and Susan springing forward, the brightly lit arcade in the background. The handheld camera, tilting erratically, moves back to keep pace. Soon many figures are rushing toward the scene of the explosion, first laterally, then increasingly into the camera. Shouts in Spanish: What happened? I don't know! Garish, flickering light: on the right, the basin of a decorative fountain is full of flame; further on, the upended wreck of the convertible burns on the left.*

SUSAN (*shouting, as they run*): Mike, what happened?

VARGAS: That car that just passed us exploded!

SUSAN: The car? How could it do that?

VARGAS: I don't know. I'll have to try to find out. (*Pausing, turning to her and patting her arm, the burning fountain on the right.*) You'd better not come any closer. There's . . . We'll have to postpone that soda, I'm afraid. (*Walks forward toward upended car on left.*)

SUSAN (*following*): Mike, couldn't I . . . ?

VARGAS (*turning back toward her*): Susie, please be careful!

He edges her off the right of the frame. Two fire trucks, sirens screaming, followed by a police car, come hurtling toward the camera on the left. The first truck passes off in the left foreground; the other turns to pause in the foreground, facing right.

4. MS: *Vargas with Susan, fire truck and bustle behind.*

VARGAS: This is going to be very bad for us.

SUSAN: For us?

VARGAS: For Mexico, I mean. Anyway, there's nothing I can do over here.

SUSAN: So?

VARGAS: So I'll try not to be too long. (*Raises her hands to his mouth and kisses them, dismissively.*) Go on, darling . . . (*edging her off toward the right*).

5. LS: *Vargas and Susan on right, fire truck driving up on left.*

VARGAS (*shouting over the confusion*): . . . you wait at the hotel.

They both leave the frame on the right, but the camera picks them up again as the truck swings around to park, its bumper and headlight in extreme low angle CU *in the left foreground. In the right background, burning wreckage. We see Susan emerge from behind the truck and, silhouetted in front of the flames, walk off to the right (her high heels giving her a hard time).*

6. *Vargas emerges from behind the silhouetted wreck in the right foreground, passing from right to left in front of the flames until he is in* MS. *The back of a head enters the frame from the foreground.*

    VARGAS: Blaine! (*Shaking his hand.*) I thought you were back in Washington.

    BLAINE: I leave tomorrow.

    The two men are in MS, *facing camera, flames behind. A curly-haired bespectacled man approaches from the left rear and passes for a moment between them.*

    BLAINE: You know Schwartz from the local DA's office?

    VARGAS: How do you do sir.

    SCHWARTZ (*distracted*): Hi. (*He passes between them, off in right foreground.*)

    VARGAS: Can you tell me who's in charge here?

    BLAINE: I can't even tell you what happened. Why aren't you back in Mexico City? (*They turn and walk away from the camera.*) Isn't that dope trial coming up?

7. MS, *moderately low angle: Blaine and Vargas walking toward camera.*

    VARGAS: Grandi's? (*They pause.*) Yes, Thursday. I hoped to go back in the morning plane. But now . . .

    BLAINE: You mean this business?

    VARGAS: I'm afraid so.

    BLAINE: That bomb came from the Mexican side of the border.

    As the conversation becomes edgy, blurred figures pass by in the foreground, moving from right to left.

    VARGAS (*after a pause, turning to him*): Car did.

    BLAINE (*turning away*): Bomb.

8. MS: *the camera follows Susan as she makes her way with difficulty through the crowds in Los Robles, crossing the street and moving from left to right, against the traffic, dodging cars. Loud Latin music. She passes behind Pancho, at first seen only as a black leather midsection lounging against a*

pillar of the arcade in the left foreground. Then the camera swings up and back to reveal him in MS, *staring after Susan: conventional leather-jacketed "hood," impassive Latin face. He draws on his cigarette, discards it, and strides forward after Susan.*

9. LS: *Pancho follows Susan. As she steps out of the arcade into traffic, he pulls her back from in front of a truck that looms up suddenly in the right foreground. She shakes herself loose and begins to cross again, determinedly swinging her white sweater over her shoulder. He follows and speaks to her in Spanish, taking a letter from his pocket. They are now in low angle* MS. *A crowd begins to gather.*

MEXICAN MAN (*half-entering frame from right foreground*): Lady, he says you don't understand what he wants.

SUSAN: I understand very well what he wants! (*She strides off the left foreground.*)

SECOND MEXICAN MAN (*left foreground, turning to look after her*): He save your life, lady.

10. *Low angle* MS: *Susan facing camera.*

SUSAN: Tell him I'm a married woman!

(*Pancho enters the frame from the foreground, stands leering over her on the left.*)

SUSAN: And my husband is a great big official in the government . . . (*A second man joins them on the right.*) . . . ready and willing to knock out all those pretty front teeth of his.

As she turns to walk away, back to camera, a third man enters from the foreground.

THIRD MAN: That's it, lady. Your husband.

SECOND MAN: That's what he wants to talk to you about.

Pancho goes to her, the camera following to a MS *of Susan and Pancho with the two men looking on from either side. Pancho speaks to her in Spanish and gives her a letter.*

SUSAN (*reading, as the man on the left peers over her shoulder*): "Follow this boy at once. There's something very important for Mr. Vargas." (*Looking up, resolutely.*) Well, what have I got to lose? (*To man on left, who grins and shrugs.*) Don't answer that! (*Resolute again.*) Lead on, Pancho!

He replies in Spanish and leaves in the left foreground.

SUSAN (*quizzically*): Across the border again?

She shrugs and follows off left foreground, followed in a moment by the other two men.

11. *Moderately high angle* MS *of street at scene of explosion. Police are clearing the way for a limousine that arrives, lights into camera, horn honking, followed by a police car.*

12. MS *of crowd, including a uniformed policeman, Vargas (who crosses and leaves frame on right), the coroner, and Menzies, a boyish-acting, middle-aged police sergeant.*

    MENZIES (*excited, pointing to right*): Hey, doc, here comes the DA!

13. MLS: *Schwartz, entering from foreground, trots back to open the door of the limousine. District Attorney Adair emerges, an exaggeratedly courtly figure in evening dress. Schwartz takes his arm and the camera tracks back as they come forward to inspect the wreckage.*

    ADAIR: Where's Captain Quinlan?

    SCHWARTZ: I got him out of bed at his ranch. He's on his way.

    ADAIR: Old Hank must've been the only one in the county who didn't hear the explosion. (*Turning to the wrecked car on the left.*) Terrible thing, isn't it? (*Looking up.*) Has the daughter been told?

14. *Police Chief Gould rushes into a low angle* CU *on the left. On the right, in the background, the horizontal stream of a firehose plays on the burning fountain.*

    GOULD: They're bringing her over right now . . .

    MENZIES (*dashing abruptly across the frame in low angle* CU, *in right, out left*): That's right!

    GOULD: . . . to identify her father's body.

15. LS: *Marcia Linnekar arrives, accompanied by two uniformed policemen, from behind silhouette of wreckage on right: smoke and steam billowing in the background.*

16. *Low angle* MS: *Facing the camera, the coroner stoops over Linnekar's body (not visible), as several others, standing behind him, look on.*

    ADAIR (*appearing from behind, sententiously*): An hour ago Rudy Linnekar had this town in his pocket.

    CORONER (*standing, raspy cynical voice*): Huh! Now you can strain him through a sieve. (*Tosses his cigarette down toward the corpse.*)

17. *Marcia Linnekar, accompanied by police, walks directly toward camera into* MS: *dark-haired, evidently rich and well-bred.*

MARCIA (*staring down*): I guess that's my father.

MENZIES (*approaching from behind, on the right*): Now Miss Linnekar, can you identify the roommate?

MARCIA (*turning away, then back, bitterly*): I'm not acquainted with my father's girl friends. (*Turns away from camera to leave.*)

MENZIES: Okay, Miss Linnekar.

18. LS *of steaming wreckage. Camera moves right to show a car careening around from behind it and moving toward us and off in the left foreground.*

19. CU: *Adair, Schwartz, with plainclothes policeman in the center behind.*

ADAIR: Well, here comes Hank at last. Vargas, you've heard of Hank Quinlan, our . . .

20. *Low angle* MCU: *Vargas.*

ADAIR (*off*): . . . local police celebrity.

VARGAS: I'd like to meet him.

21. CU: *coroner, with uniformed policeman, other figures, in background.*

CORONER: That's what you think!

22. *Very low angle* MS *of Quinlan slowly thrusting open the car door: a grossly corpulent figure in an overcoat, a huge cigar in the middle of his puffy face. The camera rises as he gets to his feet and lurches into* MCU. *Menzies enters from right foreground, stands to the left of Quinlan.*

QUINLAN (*without preliminaries*): Did they, uh, toss it in, or was it planted ahead . . .

23. *Brief* LS *of wreckage.*

QUINLAN (*off*): . . . of time?

24. MCU: *Menzies and Quinlan, as at conclusion of 22.*

MENZIES: Who?

QUINLAN: Whoever did it, you jackass!

25. MS: *Quinlan with back to camera, Chief Gould on left.*

GOULD: You figure it was a bomb then, Hank?

QUINLAN: Well, Chief . . . Rudy Linnekar *could* of been struck by lightning. (*The camera follows as Gould crosses right, revealing Menzies, back to camera, beside Quinlan.*) Where's the daughter?

26. *Low angle* MCU: *Gould, Menzies (behind, in center), Quinlan.*

MENZIES (*grinning eagerly*): Marcia? Got her right here, waiting for you, Hank!

QUINLAN: Let her go.

GOULD: You don't even want to question the daughter?

QUINLAN: Let her go and put a tail on her.
27. CU: *Adair, plainclothes policeman, Schwartz, as in 19.*
　　QUINLAN (*off*): Let's see if there was some jane that . . . (*Adair moves forward.*)
28. MS: *Adair to Gould and Quinlan, entering from left foreground.*
　　QUINLAN: . . . Rudy Linnekar . . .
　　ADAIR (*over*): Oh, some stripteaser . . .
　　QUINLAN: Well, what do you know, the DA! In a monkey suit!
　　ADAIR: Well . . .
　　QUINLAN (*to Gould, on the left*): You too. You got one of them suits.
　　ADAIR: We were all at the banquet.
　　QUINLAN: A political rally?
　　ADAIR (*jovial*): No, Tootsie's Steak House!
　　QUINLAN: G Men . . . T Men . . . Quite a little tea party, all for Rudy Linnekar's . . .
29. *Low angle* MCU: *Vargas approaching. In the background, a billboard: "Welcome Stranger! to picturesque Los Robles the Paris of the Border."*

QUINLAN (*off*): . . . bonfire. Yeah, I hear you even invited . . .
Vargas leaves the frame in the right foreground.

30. MS: *Gould, Quinlan (in center, slightly back, dominating the pyramid), Adair, as at conclusion of 28.*

QUINLAN: . . . some kind of a Mexican.

31. *Low angle* MCU: *Vargas, turning to face them.*

ADAIR (*off*): Oh, I . . .

32. MS: *Gould, Quinlan, Adair, as in 30.*

ADAIR: . . . don't think Mr. Vargas claims any jurisdiction.

QUINLAN (*as we hear a siren in the background*): I should hope not. Two people, Americans, are blown to ash with dynamite, practically in my own . . . police station . . .

VARGAS (*off*): I wonder . . .

33. *Low angle* MCU: *Vargas, as in 31.*

VARGAS: . . . what makes you so very sure it was dynamite?

34. MS: *Gould, Quinlan, Adair, still as in 30.*

QUINLAN: My leg.

35. *Low angle* MCU: *Vargas, as in 31.*

VARGAS: Your what?

MENZIES (*off*): His game leg.

36. CU: *Menzies, with Schwartz on extreme right, police car with blinking light in background.*

MENZIES (*beaming, to Schwartz*): Sometimes he gets a kind of twinge, like folks do for a change of weather. (*Turning into camera to face Quinlan.*) "Intuition," he . . .

37. CU *of Quinlan, smiling complacently.*

MENZIES (*off*): . . . calls it.

SCHWARTZ (*off*): Vargas has a theory that the murder itself . . .

38. *Low angle* MCU: *Vargas, as in 31.*

SCHWARTZ (*off*): . . . was committed . . .

39. CU: *Menzies, Schwartz, as in 36.*

SCHWARTZ: . . . outside of our jurisdiction.

40. MS: *Gould, Quinlan, Adair, as in 30.*

GOULD: Of course, we're all of us going to cooperate . . .

VARGAS (*off, overlapping*): Don't worry, captain . . .

41. *Low angle* MCU: *Vargas, as in 31.*

GOULD: . . . with Mr. Vargas here.

VARGAS: . . . I'm merely what the United Nations would call an observer.

42. MS: *Gould, Quinlan, Adair, as in 30.*

QUINLAN: You don't talk like one, I'll say that for you. A Mexican, I mean.

VARGAS (*off*): Captain, . . .

43. *Low angle* MCU: *Vargas, as in 31.*

VARGAS: . . . you won't have any trouble with me.

44. CU: *Quinlan, as in 37.*

QUINLAN: Your bet your sweet life I . . .

45. *Low angle* MCU: *Vargas, as in 31. He smiles edgily.*

QUINLAN (*off*): . . . won't!

46. CU *of Quinlan, as in 37: Quinlan stares Vargas down.*

47. LS: *a deserted street in Los Robles, stretching back, with its illuminated arcades, into deep perspective. Raucous jazz, partly "street sounds," partly "score." The camera follows Susan as, running to keep up, she follows Pancho diagonally (right to left) across the street toward the brightly lit Hotel Ritz. As they get to the entrance, a silhouetted figure runs in from the left foreground and stops them.*

GANG MEMBER (*pointing to the right*): Hey lady, look at the pretty baby! *As Susan turns, Pancho puts his arm around her shoulder.*

48. MS: *a Mexican woman holds up a baby ("Figlia mia") as another gang member ("Sal") darts behind her to photograph Susan. Exploding light bulb.*

49. MS: *Susan and Pancho turn to enter the hotel, Pancho dismissing the first gang member with a nod. The camera pans to the left to observe them, through the hotel's plate glass window, as they enter the lobby.*

50. MS *inside hotel. Pancho and Susan enter from the left. Pancho speaks in Spanish to Uncle Joe Grandi, who steps forward from the right background, where he has evidently been peering out through the curtains on the door.*

51. *Low angle* MS *of Grandi: a seedily dapper little man with greasy hair and a pencil moustache.*

GRANDI (*hands prissily on his hips*): My nephew says you call him Pancho. (*Stepping forward, threateningly.*) Why?

52. MS: *Pancho, Susan, Grandi.*

GRANDI: Why you call him Pancho? (*He paces between Pancho and Susan to the foreground center, staring in* CU *into camera: for the moment Pancho is no longer in the frame.*)

SUSAN (*over his shoulder on the left*): Just for laughs, I guess. This note (*extending it*) says you have something for my husband.

Grandi turns and paces back between Susan and Pancho, adjusting the collar of his shirt. He waves away Sal, the photographer, who looks in from the sidewalk through the hotel's window.

GRANDI: Yeah! So you're Vargas, eh? You know who I am?

The camera follows him to the right.

53. *We see Grandi's reflection in the mirror on the wall, adjusting his string tie, before his back and shoulders enter the frame in the left foreground. Susan also appears in the mirror, as does Pancho, lounging in the background.*

SUSAN (*in the mirror*): You want me to guess?

GRANDI: My name is Grandi.

54. MCU: *Susan.*

SUSAN (*surprised*): Oh!

55. MCU: *Grandi at the mirror, as in 53.*

GRANDI: You've heard that name before, hm?

SUSAN (*in mirror*): Aside from the case my husband's been working on, isn't Grandi what that night club is called?

GRANDI (*smoothing his eyebrows*): Yeah. (*He turns around and the camera follows as he paces past Susan to Pancho, who still lounges against the wall.*) Yes! Grandi's Rancho Grande. (*To Pancho.*) My gun! (*He hands it to him.*) Kind of a joke. (*He examines the gun, flipping out its cylinder with what is evidently intended to be sinister emphasis.*)

56. MS: *Grandi in left foreground, turned away from camera; Susan right, facing front. The gun is brandished in front of her white sweater.*

GRANDI (*sinister*): Get it?

SUSAN (*bravely*): I can't say it's the funniest thing I ever heard.

GRANDI (*crossing back to the mirror on the wall behind Susan, the gun stuffed in the waist of his trousers*): The name ain't Mexican. I got a permit for this thing.

57. MCU: *Grandi at mirror, as in 55.*

GRANDI: The Grandi family's living here in Los Robles a long time.

(*Attaching cuffs to his shirt sleeves.*) Some of us in Mexico, some of us on this side. (*He puts a huge cigar in his mouth.*)

SUSAN (*in mirror*): Must be convenient for business.

GRANDI: Yeah? (*He turns to the left to face her, cigar protruding aggressively. The mirror reflecting Susan and Grandi's back is still visible over his shoulder on the right.*) What business?

SUSAN (*in mirror still*): Grandi business!

GRANDI: Yeah?

SUSAN (*in mirror*): Yeah!

GRANDI: Yeah?!

SUSAN (*in mirror*): Yeah, yeah, yeah!!

The camera pans to reveal both of them CU, *his cigar almost in her face.*

SUSAN: You know what's wrong with you, Mr. Grandi? You've been seeing too many gangster movies.

He lunges with his cigar, she swats it aside.

SUSAN: Mike may be spoiling some of your fun . . .

GRANDI (*over*): Mike?

SUSAN: My husband. (*Sarcastic.*) Yeah! And if you're trying to scare me into calling him off . . . (*Grandi turns away sulkily.*) Let me tell you something (*shaking finger*), Mr. Grandi. (*Drawing a breath as Grandi turns back.*) I may be scared, but he won't be.

58. MS: *Pancho, impassive in black leather, lounges against wall.*

GRANDI (*off*): Who wants to make trouble?

SUSAN (*off*): Trouble? As a matter of . . .

59. MS: *Pancho in background, Grandi in mid range, facing camera, Susan in right foreground, turned 3/4 away from camera.*

SUSAN: . . . fact, my husband's looking for me, just about now, and that's *bound* to mean trouble.

Pancho smirks, laughs; Grandi turns toward him.

SUSAN: What's so funny about that?

Pancho speaks in Spanish to Grandi.

GRANDI: Ah? (*Turning back to Susan.*) He wants to know if your husband . . . husband is jealous, signora.

60. MCU: *Susan into camera, back of Grandi's head in left foreground.*

SUSAN: You silly little pig!

Grandi turns into profile, blinking incredulously, then back to her.

GRANDI: Who are you talking about?

SUSAN (*quietly*): I'm talking about you, you ridiculous . . .

61. *Moderately low angle* MCU: *Pancho and Grandi, deep shadows.*

SUSAN (*off*): . . . old-fashioned, jug-eared, lop-sided Little Caesar.

GRANDI (*slowly, threatening*): I didn't get that, signora. You'll have to talk slow.

SUSAN: I'm . . .

62. MCU: *Susan, as in 60.*

SUSAN: . . . talking slow, but in a minute I'll start to yell.

63. MS: *Pancho, Grandi, Susan, as in 59.*

GRANDI (*sinister*): I wouldn't do that, signora. (*Stares at her, then elaborately shrugs and grins, turning away and leaving the frame in the left foreground.*)

64. MCU: *mirror on right, in which we see Susan with Grandi striding forward; then Grandi himself enters frame from left foreground.*

GRANDI: Just a little while ago, this was a quiet, peaceful town here! (*Turning back to left, cigar thrust angrily in his mouth.*) And now this Vargas comes along! (*He charges off left foreground.*)

SUSAN (*in mirror*): Mr. Grandi!

65. *Low angle* MS: *Pancho, Grandi.*

SUSAN (*off*): Mr. Grandi, you said you had something for my husband. Don't you think it's . . .

66. MCU: *Susan faces camera on right, Grandi turned toward her in profile in left foreground, as in 60, though differently framed.*

SUSAN: . . . time you gave it to me?

GRANDI: I think it's time for him to lay off my brother in Mexico City! That's advice!

67. *Low angle* MS, *Pancho, Grandi, as in 65.*

GRANDI (*throwing down cigar butt*): That's what I got for him!

68. MCU: *Grandi, Susan, as in 66. Grandi turns furiously from Susan and leaves frame in left foreground. She looks apprehensive.*

69. MS: *Grandi in left foreground, brushing off his jacket; Susan facing camera on right.*

SUSAN: Then the conference is over? (*Grandi puts on his jacket.*) I'm free to leave?

70. *Low angle* MS: *Grandi on left, Pancho on right, reversing 67.*

GRANDI (*jacket half on, oily*): Free? Nobody was holding you or keeping you, Mrs. Vargas. (*Pulling jacket on with emphasis and moving toward camera.*) Nobody laid a hand on you.

71. MS: *Susan.*

GRANDI (*off*): You were just paying us a little visit.

The camera moves back with Susan as she edges to door, unfastens latch and begins to back out.

SUSAN: Well . . . goodbye all . . .

72. *Extreme low angle* MCU: *Grandi, Pancho. Grandi licks his lips in menacing way. Blare of jazz from outside as door is opened.*

73. MS: *Susan at the door. She backs out and closes it in front of her.*

74. MS: *the camera tracking with Susan as she emerges from the hotel. The gang members involved in taking the photograph are waiting for her. One leans against a pillar of the arcade in the left foreground; the other is behind Susan, further down the arcade. Both begin to follow as Susan*

looks back apprehensively and Pancho watches through the hotel's plate glass window.

75. LS: *another street in Los Robles. Quinlan lumbers across the street and through arcades, with Menzies and Adair trailing behind. The camera follows them, and in the course of the shot they move into* MS.
ADAIR: Quinlan, we just can't cross over into Mexico like this!
QUINLAN: Thousands do, every day.
ADAIR: Tourists, but . . .
QUINLAN: So, we're tourists.
MENZIES: Captain Quinlan wants to check on the girl that was with Linnekar in the death car.
ADAIR: I know. She was one of the stripteasers. I think I told you.
By now they have turned down another street and are walking away from the camera.
QUINLAN: Naw. Pete told me, before I left the ranch.
MENZIES: That's right!
QUINLAN: And I told him that I wanted to see all the stripteasers in the joint.
He goes on ahead in the center, while the other two pause in the foreground.
ADAIR: This is Mexican territory. What can we do?
Turning back toward the camera, they are joined by Schwartz and Blaine on the left.
MENZIES: There's no law against visitors asking questions is there, Mr. Vargas?
But Vargas is not there. Facing the camera, all four look around for him.
MENZIES: Hey, where'd he go?
76. MLS: *Susan in left foreground rushes into Vargas's hotel. Through the plate glass door we see him waiting inside.*
VARGAS (*striding forward*): Susie, where in the world . . .
77. MCU: *Vargas and Susan, inside hotel, half-embracing.*
VARGAS: . . . were you?
SUSAN: Oh, Mike darling!
VARGAS: What happened?
SUSAN: Just wait till I tell you. The craziest thing . . .
He hustles her off camera in left foreground. Through the glass door behind, the four men in the street can be seen watching curiously.

78. MS *in street: Blaine, Schwartz, Menzies, Adair, as at end of 75.*
   QUINLAN (*approaching from behind*): Who's the jane?
   ADAIR: His wife.
   QUINLAN: Well, whatta you know! She don't look Mexican either.
   He turns back and leads the others away from the camera, toward the strip joint.
79. MS: *Vargas and Susan, facing each other, in front of blank interior wall of the hotel lobby. Stationary camera.*[1]
   SUSAN (*shrugging*): That's all I remember, Mike. He said his name was Grandi, I remember that.
   VARGAS: Well, this "kid" . . . who *was* he?
   SUSAN: I don't know. And I don't want to know. All I want to do is to get out of here.
   VARGAS (*gripping her*): Look Susie, I'll get you out of here. Right away. But I . . . I can't just walk away from all this. I've got some questions of my own to get answered too, you know.
   SUSAN: Of course. (*Folding her arms.*) Even on his honeymoon the chairman of the Pan American Narcotics Commission has . . .
   VARGAS (*over*): Susie!
   SUSAN: . . . his sacred duty to perform!
   VARGAS: You know it's more than just a high sounding title. Now they're pushing my wife around!
   SUSAN: Can't we forget about that?

80. LS: *the arcade outside the hotel. A gang member (Risto) comes running down the arcade from the left and flattens himself against the wall beside the hotel's plate glass window. When Vargas emerges, Risto follows, the camera tracking back rapidly to show Vargas in LS, the boy in deep focus behind, running from pillar to pillar of the arcade. Finally Vargas passes out of the frame in the right foreground. "Cool" jazzy vibraphone music distantly heard from the strip joint.*
81. LS, *stationary camera: Risto emerges from the end of the arcade, hesitates a moment, and then turns into the street, running toward the camera.*
82. LS: *the camera travels back as Vargas crosses the empty street, moving toward the right foreground, Risto following in deep focus behind.*
83. *Moderately high angle* MLS: *Quinlan and the others approach the strip joint, moving from left foreground toward right background.*

QUINLAN: The key to this whole thing is the dynamite. The killer didn't
  just want Linnekar dead . . .
84. MLS: *the camera moves with Vargas as he strides along a wall toward the*
  right foreground, casting his shadow before him. We see Risto's shadow on
  the wall behind him before we see the boy himself, deep in the background.
  QUINLAN (*off*): . . . he wanted him destroyed. Annihilated.
  SCHWARTZ (*off, calling*): Over here, Vargas. We're going in the back way.
  Vargas moves into MS *as Risto's shadow passes him. He pauses at the*
  doorway of the strip joint with Menzies.
  RISTO (*off, whispering hoarsely*): Senor Vargas . . .
85. MCU: *Risto, wearing white gloves, carrying a vial of acid.*
  RISTO: Senor Vargas.
86. MLS: *the camera follows as Vargas turns and walks back, right to left,*
  across deserted lot, papers blowing in the wind. Vibraphone still playing.
87. MS: *Risto with vial. He looks frightened.*
88. MS: *Vargas pauses in front of a poster of Zita, the stripper.*
  VARGAS (*looking around*): Yes?
89. MS: *Risto throws the acid, lunging into camera.*
90. *Very brief* CU: *we see the vial, the acid streaming from it, then Risto's*
  white-gloved hand in motion, gripped by Vargas's two hands.
91. *Low angle* MS: *acid strikes the poster, scorching Zita's face. Struggling,*
  Vargas and Risto enter the frame from the left foreground.
92. *The shot begins with a* CU *of hands locked around a pillar of the arcade:*
  Vargas is trying to get a hold on the boy, they wheel around. Then Vargas
  pursues Risto into the background, the camera following at a moderately
  high angle as they weave between upended push carts in the vacant lot.
93. *Low angle* MS: *Menzies in front of the burnt poster, looking around,*
  puzzled.[2]

94. MLS: *inside the strip joint (Grandi's Rancho Grande). Throughout this shot*
  the camera moves briskly through deep space, filled with overlapping dia-
  logue, incomplete asides. A waiter in the foreground sets down a tray;
  behind him Quinlan is at the bar drinking milk and speaking to a show girl.
  GIRL: I hardly knew him.
  Quinlan grunts, sets down his glass, and walks back, camera following,
  past Adair and Blaine with three girls, and out of the frame in the right
  background.

QUINLAN (*as he leaves*): Adair, come on.

ADAIR (MS: *beaming at two girls seated at the bar*): Yes, yes . . . (*turning to a third girl on his right*) and I'm not finished with you yet. I was . . .

THIRD GIRL (*gathering up her wrap*): The show's over. I'm going home.

ADAIR: Oh, no, no . . .

Schwartz approaches Adair from the right foreground.

SCHWARTZ: Mr. Adair, as far as I can find out, most of these people didn't even know the murdered girl.

ADAIR (*over, waving him away impatiently*): I've got no time for that . . . I've got no time for that . . .

The camera follows Adair to the right. Quinlan, in MS, is at the foot of a stairway, down which the Madame of the joint is descending languidly, followed by musicians.

ADAIR (*bustling by*): I have no . . . I must talk to this young lady.

He scurries off in right background.

MADAME (MS: *to Quinlan*): Zita? I didn't know her. She only joined the show a few days ago.

QUINLAN (*turning toward camera, removing cigar so as to take a bite of his candy bar*): Aw . . . wasting our time around here. (*Moves out of frame in foreground.*)

ADAIR (*beaming to Madame*): Oh, I wouldn't say that! Well . . . (*tipping his hat*) good night, my dear.

95. LS: *outside the strip joint. Empty, rubbish-strewn lot in foreground. Quinlan emerges, with Schwartz and Blaine. We hear the sound of a pianola.*

BLAINE: What happened to Menzies and Vargas?

SCHWARTZ: I don't know.

ADAIR (*still in the doorway, to the girls*): He'll call . . .

BLAINE: He'll show up.

ADAIR: . . . there may be some more questions.

The camera stays with Quinlan, low angle MS, as he walks alone toward the sound, moving closer to the camera.

QUINLAN (*contemplatively*): Huh . . . pianola.

ADAIR (*coming up behind*): Hey, we go this way, you know.

QUINLAN (*ignoring him*): Huh. Tanya's still . . . open for business? (*Chewing his candy bar.*)

Quinlan moves off right foreground, as Adair and Blaine look on.

96. *Tilted MS of pianola, playing.*

97. LS *of empty lot, wind-blown papers. Framed by the bannister of Tanya's place, Quinlan enters in the distance, moving from left to right, followed by Adair, Schultz, and Blaine. The camera moves to meet him as he turns to climb up onto the porch, coming into a low angle* MS, *his face in shadow. He stands framed by the circular arch of the porch, eating his candy bar. A piece of paper blows up into the porch with him; an oil derrick is visible over his shoulder.³ As he goes off left, the camera moves down to a* LS *of Blaine, Adair, Schwartz looking on. Schwartz takes a couple of steps forward.*

*98. LS: *Blaine, Adair, Schwartz, closer than in 97. Blowing papers, pianola.*
   SCHWARTZ (*smiling, shaking his head*): I don't know what Quinlan thinks she's got to do with it.
   ADAIR (*smirking*): Tanya? Oh, maybe she'll cook chili for him. Or . . . bring out the crystal ball.

99. *Moderately high angle* MS, *over Quinlan's shoulder. He opens the door and goes in: brief glimpse of interior, a bull's head prominent on the wall.*

100. LS *from within Tanya's parlor. A table with chips and cards fills the foreground: the room is full of tacky clutter—old lamps, pictures, a toy chipmunk. Quinlan enters from outer room in right rear, stands framed for a moment in the parlor door, peering in, then turns back into the hall.*

101. MS: *camera follows Quinlan, back to camera, left foreground, as he walks toward the next room. Tanya, in gypsy costume, emerges in* LS *from a room at right rear. She comes forward into* MS *without saying anything.*

102. MCU: *Quinlan looks down at her, hemmed in by hanging lamp shades in foreground and background.*

103. CU: *Tanya, framed in doorway. She deliberately takes a drag on her cigarillo, exhales into camera.*
   tanya (*after a long pause*): We're closed. (*Turns and goes off right.*)

104. MCU: *Quinlan, as in 102. He looks after her, chewing candy bar.*

105. MS: *Quinlan, back to camera, in left foreground: another bite of candy bar. Tanya reenters, coming forward from the right rear, carrying a pot, and moves into* MS.
   quinlan: You've been cookin' at this hour?
   TANYA: Just cleanin' up.
   QUINLAN (*grunting*): Huh.

106. MCU: *Quinlan, as in 102.*
     QUINLAN: Have you forgotten your old friend?
107. MS: *Quinlan, Tanya, as in 105.*
     TANYA: I told you we were closed.
     QUINLAN: I'm Hank Quinlan.
     TANYA (*looking him up and down, flatly*): I didn't recognize you. . . .
        You should lay off those candy bars. (*Turns to go.*)
        (*Quinlan grunts.*)
108. MCU: *Quinlan, as in 102.*
     QUINLAN: Uhh . . . it's either the candy or the hooch.
109. MCU: *Tanya turns back to him.*
     QUINLAN (*off*): I must say, I wish it was your chili . . .
110. MCU: *Quinlan, as in 102.*
     QUINLAN: . . . I was getting fat on. (*Pauses.*) Anyway, you're sure
        looking good.
111. MCU: *Tanya, as in 109.*
     TANYA: You're a mess, honey.

QUINLAN: (*off*): Yeah. . . .

112.   MCU: *Quinlan, as in 102.*

QUINLAN: Yeah . . . that pianola sure brings back memories.

113.   MCU: *Tanya, as in 109.*

TANYA: The customers go for it. It's old, it's new. . . . We got the
television too. (*The camera pans with her as she paces to the right,
exhaling smoke. She remains in the same range, always frontal.*) We
run movies. What can I offer you?

114–   *Alternate* MCUs *of Quinlan as in 102 and Tanya as in 109. The dialogue*
119.   *does not overlap.*

QUINLAN: You haven't heard anything about that bomb, have you?

TANYA (*exhaling*): That happened on your side of the border.

QUINLAN: In a place like this you hear things.

TANYA: I heard the explosion.

QUINLAN: Yeah . . . Well, when this case is over, I must come around
some night and sample some of your chili.

TANYA: Better be careful. It may be too hot for you.

120.   MCU: *Quinlan, as before. He turns left with a grunted half assent and
begins to leave.*[4]

MENZIES (*off*): Hank . . .

*121.   MS: *Menzies, seen from behind, rushes in the front door of Tanya's place.*

MENZIES: . . . oh, Hank! Come out here!

*Quinlan limps forward, the bull's head prominent on the wall behind
him.*

QUINLAN (*surly*): What do you want?

MENZIES: Looks like our friend Vargas ran into some trouble.

QUINLAN (*going out door and off left foreground*): Yeah? What
kinda . . .

*122.   MS: *Tanya in doorway, looking after Quinlan.*

QUINLAN (*off*) . . . trouble? (*Further away.*) Where did this happen?

MENZIES (*off, distant*): In the alley, behind the nightclub.

QUINLAN (*off still*): Yeah?

*123.   *In the foreground, Menzies and Quinlan, seen from behind, are going
down the steps of Tanya's porch to join Blaine, Schwartz, Adair, and
Vargas, who are waiting below. The camera follows. Their voices
intricately overlap.*

ADAIR (*sputtering*): What . . . what . . . what . . .

QUINLAN (*over*): What happened to Vargas?

ADAIR: . . . happened? What was it, Al?

QUINLAN (*over*): Vargas!

*124. *Low angle* MS: *Blaine, Schwartz, Adair, Vargas.*

VARGAS: Nothing!

QUINLAN (*off*): Oh no?

ADAIR (*to Schwartz*): Al!

VARGAS (*deliberately*): Certainly nothing to do with the bombing affair.

QUINLAN (*off*): Oh yeah!

MENZIES (*who has joined the group, in rear center*): Somebody threw acid at Vargas.

VARGAS: It doesn't matter!

Quinlan enters, back to camera, from right foreground.

ADAIR: Now . . .

VARGAS: He missed me. (*He paces out of the frame in the right foreground.*)

ADAIR: . . . who was it, Al?

SCHWARTZ: I don't know . . . he got away.

ADAIR (*waving hands impatiently*): Oh . . . (*Goes out right foreground after Vargas.*)

QUINLAN: Uh . . . it was one of the Grandi kids.

VARGAS (*off*): What makes you so sure of that, captain?

QUINLAN: Intuition.

*125. *Low angle* MS: *Schwartz, Adair, Vargas.*

VARGAS (*incredulously*): Intuition?

QUINLAN (*entering from left foreground*): Uh . . . Vargas and his keystone cops seem to be giving the Grandi family . . .

*126. *Low angle* MS: *Quinlan in center, Menzies on left, Vargas facing them in right foreground.*

QUINLAN: . . . quite a few headaches . . .

VARGAS (*over*): Captain!

QUINLAN: . . . lately. (*To Vargas.*) Yes?

*127. MCU: *Quinlan in profile, left foreground, Vargas facing him on right, Adair between.*

VARGAS: Does your intuition also tell you about my wife?

ADAIR: Wife?!

VARGAS: She was accosted in the street a little while ago and led across to some . . . dive on your side of the border.

*128. *Low angle* MS: *Menzies, Quinlan, Vargas, as in 126.*

QUINLAN (*smirking*): Uh . . . the Vargas family seems to be gettin' into quite a *lot* of trouble tonight. (*Laughs, then suddenly sharp.*) Can you describe this man?

*129. MCU: *Quinlan, Adair, Vargas, as in 127.*

VARGAS: Well, the first one seems . . .

QUINLAN (*over*): Oh, the first one?

VARGAS: . . . to have been young and good-looking.

QUINLAN (*over*): Then, there were two men?

VARGAS: Not exactly.

*130. *Low angle* MS: *Quinlan in center, Menzies behind on left.*

QUINLAN (*muttering*): Not exactly. . . . You say she was taken to this dive by force?

*131. MCU: *Quinlan, Adair, Vargas, as in 127.*

VARGAS: Not by force, no.

QUINLAN (*knowingly*): Oh . . .

VARGAS: One of the Grandi's was there waiting—short, fat . . .

*132. *Low angle* MS: *Quinlan and Menzies, as in 130.*

VARGAS (*off*): . . . with a moustache.

QUINLAN (*over, to Menzies*): Uncle Joe.

VARGAS: . . . That's Susan's description . . .

*133. MCU: *Vargas.*

VARGAS: . . . I haven't run into him, I . . . (*abruptly responding to Quinlan's aside*) What?

*134. *Low angle* MS: *Quinlan and Menzies, as in 130.*

QUINLAN: They call him Uncle Joe . . . Grandi.

MENZIES (*over his shoulder*): That's right!

*135. MCU: *Quinlan, Adair, Vargas, as in 127.*

QUINLAN (*peremptory*): Go on!

VARGAS (*flustered*): What? . . . What do you mean, go on? I've told you what happened. Aren't you going to do something about it?

*136. MS: *Menzies and Quinlan on left, Vargas, back to camera, in right foreground.*

QUINLAN (*grinning*): If you're making a charge, I've got to ask the complaint. Or isn't that police procedure in Mexico?

*137. MCU: *Vargas in center, Quinlan, back to camera, in left foreground.*
 VARGAS: Procedure!
 QUINLAN: You say your wife was attacked.
 VARGAS: I did not say she was attacked!
 QUINLAN (*over*): Did you say she was . . .
*138. *Low angle* MS: *Quinlan and Menzies, as in 130.*
 QUINLAN: . . . molested?
 VARGAS (*off*): Not physically molested, no.
 QUINLAN: Was obscene . . .
*139. MCU: *Quinlan, Adair, Vargas, as in 127.*
 QUINLAN: . . . language used?
 VARGAS: I don't think so.
 (*Adair, between them, begins to look concerned.*)
 QUINLAN (*over*): How do you explain the fact that your wife allowed
  herself to be picked up by this . . .
 VARGAS (*over*): She was not picked up!
 QUINLAN: . . . good-looking . . .
 ADAIR (*breaking in, placating*): Now, Hank, I think . . .
 QUINLAN (*responding to Vargas's protest*): Oh?
 ADAIR: . . . we're getting off on the wrong tack here . . .
 QUINLAN: Then this good-looking man *was* a friend of hers?
 VARGAS: Obviously not!
*140. MS: *Menzies, Quinlan, Vargas, as in 136.*
 QUINLAN (*breaking into laughter, turning to Menzies*): You wouldn't call
  that gettin' picked up in the streets!
 ADAIR (*off, over*): Now, now, now, we mustn't forget, must we . . .
*141. MCU: *Quinlan, Adair, Vargas, as in 127.*
 ADAIR: . . . that Mr. Vargas is not on the witness stand?
 QUINLAN: Uhhh . . .
 ADAIR (*nervous laugh*): Hank's a born lawyer, you know.
 QUINLAN (*emphatically*): Lawyer! I'm no lawyer. All a lawyer cares
  about is the law!
 VARGAS: Captain! You *are* a policeman, aren't you?
*142. *Low angle* MS: *Quinlan, Menzies, as in 130.*
 QUINLAN: Mmm . . . Aren't *you?* You don't seem to be very fond of
  the job.
 VARGAS (*off*): There . . .

*143.   MCU: *Vargas faces camera in center, Quinlan in left foreground faces him.*
VARGAS: . . . are plenty of soldiers who don't like war.

*144.   *Low angle* MS: *Quinlan, Menzies, as in 130.*
QUINLAN: Hmmm . . .
VARGAS (*off*): It's a dirty job . . .

*145.   MCU: *Vargas, Quinlan, as in 143*
VARGAS: . . . enforcing the law, but it's what we're supposed to be doing, isn't it?

*146.   *Low angle* MS: *Quinlan, Menzies, as in 130.*
QUINLAN: I don't know about you. But when a murderer's loose, I'm supposed to catch him.

*147.   MCU: *Vargas. Sinister chord on soundtrack.*

*148.   *Low angle* MS: *Quinlan, Menzies, as in 130.*
QUINLAN (*withering look at Vargas*): Well, Pete . . . let's get back to civilization. (*Turning away.*)

*149.   MS: *Adair and Vargas. Adair looks up at Vargas sheepishly, then goes off left. Vargas looks after Quinlan.*

*150.   LS: *Menzies and Quinlan walking away over muddy field, derricks in background. Quinlan turns to look back, glowering, over his shoulder.*

*151.   MS: *Vargas, as at conclusion of 149. Hands in pockets, deliberately calm, he half turns to leave.*
MENZIES (*off*): Let's go, Hank, it's . . .

*152.   LS: *Menzies, Quinlan, as in 150.*
MENZIES: . . . almost dawn. You gotta get some rest.
QUINLAN (*still looking back at Vargas*): Not a chance of that, partner. (*Blowing papers: we hear them on the soundtrack, together with the sound of the wind. Derrick pumping behind.*) We got a big day ahead of us! (*He turns to catch up with Menzies.*)

*153.   LS: *shadows of Quinlan, walking with cane, and of Menzies pass by on the corrugated wall of a shed, moving from left to right. The camera pans right to reveal Vargas standing just beyond the shed, many tall oil derricks silhouetted behind him against the sky. He slowly takes a few paces back, then turns to leave, off left behind the shed.*

154.   *Dissolve to a high angle* LS *of a deserted street in Los Robles. Sinister chord. Vargas crosses the street from right background: as he approaches,*

the camera moves up the building in the left foreground and over to an open window. A shadowy figure (we later see it is Pancho) stands in it with a flashlight shining. Tense bongo theme.

155. MLS: *Susan, seen through the window of her hotel, is putting on a sweater. In the darkened room, only her head and shoulders, spotlit by the flashlight beam, are clearly visible. The camera pans quickly back to the window with the flashlight.*

156. MS *inside the room. The beam of the flashlight plays on the wall, then picks up Susan, still struggling with her sweater. Annoyed, she strides forward.*

157. *In profile at right foreground, Susan looks out her window, across the empty street, to the man with the flashlight opposite. Then she turns back into the room.*

158. MLS *in the room. Susan comes back from the window, screws a light bulb into the ceiling fixture, returns to the window. The bag she has been packing is on the bed in the right foreground.*

159. MS *over Susan's shoulder, at left of frame now, as she leans out window.*
    SUSAN (*shouting*): See any better this way? (*Turns back into room.*)

160. MLS, *as in 158: Susan goes angrily to wardrobe at left and takes out her jacket.*

161. LS: *Pancho in the window, still with flashlight.*

162. LS *from outside Susan's hotel. She comes to window, leans out, light in her face.*
    SUSAN: You can turn it off now, buster. You're wasting your batteries.

163. MS *in room. Susan, walking away from window, resumes packing, sighs, then reaches up to unscrew the light bulb in the ceiling fixture.*

164. LS: *Pancho in his window, as in 161. He switches off the flashlight.*

165. CU: *Susan unscrews the bulb, plunging the room into darkness. Then the camera turns to let us see her, MS, silhouetted against the window. She throws the bulb toward the room opposite.*

166. *As we hear bulb explode, cut to MS of Vargas, entering Susan's room from door on the left, silhouetted against light from the hallway.*
    VARGAS (*coming forward*): Susie . . . What are you doing here in the dark?

167. MS: *Susan by the window, as at end of 165.*
    SUSAN (*coming forward, still silhouetted*): There isn't any shade on the window.

168. MCU: *Vargas.*
     VARGAS: Well, can we turn the light on now?
     SUSAN (*off*): No, we can't.
     VARGAS: Why not?
169. MS: *Susan.*
     SUSAN (*lifting bag off bed*): Because there isn't any bulb any more.
170. MCU: *Vargas, as in 168. Susan sweeps by behind him and out the door
     as he continues to look puzzled.*
     VARGAS: Susie . . . (*Turns to follow her out, closing the door behind
        him.*)

171. LS: *Pancho, leaning out of his window, calls down to the street.*
     PANCHO: Risto!
     *Explosive percussion on soundtrack. The camera pans quickly to very
     high angle* LS *of Risto on street below.*
     PANCHO (*off*): Risto!
172. *Very low angle* LS *of Pancho calling from window. Risto in right foreground
     looks up, then glances back uneasily over his shoulder.*
     PANCHO: Wait there. Uncle Joe is plenty mad. He wants to talk to you.
     Risto turns to rush off in right foreground.
173. *Low angle, tilted, extreme* LS *of street, arcades. Risto races toward
     camera from deep in the background.*
     PANCHO: Risto! Risto! Come back here!
174. LS: *an illuminated phone booth in the street. Uncle Joe Grandi hangs up
     the receiver and turns out the light just as Risto rushes by in front of
     the booth. Grandi chases him into deep space to the right, the camera
     following.*
     GRANDI: Sal, grab him!
175. LS: *Sal (the photographer at the Hotel Ritz) rushes forward on the right.*
     GRANDI (*off*): Stop him!
176. LS: *the camera follows as Grandi runs from left to right.*
     GRANDI: Grab him, Sal! (*He approaches Risto, backed against a wall.*)
        Who told you to throw acid at Vargas?
     Risto darts off in the opposite direction as Sal races forward in pursuit.
     GRANDI (*racing into camera*): Stop him!
177. *Low angle* MS: *Risto facing camera, Sal approaches and seizes him from
     behind. Luridly streaked sky: it is daybreak.*

178.   LS: *Sal and Risto struggling on the right; Grandi, the camera following, catches up from the left.*

    GRANDI: Who told you to throw acid at Vargas? Huh?

179.   MS: *Grandi approaches the two boys.*

    GRANDI: Hold him, Sal! (*He grabs Risto by his collars as Sal holds him from behind.*) Who is the boss of this family? (*He slaps Risto.*) Huh? Who is the boss? (*Another slap.*)

    RISTO: My old man.

    GRANDI (*pulling his hair*): Yeah, Vic. Sure. But he is in the pen. Until he gets out, who is running this outfit?

    RISTO: Oh stop it, will you? (*He gets slapped again.*)

    GRANDI: Who is the judge?

    RISTO: All right. You.

180.   LS: *Grandi, Risto, Sal framed by pillars of the arcade. Grandi gives Risto a shove and steps away toward the camera, expostulating, arms outspread.*

    GRANDI: What a setup to work with! One brother in jail, two others dead.

181.   MS: *Grandi, Risto, Sal behind in center.*

    GRANDI: And nobody left to carry on the business but a bunch of nephews . . .

    RISTO (*waving his hand at him*): Listen . . .

    Grandi flails with both hands, as if to fend off a blow, his wig getting knocked off in the process.

    GRANDI: Don't do that!

    RISTO: You lost your rug, Uncle Joe.

    GRANDI (*over, as he walks away to left foreground*): . . . half of you too wet behind the ears . . .

    RISTO: Your rug . . . you lost your rug!

182.   *Low angle* MLS: *Vargas and Susan descending the hotel's shadowy staircase, the camera turning to follow them.*

    VARGAS: This isn't the real Mexico. You know that. (*Stopping to call after Susan, who has gone ahead, out of frame.*) All border towns bring out the worst in a country.

    Susan reenters the frame, passing from left to right, the camera following, leaving Vargas behind.

VARGAS (*off*): I can just imagine your mother's face if she could see . . . (*reenters frame, having caught up with Susan, the camera following both down the rest of the stairs and into the lobby*) . . . our honeymoon hotel.[5]

183. MLS: *Susan, carrying her bag, followed by Vargas, comes down the stairs into the lobby, the camera tracking back. Their voices echo in the bare space.*

VARGAS: Susie, will you please tell me why you're leaving?

CLERK (*off, as they pass desk*): Senior Vargas.

VARGAS (*aside*): Moment. (*Following Susan into the right foreground.*) Does this mean you're taking that early plane back to Mexico?

CLERK (*in background, holding up phone*): Telefono!

SUSAN (*muttering, exasperated, as Vargas turns back to the desk*): Telefono!

VARGAS (*walking back*): Because it doesn't leave for another two hours, you know. (*He takes the phone and asks the clerk in Spanish for his briefcase, which is under the desk.*) All I can say is if you are taking that plane, I'm very glad.

SUSAN: I'm very . . .

184. MS: *Vargas at desk with phone. On the counter: his briefcase, a pottery bull.*

SUSAN (*off*): . . . glad you're very glad.

VARGAS (*on phone*): Si. (*He takes a pistol from his briefcase, checks its chamber, then returns it.*)

185. MS: *Grandi in arcade across from hotel. He paces away from camera, hands on hips.*

GRANDI (*wheeling around to face camera*): Who told you to start this funny stuff with the acid?

Risto appears, back to camera, from right foreground.

GRANDI (*scurrying around between pillars of arcade, gesturing*): Who told you?

RISTO: I just wanted to give that wife of his something to think about on their honeymoon.

GRANDI: She's gonna to get plenty, don't you worry. She's gonna . . .

SAL (*off, overlapping*): Here, you lost your rug. (*The wig is thrust forward in the right foreground.*)

GRANDI (*feeling top of head*): What?

RISTO (*passing him the wig*): You lost your rug.

GRANDI: Oh! (*Takes it and steps off camera as he bends to put it on.*)

RISTO: My old man's in no shape for the pen. If they give him ten, he dies.

186. *Low angle* MCU: *Grandi peers from behind pillar, wig askew.*

GRANDI: Yeah. And if Vargas gets hurt, what happens? My brother Vic is just as good as convicted.

Sal and Risto enter the frame as all three, MCU, *circle around the pillar.*

GRANDI: You leave Vargas to me.

RISTO (*pointing*): Uncle Joe, Uncle Joe!

GRANDI: What?

187. LS *of hotel across the street. Susan and Vargas are barely visible through its glass facade.*

188. *Low angle* MCU: *Grandi, Risto, Sal, as in 186. Intense, sinister stares before Grandi finally speaks.*

GRANDI (*stepping forward slightly, the camera tracking back*): Sal . . . (*taking envelope from pocket*). This . . . take it to her.

189. LS *of hotel, as in 187. Sal enters running from right foreground, followed after a moment by Grandi in the center.*

190. MLS *from inside lobby. Susan is waiting by the window, her white jacket folded over her arm. Sal, outside, knocks on the window, speaks in Spanish. She turns to him, gesturing incomprehension.*

SUSAN: I don't *want* any more post cards. (*Sighing, she turns and goes off right.*)

191. MS: *Susan comes out of the door of the hotel.*

SUSAN (*trying to speak Spanish*): Que es esso! (*Hopelessly.*) I don't speak any Spanish. (*Going to him, camera following.*) What is it? What do you want?

SAL: I don't know. I was told to put this in your hands. (*Hands her the envelope.*)

She looks down at it as he leaves.

192. CU: *The letter.*

"A souvenir with a million kisses. Pancho."

She turns over the enclosed photo: Susan and Pancho together outside the Hotel Ritz.

193. MS: *Vargas comes out of the hotel and to Susan.*

VARGAS (*setting down her bags*): Susie . . .

SUSAN (*over*): Mike, look at . . .

VARGAS: . . . that was the police. Quinlan has a lead. I'm sorry, I have
to meet him. Now, you *must* tell me what you want to do. If you *are*
going to Mexico City (*consulting watch*), I have time to take you to
the airport. And perhaps that would be best, just for a few days.

SUSAN: I don't think so.

VARGAS: But . . . just a minute ago . . .

SUSAN: A minute ago I said a lot of things. But now I think the best
thing is to stick close to my husband. Okay? (*She turns and leaves off
the right foreground.*)

VARGAS (*looking after, baffled, a little annoyed*): Susie . . . (*Stoops to
retrieve her bags.*)

194. *High angle* LS *of street. Susan approaches convertible in foreground,
Vargas follows from behind. The camera moves down to them as they get
into the car.*

SUSAN: So, Mike, I'm going with you.

VARGAS: Coming with me? But I have to see Quinlan at the American police station.

SUSAN (*getting into the car*): I'll wait at the motel.

VARGAS: What motel?

SUSAN: Well, there must be one somewhere on the American side of the border.

VARGAS (*loading bags into the car*): The American side of the border!

SUSAN: Oh, well, I'll be safe there . . .

195. *Tilted, low angle* MS *of Grandi (wig still askew) and Risto, watching from beneath arch of arcade.*

SUSAN (*off*): . . . you won't have to worry about me.

196. MS: *Susan and Vargas, as at conclusion of 194.*

SUSAN: Did I say the wrong thing again?

VARGAS (*getting into the car*): No . . . I suppose it would be nice for a man in my place to be able to think he could look after his own wife . . .

197. MCU: *Susan facing camera, Vargas on right, facing her.*

VARGAS: . . . in his own country.

SUSAN: Oh, Mike, if I go to the American motel, it's just for comfort . . .

VARGAS (*turning away toward camera, muttering*): Sure, sure.

SUSAN: . . . not for safety.

VARGAS (*relenting*): Whatever you say may be the . . . (*He turns back to kiss her.*)

198. CU *of car radio: Vargas turns it on.*

199. *Low angle* MS: *Grandi peers from behind arcade, turns to go off right.*

RADIO (*off*): . . . of the contractor, Rudolph Linnekar . . .

200. MLS *of Vargas's car turning around and leaving to the left, the camera rising and moving back.*

RADIO: . . . has definitely been identified with the blond night club dancer killed in the explosion a few yards this side of the Mexican border.

*201. MS: *Grandi, back to camera, darts out of the arcade.*

GRANDI: We're gonna get you where it really hurts. (*The camera moves with him as he goes left to his car.*) And without laying a hand on him!

*202. MS: *Risto, still looking abashed, against a wall with peeling posters.*

203. MS: *Grandi, facing the camera, climbs into his car. Risto looks on behind. Catching sight of his skewed wig in the rearview mirror, Grandi adjusts it, preens.*

   GRANDI (*mock pompous, grimacing*): He's got a reputation! (*Mock lyrical, after another tug at the wig.*) He's got a young bride!

204. MS: *Grandi, from the side, turning toward camera to speak to Risto.*

   GRANDI: He's gonna leave this town wishing that he and that wife of his had never been born.

205. LS: *Grandi's car pulls into street and drives off left.*

*206. *Dissolve to* LS *of Vargas's car on a hilly road. It approaches the camera, then turns to go off right.*

*207. MCU *through windshield of Vargas's car: Susan leans drowsily against him as he drives. Nondescript pop music on radio.*[6]

   VARGAS: Now don't you see, darling, if the bomb was planted in Mexico, and the accused is Mexican, what a scandal this could turn into, internationally?

*208. MCU: *Susan and Vargas, from the side, facing left.*

   SUSAN (*lazily*): Might be kind of rough on the tourist trade.

   VARGAS: Susie! One of the longest borders on earth is right here between your country and mine. An open border. Fourteen hundred miles without a single machine gun emplacement. I suppose that all sounds very corny to you.

   SUSAN (*seductive*): I could love being corny if my husband would only cooperate.

*209. MCU: *Susan, Vargas, from the front, as in 207. Susan kisses Vargas on the ear.*

   VARGAS (*smiling*): Hey . . . Susie . . .

   She puts her arm around his shoulder.

   VARGAS (*having difficulty steering*): Well . . .

   He stops the car. A long embrace.

   SUSAN: You don't mind, do you, darling, if we just sit here by this *terribly* historic border of yours, maybe for about a month? (*Turning to nestle in his arms.*) Oh, I could stay in your arms and sleep and sleep and sleep.

Honking horn off: both look up.
*210. *The car with Vargas and Susan, seen from the rear, is in the foreground.
A police car approaches from the background and stops. (Quinlan is
inside, but he never emerges.) Barren, bleached landscape, the cars
reflecting a cloudless sky.*
SCHWARTZ (*getting out of the police car*): Vargas?
VARGAS (*getting out of his car*): Hello there, Schwartz.
SCHWARTZ: Quinlan seems to be onto something new. Coming with us?
Menzies, carrying Quinlan's cane, has also got out of the police car.
VARGAS: I have first to drop my wife at the motel.
MENZIES (*coming forward on the right*): Captain Quinlan wants you to
    go with him. I'll be glad to drop your wife at the motel.
SUSAN: Oh, really, I . . . I . . .
MENZIES (*at side of car, removing his hat in a courtly gesture*): No
    trouble at all, ma'am.
SUSAN (*to Vargas, who has headed back to the police car*): Aren't you
    going to drive me?
VARGAS: I'll phone you, darling. (*To Menzies.*) What's the name of that
    motel?
MENZIES: The Mirador.
VARGAS: The Mirador!
SCHWARTZ (*from background, over*): Quinlan's in kind of a hurry,
    Vargas.
SUSAN: Don't bother to phone.
VARGAS (*leaving*): You try to get some sleep, Susie.
MENZIES (*walking around the car into extreme foreground and passing
    out of frame on the left*): That Mirador is mighty hard to find (*off*) with
    the new highway branching off the way it does. (*Reentering the frame
    on the left, he gestures abruptly toward the departing police car.*) Hey!
*211. MS: *Departing police car.*
*212. *Menzies by car, with Susan still seated, as in 210.*
SUSAN (*drowsily*): That's all right. I can find the way . . .
MENZIES (*over*): Oh gee! I forgot . . . his cane! I forgot to give him his
    cane! (*Getting into car, still gazing after Quinlan, as Susan slumps
    back on her seat.*) He really needs it, with that game leg of his. Did I
    ever tell you how he got it, huh?

SUSAN (*inattentive*): What, the cane?

MENZIES: No! His bad leg!

SUSAN: Who're you talking about?

MENZIES (*shouting, as he gets into the car*): Captain Quinlan!

*213.   MCU: *Susan and Menzies, through the windshield.*

MENZIES (*angry at her lack of interest*): He got it in a gunfight, Mrs.
Vargas, is how. He was wounded stopping a bullet that was meant
for me.

*214.   MS: *the police car drives from right to left along a hilly road. As it
draws away from the camera and off frame on the left, we see Grandi's
white convertible coming down the same road, from above.*

*215.   MS *through the windshield of Grandi's car: wig askew, he negotiates a
curve.*

*216.   MS: *Menzies and Susan, driving, seen from behind.*

MENZIES: I reckon the bravest thing Hank ever did was to give up drink.
He used to be a terrible lush, you know. But look at him now. No
sleep, still at it.

Susan rouses herself and looks around behind them, into camera.

MENZIES: Hey, he never gives up!

*217.   MLS: *Grandi's car approaches, right of frame, passes off left.*

*218.   MCU: *Grandi, driving, seen from behind. The car with Menzies and
Susan is visible a little way ahead.*

*219.   MS: *Menzies, Susan, as in 216. Susan is still looking back, then turns
around again.*

220.   MCU: *worker's hand on detonator labeled "Linnekar Construction
Company." Sound of motors, machinery. The camera pans up to reveal
Eddie Farnham, about to set off an explosion.*[7]

VOICE (*off*): Hold that second charge!

Farnham looks up: low angle MS.

VOICE (*off*): Stop that car!

221.   MS *from within police car as it arrives at construction site. Driver and
Vargas in front seat. Through the front window we see workers trying to
stop the car. Confused shouts: "Hold that car!" "Stop!" "Stop, hold it!"
The camera pans to Quinlan in the back seat,* CU, *profile facing right, as
the car halts and a foreman approaches and leans in the window to
speak.*

QUINLAN: Hey, there was a complaint about some stolen dynamite out here. You fired anybody lately?

FOREMAN: I figured you'd be asking about that.

QUINLAN: Yeah? (*Puffing cigar.*) Boy named Sanchez?

FOREMAN: Sure. He's been playing around with the boss's daughter.

SCHWARTZ (*off*): Say captain, I just recognized somebody . . .

222.   MCU *inside car, from opposite side: Schwartz and Quinlan in back seat, facing left; Vargas in left foreground in front seat; uniformed driver half in frame in right foreground.*

SCHWARTZ: . . . over there, at the blaster.

QUINLAN: The one with big ears?

SCHWARTZ: Our office prosecuted that guy for voluntary manslaughter.

QUINLAN: Get him over here. That's Eddie Farnham . . .

SCHWARTZ (*calling*): You!

QUINLAN: . . . got five to ten (*puffing cigar*).

FARNHAM (*at window*): You have to get out of here. We're going to blast again.

QUINLAN: How long you been out?

FARNHAM: Three months.

SCHWARTZ: Quick parole.

QUINLAN: Who got you this job?

FARNHAM: My lawyer. Howard Frantz.

POLICE RADIO (*over*): Come in, car ten . . .

SCHWARTZ: Grandi's lawyer.

POLICE RADIO (*over*): Come in car ten . . . Suspect now in custody . . . (*Continues to repeat over dialogue in rest of shot.*)

QUINLAN: Well, this is it.

VARGAS (*turning from front seat*): Suspect?

QUINLAN: Mmmm . . .

VARGAS: Is that the one you've been talking about? This Sanchez?

SCHWARTZ: I'd like to make out they located him, right, captain?

QUINLAN: Yeah, in Marcia Linnekar's apartment. Come on.

FARNHAM: Stand still, we're gonna blast.

223.   MLS: *Workman pushes plunger.*

224.   LS *of blast.*

225.   MCU: *Quinlan grinning through window of car.*

QUINLAN: What's wrong, Farnham? You short of dynamite?

The car pulls forward and drives off frame to the left.
226. *Low angle* MS: *Farnham, stepping forward, looks after them angrily.*

*227. MCU *through windshield of car. Susan is asleep on the seat at the left. On the right, Menzies, looking in the rear view mirror, has spotted Grandi following them. Finally he turns around to look.*
*228. *High angle extreme* LS *of road through bare, semi-desert scrub. The sun has fully risen and the emptiness is brightly illuminated. Menzies's car is in the right foreground, Grandi's approaches from the distance. Menzies abruptly brakes his car, letting it skid across the road. The camera moves down to eye level, but still extreme* LS *as Menzies gets out of the car and walks back toward Grandi's car.*
*229. *Low angle* LS: *Grandi's car, seen from behind, stops for Menzies, who is in the road gesturing.*
       GRANDI: What's wrong?
       MENZIES: What are you following us for? Get out of the car.
       GRANDI (*getting out*): A man can't take a ride in his own car? What's the big idea?
       MENZIES (*hustling him toward his own car*): You'll find out. Come on!
       GRANDI (*flailing arms*): Don't push me! Keep your hands off me!

*230. *Dissolve to* MS: *Susan still asleep in the parked car, Menzies leaning over into the car and pointing to the left.*
       MENZIES: Wake up, Mrs. Vargas. We're here. This is it.
       SUSAN (*rousing herself, dismayed*): This *can't* be it!
       MENZIES (*shrugging*): It's all the motel we've got this side of town, ma'am. The others are all on the new highway, and most of them are closed up till the season starts.
       As Susan gets out, the camera rises so we see Grandi a little way behind the car, turned away, hands on hips, staring sulkily into the distance.
       SUSAN (*seeing him*): Oh no!
       GRANDI (*turning around*): Oh yeah. (*Shrugging to Menzies, who goes around the car toward him.*) Now listen, sergeant . . . How long are you going to hold me here? I . . .
       MENZIES: Shut up!
       GRANDI: . . . didn't do nothing at all.
       MENZIES (*over*): Mrs. Vargas, can you identify . . .

*231. MS: *car in the foreground, Susan on the left, Grandi and Menzies on the right.*

MENZIES: . . . this man? (*Taking Grandi by the arm as Grandi tries to shoo him away.*)

SUSAN: Of course I can identify him, that's Grandi.

GRANDI (*over*): I didn't do anything to you, Mrs. Vargas!

MENZIES (*to Susan*): I know.

GRANDI: I'm a member of the family, sure. (*Turning to Menzies.*) But nobody has laid a finger on her.

MENZIES: Shut up! Get in the car.

*232. *High angle* MLS: *car in left foreground, Susan and Menzies on left, Grandi going around toward right to get in.*

GRANDI (*pouting*): What about my car?

MENZIES: You can leave it here.

GRANDI: What? Here? (*Coming forward, gesticulating.*) In the middle of nowhere?

MENZIES: You're coming with me.

*233. *High angle* MS: *Grandi by car door, shrugging emphatically.*

GRANDI: On what charge?!

*234. MS: *Grandi, back to camera, is in the middle of the foreground; Susan and Menzies are behind the car at the left of the frame. The camera rises to bring them into clearer view.*

MENZIES: I don't know yet. That's for Captain Quinlan to decide.

SUSAN (*stepping toward Menzies*): But what was Grandi doing way out here?

GRANDI (*over*): I was just driving.

MENZIES (*pointing to highway*): He was following us in his car.

GRANDI (*over, with steering gestures*): Just driving along.

SUSAN (*weakly*): Oh well . . . where are my bags?

MENZIES: We've already put them by your cabin, Mrs. Vargas. (*Pointing, as Grandi climbs into the car.*) There it . . .

*235. MS: *front of car in foreground, Susan on left, Menzies in center.*

MENZIES: . . . is.

GRANDI (*off*): The last one, number seven.

The camera follows Menzies as he walks around and gets into the driver's seat.

MENZIES: If you should want to change, just phone the man at the desk.

(*Closing the car door after him.*) Off season like this, I reckon you're about the only one staying here.

In the back seat of the car, at the right, Grandi smirks, giggles aloud; Menzies turns to glare at him.

*236.   MCU: *Grandi stifles a grin.*

*237.   Brief MS: *the car with Menzies in front, Grandi in back.*

*238.   LS. *The overhanging roof of the motel cabin is in the left foreground, with Susan's bags by the door: an uninviting cube of empty space. Susan stands in mid frame as Menzies starts the car, then steps forward as it passes her and disappears off to the right. She wearily picks up her bags and stands looking around the desolation as we see Menzies's car again, leaving down the road in the distance at the right. As Susan turns back to the cabin, the camera rises over the porch roof to an extreme LS of the barren landscape and departing car.*

239.   *Low angle MS inside cabin, the bare room dominated by the exaggerated rectangle of a bed on the left. Behind the bed, an angular figure peers through a window on the rear wall: the Night Man. Susan wearily enters through the door at the right of the frame, sets down her bags, and walks toward the back of the room. The figure at the window has disappeared; now country music begins to come out of a speaker on the wall.*[8]

240.   MS: *Susan, back to camera, bangs on speaker in the center of wall. The Night Man appears again in the window at the left.*

NIGHT MAN: Uh . . . uh . . . I turned the music on up for you. Up at the office.

He disappears as abruptly as he came. The camera follows Susan to the right as she goes to look out the door. She leans out just as the Night Man pokes his head in the adjacent window. This jumpy routine is repeated.

NIGHT MAN: I . . .

SUSAN: Oh! (*Exasperated, she goes back into the room, passing out of the frame on the left.*)

NIGHT MAN (*following her in,* MCU): I turned the music on up for you. I thought you'd like it.

SUSAN (*off*): Not just now.

241.   MCU: *Susan.*

SUSAN: It's past seven, and I haven't been to bed yet.

242.   MCU: *Night Man, terror-stricken in the right edge of the frame.*

NIGHT MAN: Bed?! Well, you can get into it now. I brought the sheets.

Susan goes out the door, passing behind the Night Man, who turns to shout after her, now in MS.
NIGHT MAN: If they think I'm gonna help make it, they got another think coming!
Susan returns with her bags, passing him in the foreground.
NIGHT MAN (*backing away into a corner*): I'm . . . I'm not gonna be a party to. . . . I'm the night man.
243. MS: *Susan looks at him wearily, annoyed.*
NIGHT MAN (*off*)· It's day . . .
244. MS: *Night Man gesturing out window.*
NIGHT MAN: . . . already. I'm the night man!
SUSAN (*off*): Have the day man help me make the bed.
NIGHT MAN (*sliding in panic along wall to door on right, camera following*): There ain't no day man. He's supposed to be here at six o'clock this morning. (MCU *at doorway.*) And now they . . . they phoned to tell me he ain't coming at all. They're sending a new man.

New man. If they think I'm gonna stay here and wait for him, they
. . . they got another think . . .
Susan approaches, the back of her head in the lower left of the frame.
SUSAN: Why don't *you* help me make the bed?
NIGHT MAN (*in panic*): Bed . . . ?!

245.　CU: *Susan at door, facing camera, as Night Man turns to leave in the
right foreground.*
SUSAN: Hey, wait a minute . . .

*246.　MCU: *Night Man pokes his head through window by door, looking
apprehensive.*

*247.　MS: *Susan, facing camera, at door: she looks back toward the window.*
NIGHT MAN (*off*): That . . . that friend of yours . . .

*248.　MCU: *Night Man, as in 246.*
NIGHT MAN: . . . Mr. Grandi . . . He ain't gonna leave you here for
long?

*249.　MS: *Susan, as in 247.*
SUSAN (*coming forward*): He is *not* . . .

*250.　*Susan enters from right foreground, crosses to left.* MS: *Susan on left,
Night Man on right, his head still thrust in through window.*
SUSAN: . . . my friend!
NIGHT MAN: He . . . brought you here in that . . . that car, didn't he?
SUSAN: No, he didn't. As a matter of fact, he's under arrest.
NIGHT MAN: Under arrest? Mr. Grandi? (*Giggling fit.*)
SUSAN (*nodding head*): Yes, he is.
Night Man stares, still giggling.

*251.　MS *through window: Susan looks out (speaker visible on wall behind her
on right). Superimposed on her image is a reflection of the Night Man
outside: still giggling, he ducks and begins to lope away.*

252.　MLS: *Night Man in left foreground, flat desolate landscape behind.
Hands in pockets, giggling, he turns to lope away in the distance off
right.*

253.　*High angle* LS: *police car, siren sounding, arrives at Marcia Linnekar's
apartment. Entering in the right background, it turns down a street
toward the camera, turns again to the right, the camera following and
coming down to meet it as it halts, brakes squealing, in a parking lot by
Marcia's apartment.*

254. MS *of parked car, from rear: Quinlan, Vargas, and Schwartz get out.*
     VARGAS: Captain, have you anything definite on this boy Sanchez?
     QUINLAN: Not yet . . . (*Camera follows, keeping him in foreground.*)
     I'm just going on my intuition.
     SCHWARTZ (*in right background, at curb*): Hey, I think this car belongs
     to Howard Frantz.
     QUINLAN (*in center of frame, striding back toward the apartment*):
     Yeah?
     SCHWARTZ: You remember him. He was that slick lawyer that got Farnham
     a parole.
255. MCU: *Back of Quinlan's head as he passes a window of the apartment on
     his way in.*
     QUINLAN: Yeah, he was Rudy Linnekar's attorney too.
     (*As he goes by, we see first his shadow pass over the window, then Marcia
     looking out between lifted blinds.*)
256. MS *inside Marcia's apartment: Sanchez, Marcia, Frantz look out through
     blinds. Throughout this long sequence shot, the camera constantly moves,
     groups assemble and reassemble, dialogue overlaps. Emphasis on low
     ceiling of apartment, heavy chiaroscuro.*
     MARCIA (*turning back from window*): Hank Quinlan?
     SANCHEZ (*weakly good-looking, excitable*): Quinlan! (*Pushes forward
     to look out.*)
     FRANTZ (*coming forward, smoothly*): I figured we'd have Hank Quinlan
     to deal with. (*To Marcia.*) You finished packing? (*She nods.*)
     SANCHEZ (*turning back, already agitated*): I've heard about that guy!
     FRANTZ: Say nothing, my dear. Leave everything to me. (*Patting her
     arm.*) Let's get your bag.
     *He steers her off toward the left, ignoring Sanchez. As they cross, we see
     Quinlan entering the door in the right background,* MLS, *puffing a cigar.
     He walks by the expectant group without saying anything, passing them
     diagonally toward the camera and leaving the frame, low angle, at left
     foreground. Marcia, Frantz, and Sanchez are left in* MS. *Sound of door
     closing off. In the right rear, Casey (a plainclothes policeman) and a
     uniformed cop stand by the front door. Schwartz and Vargas have also
     entered inconspicuously.*
     FRANTZ: Remember, I'll do all the talking.
     SANCHEZ (*hysterical*): How do we begin? Do we play around first with

a few nasty questions, or (*turning to Schwartz and Vargas*) does he get out the rubber hose right away?

SCHWARTZ: Take it easy.

Vargas comes forward and speaks in Spanish. Sanchez replies.

QUINLAN (*off*): Vargas . . .

VARGAS (*stepping forward, removing dark glasses, low angle* MS): Yes, captain?

The camera moves with him, low angle, as he goes into the next room.

QUINLAN: I've got my orders, Vargas. I'm supposed to extend you every courtesy. That don't mean that you . . . you do the interrogating.

VARGAS: I know, captain. (*Wiping off glasses.*) That's what I told Sanchez.

QUINLAN (*changing the subject, gesturing toward camera*): You're Ed Hansen.

HANSEN (*entering from left foreground, silhouette of back*): That's right, Captain Quinlan.

QUINLAN (*camera following as he returns to the front room*): Run out and get me some coffee, Ed. And how about you, Miss Linnekar? (*Camera follows to her.*) Marcia, isn't it? You want some coffee?

MARCIA: No thanks.

QUINLAN (*sitting*): I really need it. I'm an old man, Marcia. I go a whole night without sleep, I feel it. Of course it was a lot worse for you. Terrible thing, what happened to your dad. (*Staring up at her, Sanchez looking on from right: Marcia on left taps her fingers distractedly and looks away.*) You've been living here for some time, Marcia? How long? (*Swallowing his words as he glances over to Sanchez.*)

MARCIA: Four months.

FRANTZ (*rushing in from right foreground and taking her arm*): Marcia!

QUINLAN (*standing*): You had a little quarrel with your dad . . .

FRANTZ (*over*): Perhaps I should introduce myself.

QUINLAN (*over*): . . . and moved out on your own?

FRANTZ: I'm Miss Linnekar's attorney. . . .

QUINLAN (*over*): I know who you are.

SANCHEZ (*bursting forward, over*): Shall *I* introduce myself. . . .

FRANTZ: . . . Howard Frantz.

QUINLAN: Yes, Mr. Frantz.

SANCHEZ: I'm Manolo Sanchez, and I haven't got any attorney.

QUINLAN: Uhh . . . you two been sharing this apartment?

FRANTZ: I must explain. On my advice my client is moving elsewhere.

QUINLAN: That means that she *has* been living with this man?

FRANTZ (*sweeping her away across foreground toward door in right back*): She will hold herself available for your later questions. I will be present, of course.

QUINLAN: Of course . . . Uh, Marcia . . . (*She remains midway to door.*) Where was your friend Sanchez last night?

FRANTZ: Later, captain, later. After she's rested. (*Leading her to door.*) Come, my dear.

Sanchez starts after her, shouts to her in Spanish, is restrained by officers.

QUINLAN (*camera following to right*): Casey, would you take a look in the . . . desk there? Might see some letters, or something. That is, unless you've already looked the place over.

CASEY (*sitting at desk on right*): We know better than that, Captain. We were waitin' for you.

Quinlan in left foreground smirks and grunts acknowledgement. Sanchez breaks forward, speaking Spanish. The camera follows as he crosses toward left foreground, speaking to Vargas: low angle MS of the two men. Then Quinlan breaks back into the frame from the right.

QUINLAN: I . . . uh . . . (*clearing throat*) . . . I don't speak Mexican.

Vargas and Sanchez continue to speak.

QUINLAN: Let's . . . uh. . . . Keep it in English, Vargas!

VARGAS (*crossing right between Sanchez and Quinlan*): It's all right with me. I'm sure he's just as unpleasant in any language.

MS: *Sanchez remains on left, then Quinlan, Vargas, Schwartz.*

SANCHEZ: Unpleasant? Strange? I've been told I have a very winning personality. The very best shoe clerk the store ever had!

QUINLAN: You weren't working as a shoe clerk out on that construction crew. (*Vargas begins to leave, moving toward background.*) Stick around, Vargas!

VARGAS: I intend to. (*Speaks in Spanish to Sanchez.*)

QUINLAN (*sharply*): In English! I don't like to repeat myself.

VARGAS: I merely asked him . . .

QUINLAN (*over*): Asked him!

VARGAS: . . . if I could use the telephone.

Sanchez replies in Spanish. Quinlan abruptly slaps his face.

VARGAS: In translation: "the telephone is in the bedroom, senior." That's all he said. (*Coming forward a step or two.*) Also he told me he thinks he is in for some sort of third degree. I assured him he had nothing to worry about. (*Crosses and out left foreground.*)

QUINLAN (*looking after him*): Casey. Go in with Vargas. Maybe he don't know how to use an American telephone.

CASEY (*coming forward on right, showing letters*): Think I ran on to something here, captain. Some love letters.

QUINLAN (*muttering*): Oh? You can read them in the bedroom. I don't want to leave that Vargas guy alone.

CASEY (*crossing in foreground toward left*): Okay.

QUINLAN: Save the good stuff for me.

The camera follows Casey, who is reading the letters as he goes into the bedroom.

QUINLAN (*off*): Now, in English.

SANCHEZ (*off*): What do you want to know?

QUINLAN (*off*): Everything, boy. The works. Let's start with . . .

Casey looks in on Vargas at the basin of the adjoining bathroom.

CASEY (*lifting phone off its stand by the door*): Want me to call the motel, Vargas?

QUINLAN (*over, off*): . . . the shoe store.

VARGAS (*leaning into the bedroom*): Later.

QUINLAN (*over, off*): That's how you happened to meet Linnekar's daughter, isn't it, in the shoe store?

SANCHEZ (*off, hysterical*): Yes, selling her shoes . . .

QUINLAN (*off, over*): Huh!

SANCHEZ (*off*): . . . and I've been at her feet ever since!

The camera follows Casey as he moves off left, then tracks into the bathroom where Vargas is leaning over the basin. It moves in on a shoe box on the shelf to the left of the basin, leaving Vargas half out of the frame on the right.

QUINLAN (*off*): Then the construction job. You stayed just long enough on that one to get your hands on some dynamite.

On the word dynamite, we see Vargas's arm (he is groping for a towel) knock the shoe box into the tub. The camera remains on it for an instant, then Vargas, moving into the foreground, retrieves it.

QUINLAN (*off, mock jovial*): What are you scared of boy? I'd only slap you again if you got hysterical again. Wouldn't be anything brutal. Why, even back in the old days, we never tried to hurt people in the face. It marks 'em up.

During this, Vargas replaces the box, then moves right, wiping his face, toward the doorway, where Schwartz appears.

QUINLAN (*off, suddenly savage*): We gave it to 'em like this! (*Sound of a punch, Sanchez's groan.*)[9]

SCHWARTZ (*shaking his head*): Boy's getting a rough deal.

VARGAS (*back to camera*): He could even be innocent, you know.

SCHWARTZ (*smiling*): Intuition?

VARGAS: Why not? (*Putting on his watch, turning into profile.*) Quinlan doesn't have a monopoly on hunches.

SCHWARTZ: Well, who do *you* like for the killer?

VARGAS: Too early to tell. . . . That ex convict . . .

SCHWARTZ: You mean out on that highway job? Farnham?

VARGAS: Maybe.

SCHWARTZ: Wait a minute . . . Some dynamite *was* stolen!

VARGAS (*the camera following him right into the bedroom, just as Quinlan, followed by Sanchez, comes in from the living room, at the right rear*): That construction crew is working for Linnekar!

SCHWARTZ: Amigo, I think you're on to something.

QUINLAN (*from background, deeply shadowed*): Uh . . . quite an apartment . . . for a shoe clerk. (*To Sanchez, on his right.*) Who pays for it? Marcia?

SANCHEZ: What if she does?

QUINLAN (*coming forward, so that Sanchez is in the center between Vargas and Quinlan*): How long's this been going on, eh?

SANCHEZ: Ever since her father had me fired from the last job, if you want to know.

QUINLAN: Naturally he objected to having a Mexican shoe clerk for a son-in-law, so naturally you . . .

SANCHEZ (*over*): Naturally!

QUINLAN: . . . you had to put him out of the way.

SANCHEZ (*hysterical*): Naturally! (*Exclaiming in Spanish, he turns and walks back, leaving Vargas and Quinlan facing each other in the foreground.*)

QUINLAN (*beaming*): Just because he speaks a little guilty, that don't make him innocent, you know.

VARGAS: You can show motive, yes. But won't you need a bit more than that?

QUINLAN: Yeah, we'll get it. (*Smiling, he turns and walks away from the camera.*) Oh, there's my coffee. (*Hansen enters through door on right and hands it to him.*)

QUINLAN (*looking after him as he goes off right*): Didn't you bring me any doughnuts . . . or sweetrolls?

VARGAS (*crossing foreground to Quinlan on right*): You'll have to put him on the scene of the crime.

QUINLAN: We will.

SCHWARTZ (*entering from left*): You got to have some evidence.

QUINLAN (*as Vargas walks back to door in next room, right rear*): We'll get it. (*Looking off right foreground to Hansen.*) Well?

HANSEN (*off*): Well, you didn't ask me to get any doughnuts, captain.

QUINLAN (*looking after Vargas*): Where you goin'?

VARGAS (*by door right rear*): This is not my case, captain.

QUINLAN: What finally convinced you of that?

VARGAS: This is not my country, that's all. I'm not convinced. (*He goes out the door.*)

QUINLAN (*muttering*): Well ain't that a shame!

257. MLS *outside the apartment: Vargas emerges on porch, low angle.*
VARGAS (*to cop on duty beside door*): Is there another phone near here?
COP: Right across the street.
The camera tracks with Vargas, left to right, as he walks across the street, putting on his dark glasses. We can see his car, with Menzies and Grandi, turn into the street behind him—just as a mother pushes a crying infant in a pram in the foreground, right to left. Vargas doesn't take any note and walks ahead into a shop in the right foreground.

258. MS *inside shop: Vargas enters on left.*
VARGAS: Excuse me. Madam, could I use your telephone please?

PROPRIETOR (*at right, near window, standing*): Right in front of you.
VARGAS (*going to phone*): You have a phone book?
PROPRIETOR (*coming to him as he sits down*): I'm blind, mister. You'll have to ask for information.
VARGAS: Oh, I'm . . . sorry.
He sits with phone in right foreground and dials. Through the window behind him, we see Grandi in the street, gesticulating violently with Menzies, who is carrying Quinlan's cane. Then they go into the apartment.
VARGAS: Hello? I'd like the telephone number of the Mirador Motel.

259. *High angle* MS *from porch of Marcia's apartment: Grandi climbs steps toward camera, followed by Menzies.*
GRANDI: What is this place you're taking me to?
Camera tracks with the two of them on the porch.
MENZIES: Get going.
GRANDI: Now listen, this is a coincidence . . .
MENZIES: Now go on!

260. LS *inside apartment: Hansen by door reading paper, Casey and Schwartz seated on left, Sanchez in right rear by window. Grandi, followed by Menzies, bursts in door at left rear.*
SANCHEZ: Who's this?
GRANDI: Who are you? (*Cringing.*) Don't push!
MENZIES (*coming forward*): Where's Captain Quinlan?
CASEY (*standing, pointing left*): He's in there makin' a search.
GRANDI (*aside*): What am I doing in here?
MENZIES (*the camera tracking back from him as he heads left for the bedroom*): Oh, Hank . . .
QUINLAN (*off in bathroom at left, irritably*): What's the idea, barging in on me like this? (*Back to camera, in* MCU, *he lurches across the frame from left to right.*)
MENZIES: I'm sorry, Hank . . .
QUINLAN (*the camera following him into the living room,* MS): What have you got in here?
MENZIES (*following*): . . . I forgot to give you your cane.
QUINLAN (*to Grandi, who is standing in extreme right foreground*): All right, sit down. (*He sits.*)
MENZIES: Queer thing, Hank . . .

QUINLAN (*over, taking his cane*): I know him.

MENZIES: . . . when I was taking Mrs. Vargas to the hotel, I picked this guy on the way.

QUINLAN: Yeah, I know. It's Uncle Joe Grandi. Why'd you bring him in here?

MENZIES: For some crazy reason he was following me in his car.

QUINLAN: He was tailing *you*?

MENZIES: Yeah.

Quinlan laughs. Grandi begins to join in, is quickly squelched.

GRANDI (*standing up*): Why would I be following a cop? He's an idiot!

QUINLAN: Maybe because you thought he was a Mexican cop, because you thought he was Vargas. He was driving Vargas's car.

MENZIES (*seeing the light*): Oh!

QUINLAN: Right?

GRANDI (*sulking*): So you're right. So I thought I was following Vargas. So what?

QUINLAN (*walking away, off left*): Sit down!

GRANDI (*sitting*): It's a free country.

QUINLAN (*off*): Shut up.

(Sanchez steps forward, looking after Quinlan.)

261. *Dissolve to* MCU *of speaker in Susan's motel room: "easy listening" music.*

262. MS: *Susan in her negligee, sitting with raised knees on the bed, wearily drying her hair. When the phone rings, she leans back against the pillows to answer it.*

   VARGAS (*on phone*): Is this the Mirador Motel? I'm trying to . . .

   SUSAN: Yes, it's the Mirador Motel, and it's me.

263. MS: *Vargas seated at phone on left; blind woman,* MCU, *in right foreground, staring blankly ahead.*

   VARGAS: Oh. . . . Darling, the news is bad. Quinlan is about to arrest that boy Sanchez, and . . .

264. MS: *Susan, as in 262.*

   SUSAN: Oh Mike, is that why you called? To tell me somebody's been arrested?

265. MS: *Vargas, blind woman, as in 263.*

VARGAS: No . . . that's not really why I called. It's . . . (*He turns away, confidentially, as if from the blind woman's attention.*)

266. CU: *Vargas with phone, facing camera on right. On left, a sign above a shelf: "If you are mean enough to steal from the blind, help yourself."*
VARGAS (*murmuring*): It's to tell you how sorry I am about all this . . .

267. CU: *Susan's head on pillow, dreamily staring into space, cradling the receiver.*
VARGAS (*on phone*): . . . and how very very much I love you. (*A pause.*) Susie?
SUSAN: I'm still here, my own darling Miguel.

268. CU: *Vargas, as in 266.*
VARGAS: Oh, I thought maybe you'd fallen asleep.

269. CU: *Susan, as in 267.*
SUSAN: I was just listening to you breathe. It's a lovely sound. (*Sighing.*) But I *am* sleepy.

270. CU: *Vargas, as in 266.*

VARGAS: Oh . . .

271. MS: *Vargas, blind woman, as in 263.*

VARGAS: . . . of course you are. (*Standing, public voice.*) Well then, I'll be calling you back later. Good-by for now.

272. MS: *Susan on bed, holding receiver.*

SUSAN: Mike?

She reaches over to jiggle phone for operator, sitting up in the bed, facing the camera.

SUSAN: Hello?

VOICE (*on phone*): Yes?

SUSAN: Oh. I just wanted to tell you I'm awfully tired. . . . Excuse me, this is Mrs. Vargas talking.

VOICE (*on phone*): I know. Couldn't be anybody else.

SUSAN: Oh?

VOICE (*on phone*): You're the only guest we got here just now. In the whole place.

SUSAN: Oh? Well, as I started to tell you, there's no sign to put up outside the door, and I just wanted to make sure I wouldn't be disturbed. . . . Oh, that is, if you're the one who's in charge.

273. CU: *Pancho on phone, extreme left. At first we see only the back of his head and the collar of his leather jacket; then he turns into profile.*

PANCHO: Don't you worry, Mrs. Vargas. I'm the one who's in charge here. (*Turning to face camera, low angle*) Nobody's going to get through to you . . . unless I say so.

*274. MS: *Vargas strides right to left, crossing street.*

VOICE (*off*): Oh, Vargas.

The camera moves so we can see, in LS, *the uniformed cop stationed outside Marcia's apartment.*

COP: Sergeant Menzies wanted me to give you this. (*Throwing them.*) Your car keys. (*Off left.*)

VARGAS (*going up steps to apartment*): Thanks.

275. LS: *Vargas up stairs.*

276. MS: *Vargas on porch, heading for door.*

277. *Low angle* MS, *inside apartment: Schwartz and Menzies seated in foreground, Vargas enters in rear center.*

SCHWARTZ (*getting up*): Well . . . I was beginning to think we'd lost
you for good, amigo.

VARGAS: I had a phone call to make.

*Sanchez enters, back to camera, from right foreground, speaking in
Spanish to Vargas.*

VARGAS: English . . . English!

*The camera moves in for their conversation. Vargas and Sanchez are in
low angle* MS, *lit from below, circling one another. Menzies, still seated,
is in profile on extreme left.*

SANCHEZ: They've got me measured for the fall guy.

MENZIES: Now just a minute . . .

SANCHEZ: Sure! I'm the fortune hunter who hypnotized Marcia, who
made her kill her father for his money! Why, if I had that kind of
power, I wouldn't be where I am today, believe me!

MENZIES: You mean you don't care about the money?

SANCHEZ: Why should I lie? If it hadn't been for the money I wouldn't
have given her a tumble.

MENZIES: Oh, no?

SANCHEZ: But I told her that right at the beginning. But still she
wanted. . . . Why bother? You wouldn't believe it! (*Turns away from
camera, flinging himself toward rear center.*)

VARGAS: Try me. I'm a good listener.

SANCHEZ (*coming back to him*): Well . . . instead of the man chasing
the girl, suppose she was the one, suppose she asked him to marry
her. What should he do? Draw himself up and say, "No, my dear, you
and I could never be happy together because of your money!"? What
would you do, Vargas?

(*Sound of door opening, off camera.*)

VARGAS (*removing dark glasses*): The question is, what did *you* do?

QUINLAN (*off*): Yeah, what *did* you do, boy?

All three turn to look at him, into the camera, low angle.

SANCHEZ: Well, you know what I did . . .

QUINLAN (*off, over*): Yeah, I know, but I wasn't asking me.

SANCHEZ (*over, moving toward camera, low angle, as Vargas looks
on*): . . . Captain Quinlan. Marcia and I made a bomb . . .

QUINLAN (*off, over*): That's right, you made a bomb . . .

SANCHEZ (*over*): . . . and we blew up her father, of course!

QUINLAN (*laughing, the bulk of his shoulder almost obliterating the frame as he enters from left foreground and crosses to right*): You're admitting it!

VARGAS (*shaking Sanchez*): Don't you see, you don't help yourself by treating this as a joke.

QUINLAN (*over*): He confesses!

All three are now in low angle MS: *Sanchez, Vargas, Quinlan.*

QUINLAN: Uh . . . you finished? Anything more you want to say, Vargas?

VARGAS (*turning to him*): No, captain.

QUINLAN: No? Good. Well, Pete . . .

MENZIES (*off*): Yes, captain?

QUINLAN: . . . since you're here, I wish you'd search the place. (*Crosses in front of Vargas and Sanchez, sits at left.*) I'm too tired to go on with this. (*Menzies has come up from behind and off the left foreground.*) Sanchez's desk we've looked into. . . . Take the bedroom and . . .

MENZIES (*off*): Okay, Hank.

QUINLAN (*apparently casual*): . . . and the bathroom.

Quinlan is seated in left foreground; Sanchez and Vargas standing in the center; Grandi seated in right foreground.

QUINLAN (*muttering*): And make it thorough.

GRANDI: Now, listen . . . (*Standing.*) How long do I have to sit here? I wasn't breaking no laws. I was just . . . (*Steering gestures again.*)

Quinlan rises threateningly. Grandi subsides into his chair.

GRANDI: I don't even know these people.

QUINLAN: You know Vargas, don't you?

GRANDI (*groaning*): Aww . . .

QUINLAN: Uncle Joe Grandi. Another Grandi. Yeah . . . you nabbed his brother on a narcotics rap.

VARGAS (*coming forward*): I don't know this Grandi.

GRANDI: Yeah. (*Seated in right foreground, Vargas and Quinlan standing over him.*) I got nothing to do with you.

QUINLAN (*over*): Shut up!

GRANDI (*into camera*): I'm an American citizen! (*Standing and turning back to them, so all three are in* MS, *Grandi between the other two.*) Now listen. (*To Quinlan.*) Vic was arrested in Mexico City, captain.

Vargas is gonna testify at his trial Thursday. It's got *absolutely* nothing
to do with me.

QUINLAN (*coming forward and off left foreground*): You just try any
rough stuff, Uncle Joe, and you'll find . . .

GRANDI (*over*): . . . he's a big shot in the Mexican government. (*To left
foreground, following Quinlan.*) Listen . . . anybody lays a hand on
Mr. Vargas between (*Quinlan returns from left foreground, the back of
his shoulder obliterating the frame until he passes to the right and into
a low angle* MS) now and Thursday, and my brother Vic is just as good
as convicted.

QUINLAN: (*grunts*)

MENZIES (*off*): Hank!

QUINLAN: Yeah, what is it?

MENZIES (*off, jubilant*): I've found it!

QUINLAN: Found what, partner? (*Crosses the frame again, off left
foreground: Grandi and Vargas looking after.*)

MENZIES (*off*): Come here and look!

GRANDI: I don't even know this Sanchez.

QUINLAN (*off*): All right, boy. Boy, come in here.

*Sanchez comes forward between Grandi and Vargas and goes off left
foreground. The camera stays with Vargas, moving into* MCU. *He lights
a cigarette as he listens.*

QUINLAN (*off*): Now, in English. Just how much dynamite was it you
stole?

SANCHEZ (*off*): What good would it be to tell you that I've never seen
any dynamite?

QUINLAN (*off*): Poor Rudy Linnekar, he did all he could to keep you
away from his daughter. But she stands to inherit a million bucks so
naturally you just moved in here.

SANCHEZ (*off*): Marcia and I were married . . .

MENZIES (*off, over, disbelieving*): Aaaah . . .

SANCHEZ (*off*): . . . secretly!

QUINLAN (*off, over*): A million bucks. Ain't no secret about that.

MENZIES (*off, over*): You got scared he'd change his will . . .

The camera draws back as Vargas, now in MS, *takes a few steps forward
toward the interrogation, looking intent.*

SANCHEZ (*off*): Why don't you let up for a minute?

QUINLAN (*off*): Then you got yourself this highway job . . .

MENZIES (*off*): You broke into the explosive bin and stole . . .

SANCHEZ (*off, over*): That's a lie!

QUINLAN (*off*): And stole ten sticks of dynamite!

SANCHEZ (*off*): No! No!

MENZIES (*entering from left foreground, to Vargas in* MCU): Well, Hank has done it again! (*Turning to look, grinning, at Quinlan off left.*) He's nailed his man!

QUINLAN (*off*): Thanks to you, partner.

MENZIES: Me! (*Gesturing boyishly.*) Nah! (*Going back to the uniformed cop and Casey, behind Vargas.*) If that dynamite had been a snake there in the bathroom, it would have bit me! (*Laughter.*)

VARGAS (*puzzled, to himself*): Bathroom?

QUINLAN: I promised Chief Gould (*lurching into the frame from left foreground and facing Vargas, in* MCU) I'd keep you informed, Vargas, so I'm doing it. This is it. We've broken the case. Rudy Linnekar was blown up with eight sticks of dynamite and Sanchez stole ten, that leaves two, and we found 'em both. You heard that, boy. (*Staring at him off camera in left foreground.*) We found the dynamite.

SANCHEZ (*entering from left foreground, faces Quinlan between Quinlan and Vargas*): That's impossible!

QUINLAN: Well, we *found* two sticks . . .

MENZIES (*coming forward, over*): Black Fox, the identical brand!

QUINLAN (*over*): . . . That's the right number and the right brand.

SANCHEZ: Where did you find this?

QUINLAN: Right here, in your love nest.

SANCHEZ: Where?

MENZIES: Where you had it stashed, of course.

SANCHEZ: What are you trying to do?

QUINLAN: We're trying to strap you to the electric chair, boy.

MENZIES: We don't like it when innocent people are blown to jelly in our town.

QUINLAN: There was an old lady on Main Street last night picked up a shoe . . . and the shoe had a foot in it. We're going to make you pay for that, Sanchez.

SANCHEZ (*turning to Vargas on the right*): They're trying to railroad me.

QUINLAN (*sarcastic*): Yeah.

SANCHEZ: I don't know why. I never stole any dynamite. (*Speaks in Spanish to Vargas.*)

VARGAS (*to Quinlan*): You'll have to stop him yourself.

QUINLAN (*over*): From now on, he can talk Hindu for all the good it'll do him.

VARGAS: He swears on his mother's grave that there has never been any dynamite in this apartment.

QUINLAN (*not looking at them*): Sure, sure. Take him in and book him.

HANSEN (*entering from right foreground and hustling Sanchez to door at rear*): Let's go.

VARGAS (*appraisingly, hands in pockets*): You say you found this dynamite in the . . .

QUINLAN (*over*): Yes.

VARGAS (*over*): . . . bathroom?

QUINLAN: Pete found it. (*Menzies comes forward.*) Show him the dynamite, Pete.

MENZIES (*passing between them, off left foreground*): Right here.

SANCHEZ (*in back, by door, turns to Vargas*): Can't you do something to help me? (*He is hustled out the door by Hansen, Casey, and the uniformed cop.*)

QUINLAN (*grinning, to Menzies off camera in left foreground*): What are you scared of, partner? (*Taking shoebox that is handed in from foreground.*) That stuff isn't nearly as easy to blow up as people seem to think. (*Examining one of the sticks, muttering.*) It doesn't go off quite that easy.

VARGAS: You found the dynamite in *this* box?

GRANDI (*darting forward between them*): Dynamite?

QUINLAN (*stares down Grandi who retreats; then to Vargas*): Yeah. (*Quietly, looking away.*) Pete found it. I told you that.

VARGAS: Captain.

QUINLAN: Yeah.

VARGAS (*slowly, with emphasis*): I looked at that box. Just now. There wasn't anything there.

QUINLAN (*after a long pause, softly*): I know how you feel.

VARGAS: Do you?

QUINLAN: Sure I do. You people are touchy. (*Siren off: the police car leaving with Sanchez.*) It's only human you'd want to come to the defense of your fellow countryman.

Vargas pauses thoughtfully, then turns and goes to the door in the right rear, which Grandi obsequiously opens for him.

QUINLAN (*turning around and crossing to right*): Vargas! (*Vargas stops, turning back at door.*) Vargas, don't worry.

VARGAS: Why should I worry?

QUINLAN (*walking back to him, the camera following*): Uh . . . you go right ahead and say anything you want to. Folks will bear your natural prejudice in mind.

The camera moves in to a tight MCU *of the two men by the door.*

VARGAS: I saw that shoebox ten minutes ago . . .

QUINLAN (*breaking in*): Yeah, well, maybe you didn't notice.

VARGAS: I knocked it over on the bathroom floor. I couldn't very well have failed to notice two sticks of dynamite.

QUINLAN: Tell any story you want to, Vargas.

VARGAS: The shoe box was empty!

QUINLAN: Go on saying it's empty. Folks will understand.

VARGAS: I'm saying more than that, captain. (*Pause.*) You framed that boy.

Quinlan, enraged, raises his cane as if to strike him.

VARGAS (*shouting*): Framed him!

When Vargas does not flinch, Quinlan slowly lowers the cane. Vargas turns to go out door.

278. MS *on porch: Quinlan, framed in doorway, looks after Vargas, into the camera. Schwartz passes him out onto the porch to the left, back to camera.*

MENZIES (*coming forward on right*): What's the matter with him, Hank? Is he . . . is he crazy?

QUINLAN (*dazed*): Yeah, that must be it. Crazy.

MENZIES: Hank, what are we going to do with this Grandi guy? Take him in?

Grandi enters frame in left foreground, back to camera.

QUINLAN (*as if stunned, not grasping what Menzies has said*): Grandi?

SCHWARTZ: I, uh, I think you ought to realize, Quinlan, when a man of
Vargas's position is willing to testify . . .

QUINLAN: Who are you working for? The Mexican government?

SCHWARTZ: I'm working for the District Attorney.

*He leaves off left and the camera pans to show him crossing the street
toward Vargas's car. Quinlan, in shadow on the porch, shouts after him.*

QUINLAN: Well listen! I've got a position in this town. A reputation!
Who's Vargas?

MENZIES (*extreme right foreground*): Vargas is kinda important too,
Hank. Somebody's going to have to give in on this thing.

QUINLAN: Either that, or somebody's going to be ruined.

GRANDI (*entering again from left*): Captain Quinlan.

QUINLAN: What do you want?

279. MS: *Vargas in front seat of car on left, Schwartz standing on right.*

VARGAS: Schwartz, you saw that shoe box in the bathroom. You know it
was empty.

SCHWARTZ: Well, now, I didn't happen to see it myself, but . . . (*turning
to get into car*) but I believe you!

*The camera rises and moves back as they drive off, moving away from
us.*

280. MS: *Quinlan on the porch, back of Grandi's head in bottom corner at
right. Quinlan nods, and they move down onto the sidewalk, the camera
following at high angle. Grandi, talking excitedly, scampers and backs
away from Quinlan as he walks, back to camera, down the street.*

GRANDI: We are both after the same exact thing, captain. If Vargas goes
on like this, shooting his face off, like he was just . . .

*Chiming bells are heard here and, repeatedly, throughout the rest of the
scene.*

QUINLAN: Yeah, move on along. Stop making trouble.

GRANDI: Trouble! Who's the one who's making trouble? Vargas!

They pause, MLS, *in the middle of the street.*

GRANDI: Sure! For my brother, Vic, in Mexico City. For you here.

QUINLAN (*turning away, toward camera*): Aw . . . go peddle your
papers, Uncle Joe.

GRANDI (*expostulating*): What? You just said it yourself. Somebody's
reputation has got to be ruined. (*Chiming bells.*) Why shouldn't it be
Vargas's?

Menzies enters in right foreground.

QUINLAN (*turning around to him, hostile*): What are you waitin' for?

MENZIES: Nothing, Hank, I was just . . . (*gesturing vaguely*).

QUINLAN: Well, we've got work to do.

MENZIES: Okay, Hank, okay. (*Hurt and bewildered, he turns and leaves in the right foreground.*)

281. MCU: *Quinlan in right foreground, Grandi further back on left, looking up at him.*

QUINLAN: What do you want?

GRANDI (*coming closer, leering up into his face*): Nothing, captain. Nothing that you don't want too.

QUINLAN: Come on, spit it out, Grandi.

GRANDI: Captain, we cannot stand out here in the street. Why don't we go somewhere nice and private, eh? Where we can sit down and have a drink?

QUINLAN (*troubled*): I don't drink.

282. *Low angle* MS: *the window of Marcia's apartment. The blinds are raised and Menzies looks out.*

283. *High angle* LS *through the window from inside. Menzies' head and shoulders in silhouette at right foreground, watching Grandi and Quinlan on the street: they cross it together.*

284. MS *of window from outside: Menzies inside on right, watching sadly; Quinlan and Grandi reflected on the window pane as they cross the street, arm in arm. Sound of chiming bells.*

285. *Dissolve to* LS *of desolate landscape reflected in window of Susan's motel. Loud rock and roll. Susan opens the shade on the window and we see her looking out wearily.*

286. *High angle* LS *of barren landscape, the motel visible in left rear. Sound of hot rods off.*

287. *Low angle* LS: *the highway. A hot rod moves across the frame, right to left, and the camera turns to follow it down the road.*

288. MS: *entering right foreground, the hot rod arrives at the motel. The camera rises to follow it as it turns down between the cabins.*

289. MS *framed by eave of motel porch. Two hot rods approach simultaneously: one moving left to right between cabins, the other approaching the camera from rear.*

290. *Inside Susan's cabin: on the right, the back of her head; on the left, an opening door through which we see one of the hot rods, moving from left to right. The camera pans to the right as Susan turns to see it, through a window, parking outside. She walks toward the window as gang members pile noisily out of the car.*

291. CU *of Vargas's car radio. We hear Quinlan's name spoken by an announcer speaking in Spanish. A finger changes the station: Latin music.*

292. MS: *Schwartz and Vargas in the car, speeding toward the camera. The camera moves with the car, as the narrow city streets seem to rush back behind them in exaggerated perspective.*[10]

    VARGAS: Look, Schwartz . . .
    SCHWARTZ: Al.
    VARGAS: Al. We must show where Quinlan himself got the dynamite. If you're really with me on this, we have still to get some proof.
    SCHWARTZ: We've got your word.
    VARGAS: Let's do better than that. In your country also, when explosives are purchased, some record is kept, no?
    SCHWARTZ: Sure. And we're going to the right place to look it up. . . . Hey, how about Quinlan's ranch?
    VARGAS: Where is that?
    SCHWARTZ: Just outside town. While you're looking up the dynamite records, I might go out there.
    VARGAS: Al, there is one thing that worries me still.
    SCHWARTZ: What's that?
    VARGAS: I could be wrong about this. That could be very bad for you.
    SCHWARTZ: Let's see if you're wrong first, amigo.

293. *High angle* CU *of hand changing station on car radio.*

294. *Overhead shot of the car. The camera rises and follows as it pulls away into the distance, passing out of town between bungalows and oil derricks. Latin music still from car radio.*

295. *Dissolve to* LS *of motel cabins. Rock and roll loud even at the distance.*

296. MS: *motel switchboard, phone on desk. It rings, a hand reaches from left for receiver, stops to snuff out a cigarette, and then lifts it, revealing a leather-clad arm.*

297. *Low angle* MS: *the motel lobby. In the left foreground, an apparently*

*drugged gang member jives to the loud music. Pancho, with the phone, is
further back on the right. As he steps forward, the camera moves in to
very low angle* MCU.

298. CU: *Susan with phone, facing the camera: white nightie, hair down,
speaker on wall behind shoulder on right.*
 SUSAN: I wondered if you could turn that music off. (*She sighs, turns
right toward speaker.*)

299. MS: *Susan with phone, facing the camera. She glances at the room
behind her, full of noisy gang members, then back to receiver.*
 SUSAN: Would it be possible to ask those people next door to move, just
to another cabin? You see, I'm still trying to get some sleep.

300. *Low angle* MCU: *Pancho with phone, as at conclusion of 297.*
 PANCHO (*insinuatingly*): Where would you like me to take you, doll?

301. CU: *Susan with phone, as in 298. She takes receiver from her ear and
looks at it apprehensively.*

302. LS: *Pancho and three other gang members at motel desk. The drugged
gang member is sitting on a table in center rear, still jiving to his radio;
left of him stands Pretty Boy; a third gang member (seen earlier, in the
photograph episode) is seated at far left.*
 PANCHO: You got the stuff?
 DRUGGED GANG MEMBER (*handing him a package from his jacket*): I
brought this. Some of the other guys got more.
 Through window on the right, the Night Man is seen approaching.
 PANCHO: You got a hypo?
 THIRD GANG MEMBER (*patting his pocket*): Sure.
 *The Night Man enters dubiously through the door on the right foreground,
clutching his lunch pail.*
 NIGHT MAN: Hi.
 PANCHO: What are you doing here? (*To the drugged gang member.*)
Turn that down.
 NIGHT MAN: I'm . . . I'm the night man.
 The camera moves in as the gang members begin to circle him threateningly.
 PRETTY BOY (*coming forward*): Yeah, well you're a little early, ain't
you?
 NIGHT MAN: I thought I'd better come by to see if you needed . . .
 The third gang member, on the right, slams the door shut: the Night Man

*flinches, whirls 360 degrees. The camera continues to move in, low
angle* MLS, *as the gang members circle around him.*
NIGHT MAN: Which . . . one of you is the new day man?
*On the right, the third gang member insolently fingers the bottom of the
Night Man's jacket. On the left, Pretty Boy approaches abruptly and tells
him in Spanish to leave.*
PANCHO (*coming forward to left foreground, turning his back to the
    camera*): Beat it!
NIGHT MAN: I . . . (*gesturing*). It's a mile and a half down to the
    highway. I . . . I think I better stay.
PANCHO (*hustling him out toward left, as camera moves into low angle*
    MS): Go in the kitchen and get yourself something to eat.
*Pancho, the drugged gang member, and the third gang member all
cluster threateningly around the Night Man.*
NIGHT MAN: I . . . I . . . I brought my lunch.
DRUGGED GANG MEMBER (*bobbing up and down beneath the Night
    Man's chin*): Eat it now.
NIGHT MAN (*bobbing in time with him*): Eat it now? (*He freezes, looking
    at them apprehensively.*) I know you. You're the Grandi boys. (*The
    switchboard sounds.*) Does Uncle Joe know you're here?
PRETTY BOY (*nervously rushing forward from right and pushing the
    Night Man aside as they all move back toward the phone*): Who could
    that be?
PANCHO: Take it easy, Pretty Boy. What are you in such a sweat about?
PRETTY BOY: It's a tough rap to get caught with the stuff.
PANCHO (*making a connection on switchboard*): It's only that Vargas
    dame again. (*Into receiver:*) Yes, ma'am?
SUSAN (*on phone*): Give me State 1212.
PANCHO: Very good, ma'am. State 1212. (*Begins to dial.*)
THIRD GANG MEMBER (*on right*): Hey, hey . . . that's the police
    department!
VOICES: Huh? Yeah?
PRETTY BOY: It's the police all right!
303. *Low angle* MS, *closer than before: Pancho with phone, others around
    him.*
PRETTY BOY (*pacing, agitated*): What do we do now?

PANCHO: We do nothing. We relax and have ourselves a ball. (*Into receiver:*) I'm very sorry, Mrs. Vargas, but the telephone is temporarily out of service. I'll call you just as soon as it's repaired. (*Hangs up, smirking.*) I'd better call Uncle Joe. (*Dials.*)

304.   CU: *two shot glasses on a bar, one full. Sentimental Latin music. A bottle from left of frame fills the second and is lifted out of frame as two hands enter to pick up the glasses. The camera moves back to reveal Grandi,* MS, *smiling greasily as he emerges from behind the bar with the drinks. It follows him as he goes to Quinlan seated at a table in the right foreground, facing forward, a cigar in his weary, bloated face.*

GRANDI: So that is our little arrangement, see? (*Sitting next to Quinlan, setting down drinks.*) A real sweet set-up. And all the help we need from the law is . . .

QUINLAN (*over*): Yes, you knock somebody off (*phone rings at bar*), I don't care who it is, there won't be any little arrangement.

BARTENDER (*off*): Hold on.

As Grandi begins to rise, we see the bartender in extreme rear, holding a phone.

QUINLAN: Not with Hank Quinlan!

BARTENDER: Joe, message for you.

GRANDI: Yeah. (*He stands and starts for the phone.*)

QUINLAN (*still into the camera, half to himself*): Vargas can't hurt me.

GRANDI (*turning back, unctuously, leaning over chair*): Well, maybe not. But maybe with our little deal we can hurt him.

QUINLAN: I don't make deals.

GRANDI (*walking to phone in deep focus on left, speaking into receiver*): Yeah. The girl all right? Naw, naw, naw, just go ahead like I said. Don't worry, no matter.

QUINLAN (*turning around, over*): Something wrong out there?

GRANDI: No, no. Nothing we can't fix.

QUINLAN: We? Where do you get that "we" stuff? I haven't given you any answer yet.

GRANDI (*hanging up and coming forward, smiling*): Captain, you keep talking as though this was some kind of a deal where I asked you to get me out of a rap. (*Standing behind Quinlan, leaning over his chair.*)

No. That ain't it at all. In this thing we're partners, see? Shall we drink
to that?
QUINLAN: I don't . . .
*But he looks down to see the glass in his hand. He removes his hand
limply, stares forward, baffled. Sudden silence as the music stops.*
GRANDI (*over his shoulder*): Juanita, two more double bourbons!
305. *High angle* MS: *Grandi on left foreground leaning over Quinlan. Camera
rises still higher, to high angle* LS, *as Grandi straightens up triumphantly
and turns around toward bar.*
GRANDI: Make 'em nice and big.
He puts a coin in the juke box at the left.

306. *Dissolve to* LS *of motel: loud voices, rock and roll.*
307. MS: *the speaker on the wall of Susan's room. It is framed by light from the
window, with shadow of shade pull. Rock and roll, party sounds.*
308. MS: *Susan in bed, on her side, mottled in shadow, staring with open eyes.*

309. *Dissolve to* LS: *Chief Gould, Schwartz, Adair in arcade in Los Robles,
     walking toward camera, which tracks back before them. As they turn the
     corner into Vargas's hotel, they move into low angle* MS, *then back to* LS.
     ADAIR: All I can say is, this better be important.
     SCHWARTZ: It is.
     GOULD: I think we're out of our minds to be here in Mexico at all.
     The camera follows them into the deserted lobby.
     ADAIR (*going forward to greet him*): Well, Vargas, you sent for us.
     VARGAS (*by desk in rear*): Adair. (*Coming forward.*) Gentlemen.
       No, it isn't really true that I sent for you. Mr. Schwartz insisted that
       I might . . .
     GOULD: Let's get down to cases.
     ADAIR: You know Chief Gould, of course, Mr. Vargas?
     VARGAS (*shaking hands*): How do you do, sir.
     GOULD: Where's this so-called document?
     VARGAS (*turning toward elevator at left*): Perhaps we'd better go to
       my room.
     ADAIR: Yes, by all means, yes.
310. MS *from within elevator as Vargas opens gates.*
     VARGAS: In here, gentlemen.
     ADAIR: Go ahead.
     VARGAS: No, no, no. I'll walk.
     ADAIR: Okay.
     VARGAS: The lift is rather small, I'm afraid.
       (*Adair goes in.*)
     VARGAS (*directing him in*): Chief Gould.
     Gould and Schwartz enter: all three in MCU.
     VARGAS: Just press the button for the second floor. I'll meet you there.
       (*Closes gates and door.*)
     ADAIR (*on right*): I still don't know why Vargas couldn't come to my
       office.
     SCHWARTZ (*in center*): He has practically cabinet status with the Mexican
       government, you know.
     GOULD (*left*): Well, if he's so important . . .
     SCHWARTZ: He can't very well make a formal call on either of you

without at least going through his consulate and putting the whole
thing on an international level.
GOULD (*over, with an impatient gesture*): Okay, okay, cut out all the
fancy talk, and what does it boil down to?
ADAIR (*breaking in*): This Mexican is bringing criminal charges against
one of the most respected police officers in the country. And that's
what it boils down to!
*Schwartz opens the gate, and Adair breaks off, abashed, when he sees
Vargas already at the elevator door.*
ADAIR: Ah, well, Vargas. . . . You must be pretty quick on your feet.
VARGAS: It's just that the lift is slow. (*Leading them out.*) This way,
gentlemen.
SCHWARTZ: Thank you.
The camera follows from behind as they leave elevator, walk down hall.
311. LS *from within hotel room: bed in foreground as Vargas opens door in
center rear.*
VARGAS: After you.
*Adair, Schwartz, Gould enter. The camera follows Vargas to a nightstand
on the left.*
VARGAS: I have it right over here. (*He removes a document and hands
it to Adair, who puts on his glasses to read, sitting on the edge of the bed
at right, Gould looking over his shoulder.*) There. While you're looking
at it, perhaps you'll excuse me if I finish a call I put in. (*He picks up
phone from the nightstand, asks in Spanish for the motel.*)
ADAIR: Where'd you get this?
VARGAS (*capping receiver*): From your department of records, about an
hour ago.
GOULD (*over*): They let anybody in there.
ADAIR (*handing it to Gould*): Well, it doesn't mean anything.
VARGAS (*on phone*): Senior Vargas, si.
SCHWARTZ (*to him from left foreground*): That's your wife you're calling,
isn't it?
VARGAS: Yes.
SCHWARTZ: You know who owns the Mirador?
VARGAS: No . . . I . . .
Camera turns back to Gould, who is reading.

GOULD: "June 18. Hill's Hardware in Los Robles. 17 sticks Black Fox
brand to H. Quinlan."

ADAIR: Quinlan needed dynamite for work on his ranch. Simple
coincidence.

312. MCU: *Vargas with phone.*

VARGAS: Mr. Adair . . . (*He hears the phone ringing at the motel.*)
Hello . . .

313. CU: *a telephone receiver is removed from its cradle. Then the camera
tips up to Pancho at the switchboard, low angle* MS. *Rock and roll still.*
PANCHO: Yes?

314. MCU: *Vargas with phone, as in 312.*

VARGAS: Mirador? My name is Vargas, and I'd like to speak with my
wife, please.

PANCHO (*on phone*): I'm very sorry, Mr. Vargas. But your wife left
definite instructions . . .

315. *High angle* MCU: *Pancho with phone.*

PANCHO: . . . she's not to be disturbed.

316. MLS *in motel room: Susan kneels on bed, raps on wall, through which
     come music, screams. She sighs as the music momentarily stops. Then a
     woman's voice, hoarsely Latin, comes through the wall.*
     VOICE: Honey . . . you . . . in the next room.
     SUSAN: What is it?
     VOICE: Come to the wall so I can whisper.
     Susan leans forward against the wall.
317. CU: *Susan leans against the wall, harshly lit so that her shadow is thrown
     on the wall at her left like a negative image.*
     SUSAN: Yes. . . .
     VOICE (*whispering*): You know what the boys are trying to do, don't
       you?
     Susan looks apprehensive, but makes no response.
     VOICE: They are trying to get in there. They went to get the master key.
318. *Brief point-of-view shot: the door, its flimsy knob.*
319. CU: *Susan, as in 317.*
     SUSAN: But what for? What do they want?
     VOICE: You know what marijuana is, don't you?
     SUSAN (*after a pause*): Yes.
     VOICE: You know what the Mary Jane is? (*Pause as Susan does not
       respond.*) You know what the mainliner is?
     SUSAN: I think so. But what's that got to do with me?
     VOICE: You take it in the vein.[11]
     SUSAN: You're trying to tell me those boys are drugged? Is that why . . .
     VOICE (*hushing her*): Shhh. . . .
320. *Low angle* LS *in the next room: two women reflected in mirror of bureau,
     a frowsy blond and a tough-looking leather-jacketed brunette.*
     BLOND (*in mirror, as brunette walks to bureau from right foreground*):
       Hey, you think they're ready for that stuff yet?
     BRUNETTE (*picking up needle from bureau*): Not yet, kid.
     She comes forward as the blond enters the frame from right: low angle
     MS *of both.*
     BRUNETTE: The fun is only beginning.

*321. *Dissolve to* MS *of bar: Quinlan, seated, back to camera in right foreground.
     In the mirror over the bar, we see his reflection and also Menzies entering
     from the right.*

MENZIES (*in mirror*): Hank, I've been looking for you in every bar in town.

QUINLAN (*turning right, rumpled, unshaven*): Yeah, I've been in half of them . . .

The camera moves to the right: MS, *Quinlan's bulk silhouetted on left, Menzies facing the camera on right.*

QUINLAN: . . . only here, on the wrong side of the border.

*322.   MCU: *Quinlan finishes drink on left; Menzies faces him, silhouetted in right foreground.*

QUINLAN: I never drink on my own beat, partner.

MENZIES: Bartender . . . (*He appears in background, center of frame.*) . . . give him some black coffee, quick.

QUINLAN: I don't need black coffee.

MENZIES (*over, whispering*): He's called a meeting, Hank.

QUINLAN: Meeting?

MENZIES: Vargas. At his hotel.

QUINLAN (*confused*): Motel . . . ?

*323.   MS: *Menzies on right, facing camera, Quinlan on left.*

MENZIES: No, right here. Across the street.

QUINLAN (*the camera following as he turns away to look*): Well, I don't need any coffee. Not yet.

MENZIES (*in mirror*): Not yet?

324.   MS: *Menzies, Quinlan behind bar, facing stationary camera. Coffee has appeared in front of Quinlan.*

MENZIES: This is a swell time to be getting fried, captain.

QUINLAN (*over*): My job's over, Pete. You ought to be over at the department . . .

MENZIES: Now listen, Hank . . .

QUINLAN: . . . working on Sanchez. We've got to break this . . .

MENZIES: Vargas is telling the chief and the DA that you planted that dynamite.

QUINLAN (*to himself*): He was a fool.

MENZIES: They're taking him seriously. They came to him.

QUINLAN: No, I mean Sanchez. Dynamite's no way to kill. Did I ever tell you the smart way to kill, Pete?

MENZIES (*wearily*): Sure, sure . . . strangling.

QUINLAN: Umm. Clean, silent.

MENZIES: You told me all that . . .

QUINLAN (*over*): That's how my wife got it.

MENZIES: Come on, finish that coffee.

QUINLAN: I don't usually talk about my wife.

MENZIES: Never, when you're sober.

QUINLAN (*after a pause, glancing over at him*): She was strangled, Pete.

MENZIES (*quietly*): I know, I know.

QUINLAN: Binding cord. She was working up at the packing plant, so the killer had it right to hand. Smart. . . . you don't leave fingerprints on a piece of string.

MENZIES (*calling*): Bartender, what do I owe you?

QUINLAN: That half-breed done it, of course. We all knew that. . . .

MENZIES (*over*): My friend too.

QUINLAN (*muttering*): But I was just a rookie cop. . . .

BARTENDER (*off*): Four seventy-five.

QUINLAN: I followed around after him, eat my heart out . . .

Menzies puts a bill on the counter, a hand removes it, but the camera does not move from Quinlan.

QUINLAN: . . . trying to catch him. But I never did.

325. *Camera pans right as Quinlan stands and turns briskly toward the door:*
MS: *Menzies on left, Quinlan on right.*

QUINLAN: Then in some mud hole in Belgium the Good Lord done the job for me, in 1917. (*With new resolution.*) Pete, that was the last killer that ever got out of my hands.

MENZIES: Where are you going now?

QUINLAN: Where do you think? To Senor Vargas's meeting. (*Grinning, Menzies hands him his cane, which he has left hooked over the bar.*) He wants a dirty fight, okay, that's the kind of fight he's gonna get. (*He turns to leave as Menzies in left foreground looks on, beaming.*)

326. *Low angle* MS *at hotel: Vargas standing on left; Adair, back to camera, at window with document; Gould seated at right.*

VARGAS: Perhaps . . .

GOULD: Perhaps what?

VARGAS: Perhaps he honestly thinks that Sanchez is guilty.

ADAIR (*turning to them*): Of course he does.

GOULD: No "perhaps" about it. (*Standing and going to Vargas.*) Hank
   Quinlan is an honest cop.

VARGAS: There are all kinds of policemen.

ADAIR (*objecting*): Oh . . .

VARGAS: I don't have to tell you that. A few take bribes. . . .

327. MCU: *Quinlan, cigar planted in the middle of his face, opens the door
   into the camera, at left of frame. He takes only a couple of hesitant steps
   forward.*

GOULD (*off*): Hank Quinlan never took a dollar in his life!

VARGAS: Most are honest, yes. But even some of the honest men . . .

328. *Low angle* MS: *Gould and Vargas, Adair behind on right.*

VARGAS (*off*): . . . abuse their power in other ways.

GOULD (*over his shoulder, toward the door*): Come in, Hank.

329. *Low angle* MS: *as Gould crosses the frame in extreme foreground, right
   to left, Quinlan emerges from behind him, left to right.*

QUINLAN (*tentatively*): Well, I . . . don't know whether I'm welcome
   or not.

GOULD (*as Quinlan comes forward*): I want you to hear this.

QUINLAN: Uh . . . I've heard it already.

*The camera follows Quinlan to the right as he goes to Vargas: very low
angle* MS, *Quinlan's bulk dominating the frame.*

QUINLAN: Our friend Vargas has some very special ideas about police
   procedure. He seems to think it don't matter whether a killer is hanged
   or not, so long as we obey the fine print . . .

VARGAS (*breaking in*): Well, no, captain . . .

QUINLAN (*over*): . . . in the rule books.

VARGAS: . . . I don't think a policeman should work like a dog- . . .

330. *Tight* CU: *Quinlan and Vargas face one another in profile.*

VARGAS: . . . catcher . . .

QUINLAN (*over*): No?

VARGAS: . . . putting criminals behind bars. No! In any free
   country . . .

QUINLAN (*turning away, into camera*): Aw . . .

VARGAS: . . . a policeman is supposed to enforce the law, and the law
   protects the guilty as well as the innocent.

QUINLAN (*over*): Our job is tough enough.

VARGAS: It's supposed to be. It has to be tough. The policeman's job is

only easy in a police state. That's the whole point, captain. Who is the
boss, the cop or the law?

QUINLAN (*quietly*): Where's your wife, Vargas?

VARGAS: What? What do you mean? You know where she is as well as I
do. Sergeant Menzies drove her. She's at the motel.

QUINLAN (*appraisingly*): Oh? And you're still here?

VARGAS: Yes. I'm checking out now and joining her. Do you have a
reason for asking, captain?

QUINLAN (*over*): Nooo . . .

331. *Low angle* MS: *Quinlan walks back, away from Vargas.*

QUINLAN: No special reason, no . . .

332. *Low angle* MS, *somewhat closer: Quinlan by window.*

QUINLAN: Just wondered. (*Bending over the window sill.*) Oh, what do
you know, a mother pigeon and her nest. A pigeon egg.

He straightens up, holding it gingerly between his fingers.

VARGAS (*appearing at left*): Captain, you did buy seventeen sticks of
dynamite. . . .

QUINLAN (*over*): Ah . . . you tell your story, Vargas. I don't have to answer your questions.

VARGAS: A hired hand at your ranch says he used . . .

QUINLAN (*over*): My ranch! (*In his agitation, he breaks the egg.*)

VARGAS: . . . fifteen sticks. (*He hands Quinlan a handkerchief.*)

QUINLAN (*angrily wiping his hand*): You been spyin' out at my ranch?

333.   *Low angle* MS: *Adair, Quinlan, Vargas.*

QUINLAN: A foreigner!

ADAIR: Without my knowledge, Hank, without my knowledge!

VARGAS (*over, fiercely*): You used fifteen sticks of dynamite, Quinlan. That leaves two sticks missing, and two sticks were found in that shoe box.

The camera follows Quinlan as he lurches to the left.

GOULD (*on left*): He's just asking, Hank.

Quinlan, in a huff, takes out his badge.

ADAIR: Hank!

He throws the badge on a table off camera at the left.

GOULD: What's that for?

QUINLAN: It's for . . . It's for letting him ask. (*Off left.*)

ADAIR (*turning to follow*): Hank, wait a minute!

334.   *Low angle* MS: *Quinlan lurching into camera. The camera tracks back from him as he goes through the hall, Gould and Adair following, and into what appears to be a deserted ballroom. It is oddly lit, so that the figures are mostly in silhouette, and their voices echo in the empty space.*

QUINLAN: Thirty years! Thirty years of poundin' beats, ridin' cars. Thirty years of dirt and crummy pay . . .

GOULD (*over*): But Hank . . .

QUINLAN: Thirty years I gave my life to this department . . .

ADAIR (*over*): Now Hank! Watch your blood pressure! Your blood pressure, Hank!

QUINLAN (*over*): . . . and you allow this foreigner to accuse me!

GOULD (*over*): We were just giving you a chance to answer him.

Quinlan strides off into the left background, a tiny figure in LS. *Adair and Gould are at first in right foreground,* MLS, *then Adair is midway between Quinlan and Gould. They all shout.*

QUINLAN: Answer! Answer! Why do I have to answer him? No sir! I won't take back that badge until the people of this county vote it back.

ADAIR (*whirling around to face Gould*): Oh!!

GOULD: Hank, will you listen a minute? (*Going to Adair, pointing back over his shoulder.*) I don't want to ever see that man at headquarters for any reason at any time! Now, you've backed him up! (*Wagging his finger in Adair's face.*)

ADAIR: Me!

GOULD: You stood by while he impugned the integrity of Captain Quinlan . . .

ADAIR (*over*): I tried to stop him!

GOULD (*over*): . . . and Sergeant Menzies. Do you realize what Vargas has done? (*Striding back to Quinlan.*) He's smearing hundreds of fine men . . .

Vargas enters from right foreground and goes to Adair.

ADAIR (*turning to Vargas, over*): Are you satisfied? Have you caused enough trouble?

GOULD (*over*): . . . men ready to give their lives for the safety of the people of this town!

ADAIR: Are you satisfied? I want you to apologize!

VARGAS (*facing him in the center of the room*): To Quinlan?

ADAIR: And to Chief Gould.

VARGAS: Would you like me to get down on my knees?

ADAIR: If you have any decency you will, yes. You'll crawl!

VARGAS: Mr. Adair, I won't give you the chance to test your authority in this matter. (*Off left.*)

Quinlan goes out the door in background, followed by Adair and Gould.

335.   MS: *Vargas, on his way out, encounters Schwartz in a hallway.*

VARGAS: Al . . . have I still any credit left with you?

SCHWARTZ: Some.

VARGAS: Tell me, where can I find the records of Quinlan's old cases?

SCHWARTZ: I'll show you.

They turn to descend stairs on left.

VARGAS: I'd like to get back to my wife. I hope this won't take too long.

336.   MS: *walking toward camera, Quinlan enters elevator, followed by Gould.*

GOULD: Hank . . .

QUINLAN: Huh?

GOULD (*holding out badge*): You're not going without this?

After a pause, Quinlan slowly takes it. Adair enters the elevator and closes the gates. Low angle MCU of all three.

QUINLAN: Well . . . now I guess I can talk.

GOULD: What do you mean, Hank?

QUINLAN (*diffident*): All I wanted to tell you was . . . I couldn't really say in my own defense. . . .

ADAIR: Go on, Hank.

QUINLAN: What do you really know about this . . . Vargas?

ADAIR: Isn't he in charge of some kind of cleanup here on this side of the border? Narcotics mainly?

QUINLAN: Yeah. Narcotics. He's a drug addict! (*Turning to leave the elevator, as Adair looks aghast.*) He's got that young wife of his hooked too . . .

They leave the elevator.

337.   MLS *in lobby: Quinlan walks from left to right, followed by Adair and Gould. The camera follows.*

QUINLAN: . . . but good! If I hadn't seen that hypodermic myself . . .

ADAIR: Hypodermic! You saw it?

QUINLAN: I just said so, didn't I?

They turn and head out the door, backs to camera. Through the plate glass window we glimpse Vargas and Schwartz leaving.

QUINLAN: And so . . . that's how come he happened to imagine all those crazy things. It's typical. (*The camera follows them outdoors.*) It's what that wife of his was doing in that dive on skid row. Both a couple of junkies! Of course he's using the job (*pausing, turning to them*) as a coverup.

338.   MS: *car passing with Vargas and Schwartz. The camera pans to the right to Adair: moderately high angle* MCU.

ADAIR: You don't mean he's mixed up in this dope racket himself?

339.   *Low angle* MCU: *Gould, Quinlan, tightly framed, with arch of arcade behind.*

QUINLAN: Uh huh.

GOULD (*shaking head*): Hank, if this is just one of your hunches. . . .

QUINLAN: I don't ask you to believe it. I can prove it. I know it isn't my department, but I'd like to show you I'm not talking out of the back of my neck.

GOULD: Just be careful.

QUINLAN: Chief, I'll be very careful.

*340.   MLS, *the Hall of Records: high steel file cabinets on left wall and to right. Steel door in back center opens with an echoing clank: Schwartz enters, followed by Vargas.*

VARGAS (*voice echoing*): This takes guts, Al. Standing up to your boss this way.

The camera follows as they turn right: long perspective of file cabinets.

SCHWARTZ (*stooping by file*): After today, amigo, you can do me a favor. (*Opening drawer.*) Help me look for an office.

VARGAS (*bending over him*): How's that?

SCHWARTZ: Hank Quinlan's famous intuition might still turn out to be better than yours. (*Passing him a folder.*) If so, *my* intuition tells me I'll be going back to private practice. (*Standing and coming back with Vargas to a desk in the middle of the corridor.*) Here are the other names you want, Burger, Ewell.

VARGAS: Look, Al . . . I can finish this alone.

SCHWARTZ: Yes, and maybe you can't.

VARGAS (*pacing away to left foreground with folders, camera following*): Well, let me try anyway. I have no right to drag you further into this.

SCHWARTZ (*crossing past him toward door, camera following*): Gonna do it alone, huh? All you gotta do is solve the murder and also prove that the idol of the police force is a fraud. (*Turning back in the doorway, chuckling mirthlessly.*) Amigo, you've got your work really cut out for you! (*Leaves, closing door behind him.*)

*341. *Cut to door of Susan's motel room: loud rock and roll, still.*
342. MS: *Susan, terror-stricken, darts about her room, clutches wall.*
343. CU *of window from inside room: rising shade reveals leather-clad torso outside.*
344. CU *of window from outside: shade rises and we see Susan, wide-eyed, looking out. On the right of the frame, Pancho, in profile, stares in at her.*
345. *Low angle* CU, *Susan's point of view: Pancho looms over her through the window.*
346. CU, *window from outside, as in 344. Susan darts away, Pancho starts forward.*
347. CU *of Susan: hair flying, she races around corner toward camera, then comes to a stop, alarmed, by wall with speaker.*
348. *Tilted, low angle* MS, *Susan's point of view: the door slowly opens.*
349. MS: *Susan backs away from camera.*
350. *Opening door, as in 348: it opens wider.*
351. MS, *Susan, as in 349: she backs off and throws herself helplessly across the bed, still facing camera.*
352. *Opening door, as in 348. The third gang member appears in the doorway, his shadow thrown sharply on the now fully opened door on the right. He steps forward, low angle* MS.
353. MS: *Susan on her knees on the bed, clutching the sheet in terror.*
354. *Opening door, as in 348: the third gang member enters slowly, followed by Pretty Boy.*
355. MS: *Susan kneeling on bed, as in 353. The third gang member crosses in extreme foreground, right to left, so that the silhouette of his torso momentarily fills the frame, obliterating her image.*

356.   CU: *Susan looks in terror to the left. The third gang member's shadow passes across her face, moving left to right.*

357.   MS: *Susan on bed, as in 353. Pretty Boy crosses in foreground, right to left, obliterating image, exactly as in 355.*

358.   CU: *Susan looking left, as in 356.*

359.   *Low angle* MS *of opening door, as in 348. Pancho enters slowly, faintly smiling.*

360.   CU: *Susan, as in 356. A shadow (Pretty Boy's?) crosses her face, moving from right to left this time.*

361.   *Low angle* MCU *at door: Pancho enters, pushing door closed behind him.*

362.   MCU: *Susan, clutching sheet, staring wildly into camera.*

363.   *Abrupt cut to Tanya's place:* MS. *Pianola theme. Tanya is seated in lower right of the frame, facing away from the camera: almost lost in the clutter, but we can't miss the billowing clouds of smoke she exhales. The phone rings and she stands, goes off right to answer.*

364.   *Low angle* CU: *Menzies in a phone booth.*
MENZIES: Hello, Tanya, is Captain Quinlan there?

365.   CU: *Tanya with phone on right, facing camera; a man's hat is on the hook in left foreground.*
TANYA: Now sergeant . . .
MAN'S VOICE (*off*): Tanya! Hey, Tanya!
TANYA (*aside*): I'll be right there. (*Back to phone.*) Now what would Hank Quinlan be doing here?
MENZIES (*on phone*): It used to be he'd hole up at your place for two or three days, with a case of whiskey.
TANYA: That was years ago. Now he's on candy bars.

366.   (*Low angle*) CU: *Menzies, as in 364.*
MENZIES (*shaking his head*): Not tonight, he isn't

367.   CU: *Tanya, as in 365. We hear Menzies hang up. Tanya looks at the receiver pensively, replaces it, turns and walks toward back.*

368.   MLS: *Night Man in motel office, music blaring. He is still chewing his lunch. He walks toward window on right, camera following, and slowly pulls down the shade.*

369. *High angle* LS *of motel, barren landscape. Music still.*
370. *Low angle* MS *in Susan's room: opening door, as in 348 and following. The leather-jacketed brunette slowly comes in, followed by two other female gang members. The camera follows, low angle, as they walk into the room, left to right, staring appraisingly, and join the third gang member and another boy, all looking down at Susan.*
371. CU: *Susan, as in 356 and following.*
372. MCU: *The brunette, staring down, slowly circles Susan, moving from left to right in front of the other gang members, camera following.*
373. CU: *Susan, as in 371. The brunette's shadow crosses her face, right to left, as in earlier sequence.*
374. MS: *the motel office. The Night Man is seated in center, against wall, eating his sandwich. He stares at amplifier and speaker: the music is annoying him.*
375. MCU: *Pretty Boy and dark-haired gang member, on the right, stare down at Susan. Then they both look up left at the speaker on the wall behind them.*
376. MS: *motel office, as in 374. With a decisive gesture, the Night Man switches off the music, returns to his sandwich.*
377. *Low angle* CU, *distorting lens: Pancho looms over Susan, speaks in Spanish to the brunette.*
378. *Low angle* MS: *brunette in foreground center, dark-haired boy over her shoulder on left.*
    BRUNETTE: Lemme stay. I want to watch.
379. CU: *Susan, as in 371.*
380. CU, *distorting lens: Pancho gazes into camera, licks lips.*
    PANCHO (*whispering*): Hold her legs.
381. CU: *Susan, as in 371. A shadow falls across her face, for a moment leaving just her terrified eyes illuminated, then darkening the whole face.*
382. LS: *The gang surrounds the bed and, struggling, tries to lift Susan off.*
    SUSAN (*struggling*): Oh, oh. No! Let me go! Don't touch me! Let me go! No, no, no! Ohhh . . . !
    They pick her up and the camera tracks back as they move out into the room. Another gang member enters the room from right foreground.
    VOICE: Close the door!
    The door, in the left foreground, is slammed shut toward the center of the frame.

383. *Cut to reverse movement at Hall of Records: the door at rear right opens away from center of frame:* MLS. *Menzies enters and moves into low angle* MS. *The camera swings to follow him as he turns right, down the corridor of filing cabinets in exaggerated perspective. Vargas is at a desk on the right.*

   MENZIES: So this is where you've been all afternoon, hm? How'd they let you in here? A foreigner.

   VARGAS (*he's been ignoring Menzies*): The Hall of Records is open to the public, sergeant.

   MENZIES: What're you doing?

   VARGAS: You'll find out tomorrow morning.

   MENZIES (*grabbing papers and going back into corridor as Vargas stands in foreground*): I want to know now!

384. *Low angle* MS: *Menzies reading papers against file cabinet.*

   MENZIES (*looking up*): What's all this?

   VARGAS (*off*): Records of every case where you and Quinlan uncovered the principal evidence.

385. *Low angle* MS: *Vargas, into camera.*

   VARGAS: In each case, as you'll notice, the defense denied the existence of that evidence.

386. *Low angle* MS: *Menzies, as in 384.*

   MENZIES: What are you trying to do? Wreck him?

387. MS: *Menzies on left, facing away; Vargas approaching on right, the camera moving in as he does so.*

   VARGAS: Him? What about you? Are you telling me you never planted any evidence, sergeant?

388. *Low angle* MS: *Menzies, as in 384.*

   MENZIES: Of course not. Neither did Hank.

389. MS: *Menzies, Vargas, as in 387.*

   VARGAS (*coming closer*): It's all there. The ax in the Burger slaying. The dentures in the Ewell case.

390. *Reverse shot: Menzies on left, Vargas facing him on right.*

   VARGAS: The lead pipe . . .

   Menzies impulsively crumples papers, throws them to the floor, then stoops out of frame.

   VARGAS: Go on, tear them. (*Turning to shout off right foreground.*) It's all there in the record.

391.   CU: *Menzies rests his head mournfully on top of a file cabinet.*
    MENZIES: All these years he's spent building up a reputation . . .
    VARGAS (*off, over*): All these years he's been planting evidence . . .
392.   *Low angle* MS: *Vargas.*
    VARGAS: . . . framing suspects.
393.   MS: *Menzies, Vargas, as in 390.*
    MENZIES (*straightening up*): That's a lie!
    VARGAS: I think I can prove it, sergeant.
    MENZIES: Sure, you can smear him.
394.   LS: *Menzies and Vargas at the end of the corridor of files. Menzies walks*
    forward toward the camera as Vargas stoops to retrieve the scattered
    papers.
    MENZIES: You've ruined his whole life's work. (MLS *in left foreground.*)
    Oh yes, I . . . I don't even know where he is. That's what you've done
    to him.
    VARGAS: What *I've* done to *him*?
    MENZIES (*near tears*): Yeah, yeah, yeah, yeah, yeah. He's on an important
    case and he's disappeared. Good and drunk, probably. After twelve
    years on the wagon. That's what you've done to him.
    VARGAS (*standing and coming to Menzies, the camera drawing back*
    to leave them both in MLS): What about Quinlan, sergeant? What's
    he done? (*Collecting papers from the desk and walking forward, the*
    camera drawing back to keep him in low angle MS.) What about all
    those people he put in the death house? Save your tears for them.
    He goes off left foreground, leaving Menzies alone in right background,
    framed by perspective of file cabinets.

*395.   *Dissolve to* MLS *inside office of motel: night has fallen, the room is*
    full of shadows. The Night Man sits behind the desk, singing softly to
    himself.
    NIGHT MAN: When the roll is called up yonder . . . when the roll is
    called up yonder . . .
    Sounds off: he gets to his feet as Vargas enters on right.
    VARGAS: What seems to be the trouble?
    NIGHT MAN: Trouble?
    VARGAS: The lights. The lights seem to be out in all the cabins.

NIGHT MAN (*coming forward, peering off left foreground, nodding as if noticing for the first time*): Yes! yes! Somebody's been monkeying in with them fuses! If they think I'm gonna fix 'em, they . . . they . . . they got another think coming! (*Jumping, startled, as Vargas approaches.*) It ain't my job to fix 'em, even if I know how. I'm . . . I'm the night man.

VARGAS (*low angle* MS, *over*): Could you show me, please, to my wife's cabin?

NIGHT MAN (*long hesitation, stares blankly, shakes head*): Noooo. There . . . there ain't nobody here.

VARGAS (*patient*): You must be mistaken, sir. My wife has been registered here since this morning. (*Pause.*) My name is Vargas.

NIGHT MAN (*after another pause, weakly*): Vargas?

VARGAS: Would you look (*gesturing*), please, in the register?

NIGHT MAN (*turns to left, looking down*): The register?

He drifts back toward the desk, looking out the window. Vargas stoops behind the desk for the register.

NIGHT MAN: It might be cabin six.

VARGAS: Possibly.

NIGHT MAN (*darting around to left of desk*): Maybe seven.

VARGAS (*straightening up, with register*): Yes, here. (*Hands it to him.*)

The Night Man fidgets with it ineffectually.[12]

VARGAS (*snatching it from him*): May I? (*Reads, as the Night Man peers over his shoulder.*) There's . . . nobody been registered all week! (*Closing it and looking up sharply.*)

NIGHT MAN (*jumping back, the camera following*): No . . . no. It's . . . it's . . . it's off the season. Nobody hardly ever comes around at all. I'm . . . I'm the night man.

Vargas, exasperated, turns and goes out right foreground.

NIGHT MAN (*looking after him*): Oh, there *was* that party. . . . (*Follows him out.*)

396.   MS: *Vargas, on left, facing camera, against night sky.*[13] *Sound of wind.*

VARGAS: Party? What party?

NIGHT MAN (*into frame from right foreground*): It's a mess . . . awful mess!

VARGAS: Where?

NIGHT MAN: They think I'm gonna clean it up, they got another think coming. Terrible, terrible brawl! (*Turns to point over to the cabins, facing the camera as he counts.*)

397. MLS: *Vargas, Night Man, as before. Vargas's car on left.*

NIGHT MAN: Cabin number seven!

Vargas reaches into his car for a flashlight.

NIGHT MAN: Right in the middle of the afternoon! Cabin number seven!

They walk toward the cabins, the camera tracking back in front of them. The wind is so strong that the Night Man must hold his hat on his head.

398. LS: *framed by eaves of cabin's porch as the two men approach.*

VARGAS (*pausing*): This brawl. You mean there was some sort of a fight?

NIGHT MAN (*after a hesitation*): Fight?

VARGAS: Yes.

NIGHT MAN: No . . . no . . . it wasn't that kind of a brawl.

They continue forward, moving into MS as they reach the cabin.

NIGHT MAN (*drawing back skittishly as Vargas tries the door*): It was . . . one of them wild parties. You know the kind?

He disappears around the corner of the building: Vargas turns to follow.

399. MS: *inside room. Vanity and mirror on left, window on right. The Night Man passes by the window outside and is reflected in the mirror; then Vargas. The camera pans to the right, past the wall speaker and an open window, curtains billowing into the room, and we see the Night Man and Vargas enter through door in right foreground. The camera follows them left into the room, Vargas with his flashlight, then draws back to reveal littered bed in the foreground.*

VARGAS (*looking at mess*): This can't be my wife's room.

NIGHT MAN (*in rear, picking up robe*): This ain't her clothes, huh? Whew! It stinks in here! (*Back to window in rear, then forward again.*) Let's get some air in here! (*To the window on the right.*)

400. MS: *Night Man at window, billowing curtains.*

NIGHT MAN: It's a mess! It's a stinkin' mess! (*Turning back into the room, wrestling with the curtains.*) Everything's . . . wild parties . . .

401. MS: *Vargas enters from left foreground, bends over to pick up his briefcase.*

VARGAS: Here's my briefcase. I left it with Susan. (*Turns around toward camera as he gropes in it for his gun.*)

402.   MS: *The Night Man finds a marijuana butt, lurches toward the camera with it, into* CU.

NIGHT MAN: Ah! . . . stub here . . . (*Sniffs it, is aghast, screams.*)

403.   MS: *Vargas with briefcase, as in 401.*

NIGHT MAN (*darting quickly across extreme foreground and off left*): I'm getting out of here!

VARGAS (*finding it missing*): My gun! (*Off left, after Night Man.*)

404.   LS *outdoors: Night Man in far distance at left; Vargas entering,* MLS, *at right. Both men must shout to be heard.*

VARGAS: You haven't been here?

NIGHT MAN: Nah. . . .

VARGAS: You haven't been in that room?

NIGHT MAN: Agh. . . . I just looked in.

VARGAS: I had a gun in this case! (*Going after Night Man.*) You didn't take it?

NIGHT MAN (*screaming, from extreme distance*): What would I want with a gun?

VARGAS (*after him*): Well, somebody wanted it!

405.   *Low angle* MS: *the Night Man clings wildly to a spectral tree, facing camera.*

NIGHT MAN: If they hadn't put that Grandi boy on the desk this morning, none of this would have happened!

406.   MS: *Night Man and tree on left, in profile; Vargas approaching from center.*

VARGAS: Grandi?!

NIGHT MAN: Who . . . who do you think this belongs to, anyway?

VARGAS: Where are they?

407.   MS: *Night Man and tree, facing camera; Vargas in right foreground.*

NIGHT MAN (*gurgling*): The . . . the . . . the kids?

VARGAS: Yes!

408.   MS: *Night Man on left, Vargas in center, as in 406.*

VARGAS: Please. . . .

NIGHT MAN (*gurgling, trying to articulate, finally screaming it out*): Rancho . . . !

VARGAS: Rancho Grande!

NIGHT MAN (*triumphant*): Yeah!

Vargas rushes off left foreground as the Night Man, still clinging to the tree, turns into the camera to look after him.

409. *High angle* LS *of motel as Vargas's car turns and leaves off right.*
410. LS: *Vargas's car on the road, headlights into camera, squealing brakes as it curves away.*

411. LS: *a street in Los Robles. The neon sign of the Ritz Hotel in center rear, framed by arcade in foreground. Bustling nighttime crowd of servicemen, tourists. Bongo theme.*
412. *Cut to what seems to be black screen. Then door opens in center of frame to reveal Susan sprawled, unconscious, on an ornate brass bed, her head at its foot. As the sequence progresses (412–490), an increasingly dense and cacophonous blur of brass and bongos: suggestions of street noise, half-heard repetitions of themes from the bomb sequence.*
413. *Tilted, low angle* MS *from within hotel room. Ornately twisted foot of bed in foreground, foreshortened view of Susan; Grandi enters cautiously from door in background.*

GRANDI: You got her undressed?

414. *Reverse shot. The back of Grandi's head and shoulders in extreme right foreground; two female gang members beyond foot of bed in back.*
FIRST GANG MEMBER (*blond, husky voice*): Yeah. We've scattered more reefer stubs around.

415. MS: *Grandi seen through foot of bed, as in 413.*
GRANDI: You kids didn't use none of that stuff yourself, huh?
SECOND GANG MEMBER (*brunette, lighter voice, off*): Think we're crazy?
GRANDI: Nobody in the Grandi family gets hooked. Understand? That's the rule.

416. MS: *Grandi facing gang members, as in 414.*
FIRST GANG MEMBER: We blew the smoke in her clothes, that's all.
SECOND GANG MEMBER: Like you said, we put on a good show to scare her.

417. MS: *Grandi seen through foot of bed, as in 413.*
GRANDI: Let's hope it was good enough. (*Camera up slightly as he advances.*) When she wakes up, she's gotta think maybe something really did happen. All right, now, beat it.

418. MS: *Grandi facing gang members, as in 414.*
SECOND GANG MEMBER: What about our dough?

419. MS: *Grandi seen through foot of bed, as in 413. We see the first gang member's hand passing over the foot of the bed on her way to the door.*
FIRST GANG MEMBER: We're not doing this for fun, Uncle Joe.
GRANDI: Beat it, beat it. You're gonna get your dough tomorrow.
Both girls pass behind Grandi to the door.
FIRST GANG MEMBER (*sullen, as they leave*): Okay.
GRANDI: Beat it!
He stands looking down at Susan, then backs away from the bed toward the door.

420. MS, *in the hall: Grandi is framed in the doorway as he pulls the door open and looks out, peering up and down the hall in both directions.*
GRANDI (*turning to right*): Pssst!
The camera pans quickly to the right: empty corridor. Then in a doorway near right foreground, we see the brim of Quinlan's hat and a flask going up to his mouth.
GRANDI (*off*): Okay.

Quinlan lurches forward unsteadily, looking groggy and unshaven. The camera turns to follow, MCU, *as he turns into the room, followed by Grandi, who shuts the door after him.*

421. *Tilted, low angle* MS: *foot of bed in foreground, as in 413. Quinlan is in mid range, looking down at the bed; Grandi is at the door, coming forward behind him.*

QUINLAN (*abruptly*): Turn out the lights!

GRANDI: But why? (*Quinlan glares: he switches them off.*) Nobody can see you up here.

From now on, the scene is lit only by the flashing neon sign outdoors.

QUINLAN (*leans cane on foot of bed, begins putting on black gloves*): You sure?

GRANDI: Of course I'm sure.

422. *Low angle* MS: *Quinlan's gloved hand and torso are silhouetted in the right foreground. The camera follows as he walks around to the end of the bed, so that its foot is in front of him.*

423. *Low angle* MS: *Grandi seen through foot of bed, as in 421.*

GRANDI: Hey, what are you doing?

424. MLS: *Susan's foreshortened torso, foot of bed in foreground; Quinlan behind, menacing, still putting on gloves.*

QUINLAN: I brought you up here for a reason.

425. *Low angle* MS: *Quinlan's torso and his gloved hand in left foreground; Grandi looks up at him from behind the foot of the bed.*

GRANDI: I don't get it. (*Apprehensively, as Quinlan's arm is lifted out of frame.*) I don't even see why you wanted us to bring her . . . all the way into town here.

QUINLAN (*we still don't see his face*): I couldn't drive out to the motel. My car's known.

GRANDI: So what? You're a cop making an arrest.

QUINLAN: The vice boys will do that. (*His hand returns to the foreground, holding a large revolver.*)

GRANDI: What's that for?

Silence, then Quinlan moves out of frame to left.

426. *High angle* MS: *Susan on the bed, her face seen through the curve of its foot. She tosses uneasily, the camera swinging to follow the motion of her head.*

427. *Very low angle* MS: *Quinlan, on left, points his gun at Grandi.*

QUINLAN (*pushing him to the wall*): Turn around! (*He frisks him and tosses his gun aside.*) Get the phone!

428. MS: *Grandi, with phone in right foreground.*

QUINLAN (*off*): The phone!

Grandi takes the phone, looking scared. The camera moves into a high angle MCU *as Quinlan crosses in front of Grandi and stands looming over him in the right foreground.*

QUINLAN: Now dial 1212.

GRANDI: But that's the police station!

QUINLAN: Go on, dial it.

GRANDI: Stop with it. You're drunk. (*Dialing.*) Just stop and think for a minute.

QUINLAN: Simply answer.

GRANDI (*on phone*): Hello.

QUINLAN: Ask for Sergeant Menzies. Menzies!

GRANDI (*on phone*): Sergeant Menzies. (*Setting aside the receiver.*) Quinlan, if you turn me in, I'll have quite a story to tell.

QUINLAN (*half-chuckling*): Hmmm. Yeah, you sure will.

429. *Low angle* MS: *Grandi turned away from camera in left foreground; Quinlan facing him on right.*

QUINLAN: See if Menzies . . .

GRANDI (*on phone*): Hello, Menzies?

QUINLAN: Got him? Hand me the phone. (*Grandi hands it toward him.*) Hold it so I can talk to him. Gimme the receiver. (*Taking it roughly.*) Gimme the receiver!

430. *High angle* MCU: *Grandi on left, Quinlan in profile in right foreground, as at conclusion of 428. He holds the receiver in one hand, his gun on Grandi with the other.*

QUINLAN: Hello, Pete? (*Smiling.*) Of course it's me, partner. Any news yet?

431. *The police station. Menzies in left foreground,* MCU, *with phone. In the right rear we see Sanchez in a glass booth, being interrogated. Sound of a typewriter.*

MENZIES (*on phone*): Sanchez still hasn't broken. . . . What? (*Camera moves into tight* CU.) Vargas's wife? A narcotics rap?

432. *High angle* MCU: *Grandi, Quinlan, as in 430.*

QUINLAN (*on phone, voice slurred with drink*): Oh, one of the boys who was on this wild party came into the bar, see? Oh, just relay it to the vice boys as anonymous. The Hotel Ritz, Room 18. From what I hear, things got a little out of control. Don't be surprised . . . what they find.

433. CU: *Menzies on phone, as at conclusion of 431.*

MENZIES (*mournfully*): But what about me, Hank? What do I do?

434. *High angle* MCU: *Grandi, Quinlan, as in 430.*

QUINLAN (*harshly*): Keep after him! Break him! Break him!! (*Slams down receiver; then to Grandi:*) Put up the phone. (*Grandi nervously does so, the camera moving down to low angle* MS: *Grandi on left, Quinlan on right.*) The receiver! (*Grandi manages to get it back on the cradle.*) Gimme the key! (*Grandi hands it to him. Quinlan backs away into* MLS, *turning the lock in the door and putting the key in his pocket.*) I told you I brought you up here for a reason.

In left foreground, Grandi's head is no longer in the frame. Quinlan stands pointing his gun at him, then begins to move forward.

435. *Low angle* MS: *Grandi looks up in terror as Quinlan enters the frame from the right foreground. His bulk briefly covers the frame as he moves across toward the left, Grandi retreating before him. The camera stays with Grandi, moving into high angle, as he backs off to the right. Then, as he approaches the wall, Quinlan's dark bulk reenters the frame from the left. Back to the camera, he seizes Grandi by his tie. Grandi struggles. Quinlan lurches into the camera.*

436. MS: *Grandi, facing the camera, is thrown back against the wall. Garishly lit by light from outside, he slithers along it to the right. The camera follows as he turns to race back and clamber up to a transom over a chest of drawers.*

437. *Low angle* MS: *Quinlan advances, the camera tracking back before him.*

438. *Low angle* MLS: *Grandi, seen from behind, struggles at the transom. He rips off the curtain, picks up a mug from the top of the chest.*

439. *Very brief* MCU: *back of Grandi's head as he smashes glass of the transom with the mug.*

440. MCU *outside transom as it is smashed: we briefly see Grandi trying to scramble up.*

441. *High angle* MLS *inside room: Grandi in right foreground on chest, reaching for transom; Quinlan below, pulling at him, ripping off his shirt.*

442. *Extreme* CU: *Quinlan, lunging forward, his face distorted with fury.*
443. *Low angle* CU: *Grandi's face, flailing arms.*
444. *Low angle* MS *at transom: Quinlan in the foreground pulls Grandi down and throws him toward the camera. A huge* CU *of Quinlan briefly fills the frame as he heaves Grandi and lurches off the right foreground. Grunts and cries are lost in the blare of the soundtrack.*
445. *High angle* MS: *the bed. Grandi, shouting, an indistinguishable blur, falls into the frame from the left foreground, lands near foot of bed.*
446. MS: *from beneath the bed, through the frame of its foot, we see Grandi, falling from right to left, hit the floor, his bald head exposed.*
447. *High angle* MS: *Susan tosses on the bed. Quinlan says something inaudible.*
448. MCU, *under bed: Grandi's gun in foreground, his arm straining through the bed frame to reach it.*
449. MCU: *Grandi's face, pressing through bed frame as he strains to reach gun.*
450. MCU: *hand reaching for gun, as in 448.*
451. MCU: *Grandi's face through bed frame, as in 449.*
452. MS: *Quinlan on right hauls Grandi to his feet and flings him back against the wall.*
453. MS: *Grandi cowers against wall, shirt torn, wig askew, running his tongue around his mouth in terror.*
454. MS: *Quinlan hunches over the bed, finds a stocking, tightens it between his hands. As the sign outside blinks, the frame plunges in and out of darkness.*
455. *High angle* MCU: *Grandi cowers against the wall.*
456. MS: *Quinlan at bed, as in 454. He turns and walks back toward Grandi.*
457. *High angle* MS: *Susan seen through foot of bed.*
458. MCU: *Grandi screams. Quinlan enters the frame from the right and begins to twist the stocking around Grandi's neck.*
    GRANDI: No, don't!
459. CU: *Susan, seen from in front, tosses on the bed.*
460. *High angle* CU: *Grandi twists in the noose as Quinlan, on the right, tightens it. The camera tilts up toward Quinlan's grimacing face.*
461. CU: *Susan tossing, as in 459.*
462. *Extreme* CU: *Quinlan's grimace, lunging into the camera as he struggles with Grandi.*

463. *Low angle* MS: *Susan silhouetted on bed in foreground. Through the foot of the bed we see Quinlan approaching from right, carrying Grandi, his feet kicking.*

464. *High angle* MS: *Susan, through foot of bed, as in 457.*

465. *Low angle* MS: *Grandi's kicking legs, dangling from the top of the frame, batter the foot of the bed, in foreground.*

466. *High angle* MS: *Susan, through foot of bed, as in 464.*

467. *Low angle* MS: *Susan and bed in foreground, as in 463. Grandi's legs, no longer kicking, are lowered on the right; and then we see his head drop limply over the foot of the bed. The camera reframes slightly, and in the dark, the neon sign having blinked off, only Susan is seen clearly.*

468. *Low angle* CU: *Quinlan's shoulder as he goes out the door, his bulk for an instant almost filling the frame. Then he turns, framed in the half-closed door, and looks back.*

469. *High angle* MS: *Susan, seen from in front, tosses on the bed. Grandi's corpse dangles from top of frame.*

470. MS: *Quinlan in doorway, as at conclusion of 468. He slowly closes it. The camera zooms in to sign on the door: "STOP. FORGET ANYTHING? Leave Key at Desk."*

471. *High angle* MCU: *Susan's head, upside down, on left. Grandi's dangling head and shoulder half in the frame at extreme right foreground, as if looking down at her. First dark, then light, as neon blinks. In the light, Susan opens her eyes.*

472. *Low angle* MCU: *Grandi's head, upside down, eyes popping. First light, then dark, the face turning to shadow.*

473. *High angle* MCU: *Susan's head, upside down, as in 471.*

474. *Low angle* CU: *Grandi's head, upside down, closer than 472. Light, then dark.*

475. *High angle* MCU: *Susan's head, upside down, as in 471. Screaming, she sits up.*

476. MS: *Susan, seen from side, in silhouette, sits up, screaming; Grandi slumped on right, in silhouette. Camera follows as Susan rushes, hair flowing, toward the brightly lit window. As the light blinks on, then off again, she pulls it open.*
    SUSAN (*barely audible over blare on soundtrack*): Please help!

477. *Low angle* LS *from street: Susan on fire escape in nightgown.*
    SUSAN: Will somebody help me!

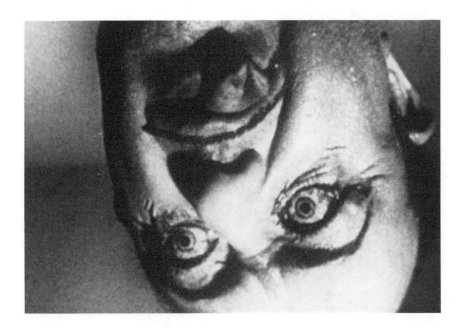

478. *Point-of-view shot from above: people in the street stare up, grinning.*
479. *Low angle* MS *from street: people pass by, a soldier waves up at her.*
     SUSAN (*barely audible*): Help! Somebody come up and help me!
480. *High angle* LS: *the street, as in 478. People wave, a woman shouts in Spanish.*
481. *Tilted low angle* LS: *Susan on the fire escape (different angle from 477).*
     SUSAN: Help me!
482. LS *on street. The camera follows Vargas approaching from the right in his car. He stops as a car pulls out of a driveway in front of him.*
483. LS *from in front of Vargas's car. The other car passes in front of Vargas, who then proceeds.*
484. *Closer shot, same direction, of car passing in front of Vargas. "Jesus Saves" sign above. The camera then moves up and to the left to observe Susan on the fire escape.*
485. MS *on the street. Rowdy, shouting servicemen in the foreground. Vargas in his car eases his way through the crowd, right to left, shouting in Spanish to people in his path.*

486. *Low angle* MLS: *Susan leans over the rail of the fire escape.*
     SUSAN (*seeing him*): Mike!
487. MS *on street, as in 485. Vargas makes his way through the crowd. Then
     the camera rises to* LS *of building, fire escape.*
488. *Low angle* MLS: *Susan on fire escape, as in 486.*
     SUSAN: Mike! Mike!
489. *High angle* LS: *Vargas's car, speeding up, moves from right to left, then
     turns toward camera as it passes customs booth on the border.*
490. MS: *crowded street on the other side of the border. The camera, tracking
     to the right, picks up and keeps pace with Vargas's car speeding away,
     left to right, knocking down a bicyclist as he leaves the frame.*

491. *Cut to Grandi's Rancho Grande.* MS *of bartenders, customers, framed
     by the spread legs of a stripper. Raucous rock and roll. Vargas rushes
     in, right to left, barely visible in the background. Then the camera draws
     back to reveal the stripper's whole figure.*
492. MS: *back room of the strip joint. Vargas, back to camera, enters from*

*left foreground, pushing his way into the smokey room through beaded
curtains in the foreground. Shouting, he asks in Spanish for Grandi. The
noise subsides: then, after a tense pause, the music resumes. The camera
tracks to left along the beaded curtain as Vargas penetrates deeper into
the crowded space of the night club. Pancho and some of the gang are
seated at a table in center foreground. By the end of the shot, Vargas has
made a circuit and approaches the camera,* MLS, *on left.*

493. MLS: *Vargas at bar on left, Pancho seated at side of table in right
foreground. Vargas picks up a glass from the bar, throws it to the
ground, and, in the sudden silence, shouts in Spanish. Pancho stands
and goes to Vargas, the camera tracking and moving in to a* MS *of the
two men. Pancho blows smoke in Vargas's face, speaks insolently in
Spanish. Vargas takes him by the collars of his jacket and, the camera
tracking right, pushes him across the room and smashes him against a
jukebox. He interrogates him angrily in Spanish:* MCU.

494. MS: *Risto, a blond girl, and another gang member look on from their
table. The blond gets up nervously and goes off left.*

495. MCU, *as at conclusion of 493. Vargas smashes Pancho's head against
the jukebox, breaking the glass. Pancho sinks to the floor. Vargas turns
to stare angrily into the camera toward the gang's table.*

496. MS: *Risto, still seated, apprehensively returns Vargas's glare, then,
losing his nerve, stands and darts out left foreground.*

497. LS *of bar in deep perspective. First we see the blur of Risto entering left
foreground. Then* LS *as Vargas pursues him down the length of the bar,
away from the camera.*

498. MS: *lateral view of bar. Vargas races after Risto, right to left, catches up
with him at door near left foreground.*

499. MLS *of club through bead curtain: shouts, confusion, shadowy figures
rush across foreground.*

500. MS: *Vargas and Risto, as at conclusion of 498. Vargas grips him fiercely,
shouts in Spanish, still asking about his wife.*

501. LS *of bar. Camera tracks back as Vargas, approaching us, carries Risto
half the length of the bar, beginning in his fury to catch up with the
camera. He pushes him back over the bar, shouting in Spanish.*

502. *Low angle* MS: *Vargas pushes Risto back over the bar.*
    RISTO: Talk English, can't you?
    VARGAS: Listen, I'm no cop now. I'm a husband! (*Throwing him*

forward and off right foreground.) What did you do with her? (*Into camera.)* Where is my wife? My wife!
A gang member approaches Vargas from behind, walking on the bar: he leaps onto his shoulders.

503. MS: *back of Vargas as he falls, grappling with the gang members, on collapsing table and chairs.*
504. MS: *Vargas and two gang members grappling against bar. Vargas punches them, one of whom falls off right; then turns to wrestle with a third who comes at him on the left from the top of the bar.*
505. MS, *from a different angle: Vargas flips his assailant to the floor, the bar beginning to topple over with him.*
506. *Low angle* MS: *the toppling bar, as Vargas drags off gang member.*
507. MLS: *back room of club, milling crowd. Camera tracks in as police arrive: whistles, confusion. Some of the crowd try to escape through the beaded curtain in the background but more cops arrive there too.*
508. MLS *through beaded curtain: crowd rushing back, cops rushing forward.*
509. LS: *the narrow corridor of the club, filled with the overturned bar. People rush out over it, moving away from camera. Vargas is left standing midway down.*
    SCHWARTZ (*off*): Vargas!
510. MLS: *crowd milling in front of beaded curtain, as at conclusion of 507.*
511. *Low angle* MS, *toppled bar in foreground, Vargas behind. Schwartz enters left, crosses foreground to Vargas: the camera rises slightly to reframe on the two men.*
    SCHWARTZ: It's your wife, Vargas. They picked her up.
    VARGAS (*gripping his shoulder*): What do you mean, picked her up?
    SCHWARTZ: The vice squad.
    VARGAS: Quinlan?
    SCHWARTZ: You better come outside with me, amigo.
    Turning to lead him out, Schwartz crosses left in front of the camera again. Vargas, anguished in right foreground, turns to follow, lurches past camera.
512. MS: *Vargas, entering right foreground, back to camera, follows Schwartz through beaded curtain. The camera follows to* MCU *of the two men.*

VARGAS: No . . . no . . . ! Tell me what happened.

SCHWARTZ: They found her at the Hotel Ritz. Half-naked on one of the
  beds. Drugged. There were reefer stubs and a heroin fix.

Vargas turns to leave through beads in background.

513. MLS: *police interrogate crowd on left. Vargas breaks through beads in
  right background, racing toward camera, followed by Schwartz.*

SCHWARTZ: Vargas!

They move into low angle MS.

SCHWARTZ (*grasping him*): The charge isn't just possession of
  narcotics.

VARGAS: What is it then?

514. *Extreme* CU: *back of Schwartz's head fills left of frame; Vargas half out
  of frame on right, face shadowed, stares incredulously into camera.*

SCHWARTZ: Murder.

The camera zooms in.

VARGAS: Murder!

The screen goes black.

515. *Cut to low angle* LS *of jail corridor. Schwartz, entering from foreground,
  back to camera, follows Vargas as he races ahead into deep space.
  Jagged musical theme. As Vargas turns right at the end of the corridor
  he shouts something [inaudible] to the matron, who approaches from the
  left. Low angle as all three approach a cell on the right.*

516. *High angle* MS: *Vargas, back to camera, on right; matron opening cell
  door on extreme left. The camera moves left as Vargas enters cell and
  goes to Susan on a cot, the matron closing the door behind him.*

517. *High angle* MS *through cell door: Vargas kneels beside the still groggy
  Susan.*

VARGAS: Susie! (*Kissing and cradling her passive face.*) Susie! Darling!
  It's all right now. Susie. Susie.

518. MLS *through bars from inside cell: coroner looks on, Menzies
  approaches from right.*

CORONER (*to Menzies*): It's all down in the report. Found evidence of a
  mixed party.

519. *High angle* MS: *Vargas and Susan, as in 517.*

VARGAS (*looking up*): Mixed party!

520. MS: *coroner, Menzies.*
      CORONER: Articles of clothing, half-smoked reefers (*turning away*),
         needle . . .
521. *High angle* MS: *Vargas and Susan, as in 517.*
      CORONER (*off*): . . . marks.
      VARGAS: Something else could produce the same effects. Demerol, for
         instance, or sodium . . .
522. MS: *coroner, Menzies, as in 520. Camera follows as coroner crosses
      right behind woeful-looking Menzies.*
      VARGAS (*off*): . . . pentothal.
      CORONER: You could smell the stuff on her. (*Goes off right.*)
523. *High angle* MS: *Vargas and Susan, as in 517. Camera tilts up as Vargas
      gets angrily to his feet.*
      VARGAS: This whole set-up stinks! Who the hell does Quinlan think he
         is, hanging a murder . . .
524. *Low angle* CU: *Menzies, looking melancholy, badly in need of a shave.*
      VARGAS (*off*): . . . rap on my wife?
      SUSAN (*off, muffled*): Mike . . .
525. CU: *Vargas, glaring into camera.*
      SUSAN (*off*): Mike. . . . (*More clearly:*) Mike?
      VARGAS (*turning and kneeling down to her again*): Susie, lie down.
      The camera moves down to a moderately high angle CU *of both.*
      SUSAN: Mike.
      VARGAS: Now it's all right, Susie.
      SUSAN: Mike.
      VARGAS: You're wonderful.
      SUSAN: Take me home.
526. *Low angle* CU: *Menzies, as in 524. He gulps as he looks on.*
      VARGAS (*off*): Yes, Susie.
      SUSAN (*off*): Mike.
      VARGAS (*off*): Susie. Susie.
527. *High angle* MS *through bars: Vargas, Susan, as in 517.*
      VARGAS: Susie . . . forgive me. (*He stands and moves out of frame on
         right.*)
      SUSAN (*sitting up, reaching after him*): Mike . . .
      (*Vargas, silhouetted in the right foreground, opens the cell door.*)
      SUSAN: . . . don't go.

528. *The cell door opens onto a* MLS *of Menzies, hands in pockets, looking on diffidently.*
VARGAS (*off*): I'm right here, Susie . . .
529. *Low angle* CU: *Menzies. He moves toward right foreground, approaching Vargas.*
VARGAS (*off*): . . . it's all right.
530. MS: *Vargas at door of cell on right, Menzies approaching on left. Menzies gestures with his head, then the camera tracks back, low angle, as he leads Vargas down the corridor. Menzies opens a door in the left foreground, wordlessly turns to Vargas, who follows him in.*
531. *Low angle* MS *in storeroom. Menzies enters, followed by Vargas. Menzies in depth at left; Vargas, back to camera, partly visible in extreme right foreground.*
MENZIES: You understand, Vargas, there's no formal charge against your wife.
VARGAS (*moving forward into frame*): Oh?
MENZIES: Even the vice boys are not pressing anything.
VARGAS (*pacing past him into deep focus on right*): Oh, the fact that Susan won't actually serve time makes everything all right! Is that it?
MENZIES: I told you I got something to show you.
VARGAS (*pacing forward again to right foreground*): Her family! Her good name! Nothing's been touched by all this . . . filth!
Menzies carefully removes a coat from a table in the left foreground. Sinister chord on soundtrack. Vargas stands staring at him for a moment, then slowly approaches the table, turning his back to the camera. He turns around again, holding Quinlan's cane. Menzies comes forward on the right, so both men are in low angle MS.
532. CU: *Vargas in profile in left foreground, Menzies further back on right, facing camera.*
MENZIES: I found it in the hotel room. Yeah, with Grandi's body.
With a sigh, Vargas moves off right foreground, leaving the camera on Menzies, looking desolate.
*533. *Dissolve to low angle* MS *of Tanya's porch: door open, pianola heard from within (not Tanya's theme). Vargas, below, stealthily crosses foreground, left to right, then reappears on the porch, moving from right to left.*

534.   MLS *inside Tanya's parlor: Quinlan slumped in chair in right
foreground. Pianola, TV, clutter.*[14]

*535.   MLS: *the wall of Tanya's parlor: peeling plaster, bull fight photos, mirror
on left. Vargas's reflection appears in the mirror. Then the camera moves
down to Quinlan in his chair,* MS, *facing the camera. He blinks groggily,
gets up into low angle* MCU: *he is standing in the right of the frame, the
bull's head prominent in the center of the wall behind him.*

*536.   MS *of window in Tanya's parlor, table with lamp, clutter in foreground.
We see Vargas in the window, passing by toward the right; the camera
then pans right to show him passing a second window.*

*537.   Low angle MCU: *Quinlan, bull behind, as at conclusion of 535. He
blinks, uncertain what he has seen.*

*538.   MS *as at conclusion of 536: Vargas disappears past second window.*

*539.   Low angle MCU: *Quinlan, bull, as in 537. Quinlan uncertain still.*

*540.   MS: *Vargas prowling in front of Tanya's, moving from right to left,
derrick visible behind him. The camera rises to reveal Menzies, with
listening device, on second-story platform of a building across from
Tanya's, facing the camera. We hear steps on the wooden stairs as Vargas
comes up to join him.*

*541.   MS: *Menzies leans over railing with listening device, facing camera.
Vargas comes up from behind. Pianola still audible.*
    VARGAS: He's still just . . . sitting in there. (*Reaching for recorder.*)
        Here, give me that.
    MENZIES (*over*): We've been waiting three hours already.
    VARGAS: We won't get a word on this as long . . .
    MENZIES (*over*): Now look, why don't we . . .
    VARGAS: . . . as he's near that piano. If you would just go in and shut
        it off.
    MENZIES (*removing jacket so he can be fitted with mike*): He'll never
        stand for that. I have to get him out of there.
    VARGAS (*assembling device on railing*): Give me the microphone.
    MENZIES (*handing it to him*): Vargas, I can take care of this thing.
    VARGAS (*wiring him*): Not without me.
    MENZIES (*his back to Vargas as he attaches device*): You know I was
        just checking with the department. You know that Grandi kid we
        picked up?
    VARGAS (*attaching wires*): Stand quietly.

MENZIES: He started to talk. He says the kids were all faking. They . . . they . . .

VARGAS (*over*): Here's the [inaudible].

MENZIES: . . . didn't give your wife any real dope. (*Turning to face camera.*) The doc says it was just that truth stuff.[15]

VARGAS (*holding recorder*): Sodium pentothal.

MENZIES: Yeah, no harm in it at all. (*Putting on his jacket.*)

VARGAS: No harm!

MENZIES: Schwartz is driving your car across the border. I told him we'd be by the bridge here. He's bringing your wife along. She's feeling fine. The doc says she can travel.

VARGAS: Sergeant . . .

MENZIES: Look, all she wants is to catch the early plane out of here.

VARGAS (*gripping his lapels*): How can I leave here until my wife's name is clean? Clean! (*Pulling back Menzies' lapels to reveal listening device.*) What do you think you're carrying that microphone for?[16] Now remember, don't cross your arms. I won't be able to get a word over this.

MENZIES (*over*): I know, I know.

VARGAS: I've got to get the truth from Quinlan.

MENZIES: Yeah?

VARGAS: All on tape!

MENZIES: He could stay there (*gesturing toward Tanya's*) the rest of the week, like he used to. (*Turning to Vargas.*) Now look, why don't you just take your wife home and let me handle this. It's my job!

VARGAS (*whispering fiercely*): It's my job too, Menzies!

Vargas turns on the device to test it.

MENZIES (*on tape*): It's my job!

VARGAS (*on tape*): It's my job too, Menzies!

Vargas switches it off.

VARGAS: You think I like it? I hate this machine. (*Crossing in back of Menzies.*) Spying . . . creeping about . . .

MENZIES (*over*): How do you think I feel about it? Hank is the best friend I've ever had!

VARGAS (*whispering still*): That's one reason for my staying.

MENZIES: Oh, you don't trust me, huh? Don't forget, I was the one that showed you that cane. I didn't have to do it, you know.

VARGAS (*grim*): Oh yes you did, sergeant.
MENZIES: Somebody could have planted it there . . .
VARGAS (*over, with a mirthless smile*): Menzies! . . .
MENZIES: . . . beside Grandi's corpse.
VARGAS: . . . you know better than that.
MENZIES: You say the reefers were planted . . .
VARGAS (*over*): You *know* better!
MENZIES: . . . why not Hank's cane?
VARGAS: You're an honest cop!
MENZIES (*turning away, into the camera*): Sure I am. And who made
me an honest cop? Hank Quinlan.
VARGAS (*going off right*): Come on, Menzies.
MENZIES (*remaining*): I am what I am because of him. (*Turns to follow
Vargas.*)

*542. MS: *Tanya doing her accounts, facing camera, table with chips and
cards in foreground. Pianola: Tanya's theme again. She looks up.*
543. MLS, *slightly tilted: Quinlan, entering from right rear, makes his way
through the clutter of Tanya's parlor.*
QUINLAN: What's *my* fortune?
544. CU: *Tanya, seated, blows smoke up into camera. She says nothing.*
545. *Low angle* MS: *Quinlan approaches camera.*
QUINLAN: You've been reading the cards, haven't you?
546. MS: *Tanya at table, as in 542.*
TANYA: I've been doing the accounts.
547. *Low angle* MS: *Quinlan, as in 545. He leans forward.*
548. CU *of table: Quinlan's hands spread tarot cards.*
QUINLAN (*off*): Come on, read my future for me!
549– *Alternates* CU *of Tanya, as in 544, and low angle* MS *of Quinlan, as in
553. 545. The dialogue does not overlap.*
TANYA (*after a long pause*): You haven't got any.
QUINLAN: Huh? What d'ya mean?
TANYA (*another pause*): Your future's all used up.
(*Quinlan half shrugs.*)
TANYA (*not unsympathetically, after a long pause*): Why don't you
go home?
554. LS *from Tanya's porch, the arch of its roof bisecting the frame. Menzies*

approaches on the right. Sound of pianola over the roar of derrick in
background. Menzies takes a couple of steps up onto the porch, into
MLS, *looks back over his shoulder.*
555. *Low angle* LS: *Vargas with recording device stands on catwalk at base*
of derrick, the camera moving in slightly.
556. *Menzies on porch steps, as in 554. He walks forward onto the porch, the*
camera moving up to a high angle MS *as he turns to whisper out through*
the arch.
MENZIES: Vargas. Vargas.
557. *Low angle* MLS: *Vargas in derrick, as in 555.*
558. CU: *the listening device, two dials, Vargas's hand adjusting. Camera*
moves right to speaker as we hear Menzies' voice.
MENZIES (*over speaker*): I don't know if you can hear me over that
piano music. But I'll get him out of there so you *can* hear.
559. *High angle* MS: *Menzies on porch, as at conclusion of 556, his head*
framed by its arch. He turns slowly to enter, off right foreground.
560. *Tilted low angle* MLS: *Tanya's parlor. In the center, Quinlan slouches*

*in a chair amidst the clutter, as we saw it in 100. In right rear Menzies
slowly enters from the front room, but withdraws as Quinlan peers
around toward him.*

561. MS: *Tanya at table, as in 542. She looks up.*
562. MLS: *Quinlan, as in 560. He looks around, gets unsteadily to his feet,
and totters back toward the passage where Menzies had appeared.*
563. MLS *from front room: on the right Quinlan is coming out from the
parlor, walking toward the camera.*
564. *Low angle* MLS: *Menzies under arch of Tanya's porch in left foreground;
small figure of Quinlan in rear right, framed by doorway.*
     MENZIES (*quietly, into mike*): I'll get him out. Away from that music.
        Be sure he doesn't see you. (*He takes a couple of steps down from the
        porch.*)
565. MS: *Quinlan in right foreground looks out uncertainly.*
     QUINLAN (*to Menzies, off left*): I must be drunk. A minute ago . . . I
        thought you were Vargas.
566. *Low angle* MLS: *Tanya's porch, as in 564. Menzies is now in extreme left*

foreground, only his torso visible, turned away from camera. Quinlan is a tiny figure in the right background, framed by the doorway and by the arch of the porch.

MENZIES: Come on out, Hank.

QUINLAN: What's that?

MENZIES: Come on out, Hank. I'm tired.

QUINLAN (*moving forward*): Who told you to come here?

MENZIES: I'm . . .

567. *Low angle* MS: *Vargas in derrick.*

MENZIES (*on speaker*): . . . tired of waiting, Hank. There's some questions you gotta answer.

568. *Low angle* MLS, *from within porch: small figure of Quinlan in door, moving forward.*

QUINLAN (*woozily*): Questions? Questions?

569. *The camera rises steeply as Quinlan, see from behind, goes down the porch steps, passing under the arch.*

QUINLAN: I need another drink.

Very high angle MLS: *Quinlan and Menzies at foot of the steps, framed by arch.*

MENZIES: You had enough.

QUINLAN: That's what Tanya keeps telling me. (*Walking off toward right.*) How much is enough?

570. MLS *inside Tanya's, pianola on left. Tanya enters from next room, in right rear, looks around inquiringly for Quinlan.*

571. *Extreme* LS: *Quinlan and Menzies enter in far distance, left to right, walking past a seedy little bungalow. Framework of derrick in foreground.*

MENZIES (*on mike*): Hank, I'm sick of chasing around trying to get it through to you.

Vargas appears with listening device in left foreground, MS, *back to camera.*

QUINLAN (*over, on mike*): You could use a drink yourself, partner.

Vargas in center foreground momentarily obscures them; camera pans to right as he turns around to follow their progress.

MENZIES (*on mike*): You gotta answer, Hank. All kinds of things. First about Vargas's gun.

QUINLAN (*on mike*): What do you know about the gun?

572. CU: *the listening device. Sound of static. Vargas's hand adjusts it.*
573. *Extreme* LS, *as in 571. Quinlan and Menzies pass base of ghostly
      derrick. The aerial of the listening device intrudes in the foreground.*
      MENZIES (*on mike*): He thinks you took it.
      QUINLAN (*on mike*): Vargas?
      MENZIES (*on mike*): Or was it Grandi that stole it?
      (*Sound of static.*)
574. CU: *listening device, as in 572. More static, as Vargas's hand adjusts.*
      QUINLAN (*on mike*): You've been talking to Vargas, huh?
575. *Low angle* MLS: *Vargas in derrick on left, facing camera; pump moving
      in right background.*
      MENZIES (*on mike*): And then you took it from Grandi?
      QUINLAN (*on mike*): You've been gettin' kinda chummy, you and that
      Mexican.
576. *Low angle* MCU: *Quinlan on left, facing camera; Menzies in right
      foreground, profile, almost out of frame.*
      QUINLAN (*live voice*): That explain that thing you're carrying around
      now?
577. MS: *Quinlan in left foreground, in profile; Menzies facing camera,
      further back, on right.*
      QUINLAN (*after short pause*): What's it called . . .
578. *Low angle* MLS: *Vargas in derrick, as in 575.*
      QUINLAN (*on mike*): . . . that thing you're wearin'?
579. MS: *Quinlan, Menzies, as in 577.*
      MENZIES (*tight-lipped*): What I'm wearing?
      QUINLAN: Sure.
580. *Low angle* MCU: *Quinlan, Menzies, as in 576.*
      QUINLAN: That halo.
      MENZIES: Halo?
      QUINLAN: Looks real pretty on you, Pete. (*Turning to walk away to
      right, behind Menzies.*) Pretty soon you'll be flapping your wings like
      an angel!
581. *Vargas on catwalk of derrick. He passes from* MS *on left foreground into*
      LS *as he moves right and back, trailing after Quinlan and Menzies, who
      are barely visible in the distance. The camera follows.*
582. CU *of listening device, being carried by Vargas.*

QUINLAN (*on mike*): Look out . . .

583. *Brief low angle* LS: *Vargas leaps from one platform to another.*

584. *Very high angle* LS: *Quinlan and Menzies walking almost directly below a catwalk, through whose framework we glimpse Vargas in center foreground, looking down and following.*

    QUINLAN (*live, but echoing in distance*): . . . Vargas'll turn you into one of these here starry-eyed *idealists.*

585. CU *of listening device, being carried by Vargas, closer than 582.*

    QUINLAN (*on mike*): They're the ones making all the real trouble in the world.

586. *Extremely low angle* LS: *Vargas walks toward camera, right to left; crazy diagonals of derrick behind.*

    QUINLAN (*on mike*): Be careful.

587. *Bird's-eye shot: Quinlan and Menzies on bare ground, walking left to right.*

    QUINLAN (*live, echoing in distance*): They're worse than crooks. You can always do something with a crook.

    MENZIES (*pausing*): You're the one who should be careful, Hank . . .

    QUINLAN (*over*): Hah!

    MENZIES: . . . dealing with crooks.

    QUINLAN: What?

588. *Structure of derrick in foreground. First the listening device, then Vargas's head, appear from below,* MCU, *facing camera.*

    MENZIES (*on mike*): Sometimes you can turn into a crook yourself. Look what happened with Grandi.

    QUINLAN (*on mike*): Partner, nobody ever called me a crook.

    The camera follows Vargas up a walkway to the right, into low angle MLS.

589. LS: *Vargas makes his way through the maze of the derrick, moving left to right. Sound of the pump moving behind him. As he goes down some steps, the camera moves down with him to reveal Quinlan and Menzies far below on the right, the derrick still in foreground.*

    QUINLAN (*voice echoing*): Look! Look up there.

590. *Very low angle* LS *of derrick, the back of Quinlan's head and shoulders in left foreground. The camera moves down to reframe on the movement of the pump, Quinlan still partly in the frame in extreme left foreground.*

QUINLAN (*live, closer*): See? That oil pump . . .

591. *Low angle* LS *of pump, from within shaft of derrick. The camera wheels up and down in time with its rhythm.*

QUINLAN (*off, softly*): . . . pumping up money . . . money. Don't you think I could have been rich? A cop in my position. What do I have?

MENZIES (*off*): Tell me about . . .

592. *Very low angle* MCU: *Quinlan, turned away, in left foreground; Menzies approaching from right; derrick rising behind them.*

MENZIES: . . . Grandi, Hank.

QUINLAN (*walking away, back to camera*): After thirty years, a little turkey ranch, that's all I got. A couple of acres.

MENZIES (*turning after him as they both leave the frame on left*): We gotta talk . . .

593. LS: *the camera follows Vargas's progress down derrick, his feet echoing on metal stairs.*

MENZIES (*echoing in distance*): . . . about Grandi.

594. LS: *the camera rises to meet Vargas walking toward it through a passageway. He ends in* MS, *center, facing directly into camera.*
QUINLAN (*on mike*): An honest cop! And then this Mexican comes along, and . . .

595. MLS: *Quinlan, followed by Menzies, enters right foreground, walks past derrick toward bungalow in left rear.*
QUINLAN (*live*): . . . look at the spot he puts me in.
MENZIES: You can't blame Vargas for what happened to Grandi.
QUINLAN (*over*): Blame Vargas!

596. CU: *Vargas, face into camera, adjusts device, glances off right. Sound of static.*

597. *High angle* LS: *Quinlan and Menzies walk right to left, framed by horizontal beams.*
QUINLAN: I blame Vargas for everything!
MENZIES: Hank, don't be crazy.
QUINLAN: Crazy!

598. CU: *the listening device. Vargas sets it down under a pipe. He is scrambling around behind, then sits behind it,* MCU, *listening.*
QUINLAN (*on mike*): If it wasn't for him, you think I'd be in a situation where Grandi could blackmail me? Then of course when I had to defend myself . . .
MENZIES (*on mike*): Defend yourself! I think you must be crazy . . .
QUINLAN (*mike*): Sure . . .
MENZIES (*mike*): . . . insane . . .
QUINLAN (*mike*): Sure, I'm crazy.
MENZIES (*mike*): Defend yourself! Hank!

599. *Overhead* CU: *Vargas's hand hovers over speaker of device.*
MENZIES (*on mike*): You murdered Grandi!
The camera zooms in on the speaker.
QUINLAN (*on mike*): Well, I left my cane by his body.

600. MCU: *Vargas and device, as in conclusion of 598. He picks it up.*
QUINLAN (*on mike*): That was sure crazy!

601. *Low angle* MLS: *Menzies, then Quinlan, walk in front of floodlit wall, right to left, casting black shadows.*
MENZIES (*live, pausing*): All right, let's start in the beginning. What about Vargas's gun?

QUINLAN (*walking past him, turning toward camera*): I was talking about . . .

602. MCU: *Vargas, as in 600. Picking up the listening device, still stooping, he moves off left. Shadows of Quinlan and Menzies are cast behind him.*
QUINLAN (*off, echoing in distance*): . . . my cane.
MENZIES (*off, echoing*): The gun!
QUINLAN (*off, echoing*): I forgot it.

603. *Tilted, low angle* MCU: *Menzies and Quinlan, walking right to left.*
MENZIES: The gun you stole from his briefcase!
QUINLAN: Gun?
As they pass out of frame to left, we see the tiny figure of Vargas in center background, coming down some steps.
MENZIES (*off*): Vargas's gun! Vargas's!
QUINLAN (*off*): Vargas, Vargas, Vargas! All you want to . . .

604. LS, *much closer than 603:* Vargas, *hurrying down steps.*
QUINLAN (*off, echoing*): . . . talk about is Vargas!

605. *Tilted* MLS: *Vargas leaps into frame from above and makes his way through girders off to the left.*

606. MLS: *Menzies and Quinlan approach the camera, a low wall in foreground.*
MENZIES (*live*): You took the gun from his briefcase, but you didn't use it.

607. MCU: *Vargas's head, facing the camera, rises from bottom of frame; he sets the receiver on a railing in front of him.*
MENZIES (*on mike*): Grandi was strangled.
QUINLAN (*on mike*): Grandi was a crook.
MENZIES (*on mike*): You're a killer, Hank.
QUINLAN (*on mike*): Partner . . .

608. MS: *Menzies, back to camera, in extreme left foreground; Quinlan facing camera on right.*
QUINLAN (*live*): . . . I'm a cop.
MENZIES: Yeah, yeah, yeah. (*The two men have moved forward into* MCU, *facing one another in profile.*) Drunk and crazy as you must have been when you strangled him, I guess you were somehow thinking of your wife. The way she was strangled.
QUINLAN: Well . . . (*grunting, turning away toward camera*), I'm

always thinking of her. Drunk or sober. What else is there to think
about? Except my job. My "dirty" job.

609. LS: *Menzies and Quinlan walking toward camera, derrick on left.*
MENZIES (*echoing*): You don't have to make it dirty, Hank.
QUINLAN (*echoing*): I don't call it dirty. Look at the record!

610. MS: *Vargas, crouching, scrambles toward canal, right to left, camera following.*
QUINLAN (*on mike*): *Our* record, partner.
MENZIES (*mike*): Sure, sure, sure.
QUINLAN (*mike*): Well . . .
As Vargas scrambles down the embankment to the canal, the camera rises to pick up Quinlan and Menzies walking across a bridge above him, high angle LS.
QUINLAN (*live*): . . . all those convictions!
MENZIES (*live*): Convictions. Sure. How many did you frame?

611. MS: *Vargas under bridge, moonlit water behind.*
QUINLAN (*on mike*): Nobody!
MENZIES (*on mike*): Come on, Hank . . .

612. *Low angle* MS: *Quinlan and Menzies walking across the bridge, right to left.*
MENZIES (*live*): . . . how many did you frame?
The camera moves down to reveal Vargas beneath arch of bridge.
QUINLAN: I told you . . . nobody!

613. *Low angle* MS: *Menzies faces camera on left; Quinlan in center foreground, back toward camera, partly obscuring him.*
QUINLAN: Nobody that wasn't guilty. (*Turning and walking toward camera.*) Guilty!

614. *High angle* MS: *Vargas, under the bridge, removes his jacket and tosses it aside.*
QUINLAN (*on mike*): Guilty!

615. CU *of receiver, as Vargas picks it up.*
QUINLAN (*on mike*): Every last one of 'em . . .

616. MS: *Menzies on left and Quinlan on right, walking toward camera.*
QUINLAN (*live, softly*): . . . guilty.
MENZIES (*stopping and turning toward him*): All these years you've been playing me for a sucker.

617. *High angle* MLS: *Vargas, on left, begins to wade out into the water.*
     MENZIES (*on mike*): Faking evidence. . . .
     QUINLAN (*on mike*): Aiding justice, partner.
618. LS: *Menzies and Quinlan walking into camera, derrick on left, as in 609.*[17]
     MENZIES (*live*): Yeah, like the ax in the Burger case.
     QUINLAN: Eh? Remember that?
     MENZIES: I was the one that found the ax.
619. *High angle* LS: *Quinlan and Menzies crossing bridge, on left, backs to camera; in lower right, Vargas, holding recording device aloft, wades out into the water.*
     MENZIES (*live, beginning to echo over the water*): Just where you planted it for me to find. Just like . . .
620. *Low angle* MS: *the camera tracks back from Quinlan and Menzies as they cross the bridge, circling one another. Their voices echo over the water.*
     MENZIES: . . . the dynamite with Sanchez. Just like you planted that dynamite.
     QUINLAN: Don't you think Sanchez is guilty? He's guilty. He'll confess. (*Pausing, turning around.*) Hey! Listen to that!
621. MS: *Vargas, below, in water to waist, looks up apprehensively.*
622. *Low angle* MS: *Quinlan, Menzies, as in 620.*
     MENZIES: Hank, I got to ask you something. . . .
     QUINLAN: Hear that? (*Moving off to left.*)
623. MS: *Vargas in water, as in 621. Apprehensive still.*
624. *Low angle* MS: *Quinlan, Menzies, as in 620.*
     MENZIES: Hear what?
     QUINLAN (*leaning off left*): An echo.
625. LS *of bridge, laterally across frame. Quinlan and Menzies, tiny figures on the left, lean over the balustrade. We hear the echo of Quinlan's last words.*
626. MS: *Vargas in water, as in 621. He reaches up for something to hang onto as he comes to deeper water.*
627. *Tilted, low angle* LS (*Vargas's point of view*): *Quinlan leans over the balustrade.*
628. MCU: *Vargas in water, hangs on, clutches recorder.*
629. *Low angle* LS. *The bridge with Quinlan peering over the edge stretches*

away into deep space on the right. Perspective is distorted so that the derrick, on the left, seems to tilt in toward the center of the frame.
QUINLAN (*live, echoing*): Vargas?
630. CU *of recorder: camera moves in on speaker.*
QUINLAN (*on mike*): I've got a feeling he's some place around here.
631. MCU: *Vargas in water, hanging on, as in 628.*
632. *Low angle* MCU: *Quinlan on left, Menzies on right, both into camera.*
QUINLAN (*live*): Close to me. I've got a hunch.
MENZIES (*flustered*): Why Vargas? Why . . . why . . . why should he . . .
QUINLAN: You sound kinda nervous, Pete. (*No response.*) My game leg. It's started to talk to me. (*Moves abruptly off right foreground.*) Vargas!
633. MCU: *Vargas, hanging on as in 628, works his way forward.*
634. LS *of bridge, like 625, but Quinlan and Menzies are now on the right.*
635. *Low angle* MCU: *Quinlan.*
QUINLAN: Maybe he's trailin' me. With a bug!
636. MCU: *Vargas, as in 628.*
637. *Low angle* MCU: *Quinlan, as in 635.*
QUINLAN: A recording . . . (*turning around abruptly:*) Hey!
638. MS: *Quinlan, back to camera, turns on Menzies.*
QUINLAN: Are you carrying a bug for him? A microphone?
MENZIES (*over*): Hank, I just . . .
QUINLAN: Don't lie to me!
MENZIES: All right. . . .
639. MLS: *the camera follows Vargas, left to right, as he begins to walk up other shore, the water only to his knees now.*
MENZIES (*on mike*): . . . now you better give me that gun, Hank.
QUINLAN (*on mike*): Where is he? Where is he?
640. MS: *Quinlan, Menzies, as in 638.*
MENZIES (*live*): How did you figure to frame Vargas with it?
QUINLAN: Framed? Who's been framed?
641. *Tilted* MLS: *camera follows Vargas below, as in 639. He holds device up to his ear.*
QUINLAN (*on mike*): Where is he? Vargas!
642. *Low angle* LS: *the bridge, Quinlan and Menzies crossing toward right foreground.*

QUINLAN (*echoing*): Where is he?

MENZIES: Hank, look, I . . .

643. MLS: *camera follows Vargas below, as in 639.*

QUINLAN (*on mike*): I'm talking to Vargas now.

644. LS: *the bridge. As Quinlan and Menzies continue to walk toward right foreground, the camera gradually rises to reveal Vargas below, on dry land now.*

QUINLAN (*echoing*): Vargas! Do you hear me? I'm talking to you. Through this . . . this walking microphone that . . .

645. MS: *Vargas, below, passes under an arch at base of bridge, the camera following.*

QUINLAN (*on mike*): . . . used to work for me!

646. *High angle* MS: *Quinlan and Menzies, backs to camera, moving right to left. Below them is the rubbish-strewn incline that leads to the canal.*

MENZIES: No, I ain't working for Vargas.

QUINLAN (*shouting, over*): Vargas! Vargas!

MENZIES: I'm working . . .

647. MS: *Vargas under arch, as in 645.*

MENZIES (*on mike*): . . . for the department, Hank.

Vargas, crouching, sets down the recorder amid the rubbish and darts out of frame in right foreground. The camera moves down to remain on the recorder.

MENZIES (*on mike*): Better give me Vargas's gun.

648. CU *of speaker: camera zooms in.*

QUINLAN (*on mike*): Okay, here it is!

MENZIES (*on mike*): Give it to me!

649. MS: *Vargas hoists himself over a wall.*

QUINLAN (*live*): Vargas!

The sound of a shot.

650. CU: *Menzies, mouth open, incredulous, falls toward camera. Vargas is barely visible in center background, over his shoulder. Sinister theme in brass on soundtrack, progressively more raucous until shot 668.*

651. *Low angle* MS: *Quinlan faces camera on left; Menzies, in right foreground, falls back toward the camera.*

MENZIES (*grasping Quinlan's hand as he sinks*): Hank? Hank?

652. CU: *Menzies falling, as in 650. Vargas now clearly visible over his shoulder on the right.*

653. *Low angle* MS: *Quinlan, Menzies sinking, as in 651.*
654. CU: *Menzies falling, as in 650. His head sinks off frame in left foreground; Vargas comes forward.*
655. *Low angle* MS: *Menzies still sinking in front of Quinlan, as in 651.*
656. *High angle* CU: *Menzies, falling sideways, turns to look up at Quinlan.*
657. *Low angle* MS: *Quinlan as in 655, alone in frame now. He looks at his bloodied hand, extended in front of him.*
658. *Low angle* MS: *Vargas looks on.*
659. *Low angle* MS: *Quinlan, still looking at his hand, walks toward the camera, past Vargas on the right. He obliterates the frame, then passes out in the right foreground, leaving Vargas.*
660. *Tilted* LS: *Quinlan, holding his arm aloft gingerly, stumbles down the rubbish-strewn incline toward the canal, framed by arch of bridge in foreground.*
661. LS: *camera follows as Vargas rushes, left to right, after Quinlan, his progress obscured by rubble in foreground.*

662. *Very low angle* MS: *Quinlan staggers down incline toward camera, extending bloody hand before him.*
663. *Very high angle* LS: *Quinlan, at left, stoops over dirty, rubbish-strewn water to wash his hand.*
664. *Low angle* MCU: *Quinlan leans into the camera, rubbing his bloody hand.*
665. *Low angle* MS: *Quinlan, seen from the side, his head truncated by the top of the frame, backs up the incline and subsides into a heap of rubbish.*
666. *Low angle* MS: *Quinlan, seen from front, comes to rest, feet extended into camera.*
667. *Tilted low angle* MS: *Vargas looks on.*
668. CU: *Quinlan's weary, bloated face into the camera. Tears run down his cheeks.*
     VARGAS (*off, quietly as music subsides*): Well, captain . . .
669. *Tilted low angle* MS: *Vargas, as in 667.*
     VARGAS: . . . I'm afraid this is finally something you can't . . .
670. CU: *Quinlan, as in 668, but now looking up at Vargas.*
     VARGAS (*off*): . . . talk your way out of.
     QUINLAN (*impassive*): You want to bet?
671. *Low angle* CU: *Vargas.*
672. CU: *Quinlan, as in 670.*
     QUINLAN: You killed him, Vargas.
673. *Low angle* CU: *Vargas, as in 671.*
     VARGAS: Come on now. Give me my gun back.
674. *Extreme* CU: *Quinlan's bloated face nearly fills frame.*
     QUINLAN: You don't understand me. You killed Pete. The bullet is from your gun.
675. *Low angle* CU: *Vargas, as in 671.*
     VARGAS: You think anyone would believe that?
676. CU: *Quinlan, as in 670.*
     QUINLAN: They always believe me. (*Ruefully.*) Anyway, they'll never believe I killed him.
677. *Low angle* MS: *Vargas.*
     VARGAS (*extending his arm toward camera*): The gun.
     Quinlan's arm, holding the gun on Vargas, enters bottom foreground of the frame.

QUINLAN (*off*): You're resisting . . .
678. *High angle* MS: *Quinlan, still seated, extends gun toward camera.*
QUINLAN: . . . arrest.
679. *Low angle* MS: *Vargas, gun in foreground, as at conclusion of 677.*
VARGAS: How could you arrest me here? This is my country.
680. *High angle* MS: *Quinlan, as in 678.*
QUINLAN: This is where you're gonna die.
681. *Low angle* MS: *Vargas, gun, as in 679. He is illuminated by approaching headlights.*
682. LS: *Car arrives from left, turns in toward camera.*
683. *Low angle* MS: *Vargas, gun, as in 679. He dives forward.*
684. *Tilted* MS: *Quinlan seated in extreme left foreground with gun; Vargas, making a run for it, leaps off frame at right.*
685. MLS: *Quinlan seated in upper right part of frame, facing camera with gun, a network of rubble in the foreground: he fires.*
686. MCU: *Vargas turns back over his shoulder into camera.*
QUINLAN (*off*): That wasn't no miss, Vargas. That was just to turn you around.
687. MCU: *Quinlan on right, facing camera, pointing gun.*
QUINLAN: I don't want to shoot you in the back. Unless you'd rather . . . try to run for it.
688. MCU: *Vargas, as in 686. He says nothing.*
689. MCU: *Quinlan aiming gun, as in 687. Just as he is about to fire, we hear another shot and he suddenly jerks forward.*
690. MS: *Menzies, with gun, breathing his last, leans over edge of bridge behind Quinlan. His head falls forward.*
691. *Low angle* MCU: *Quinlan on his back in rubbish, the fallen torso extending across frame. He grimaces in pain.*
692. MLS: *Vargas. Sound of auto horn. Camera follows as he runs, right to left, up incline.*
693. MS: *Menzies, as at conclusion of 690. His head, eyes staring, settles limply over the edge of the bridge. His hat topples off.*
694. *Low angle* MCU: *Quinlan on his back, as in 691. He peers up at the bridge.*
695. *Tilted* LS: *the bridge, Menzies sprawled over its edge at right of frame, derrick visible behind. He lets his gun drop.*
696. *High angle* LS: *the gun drops into the littered water of the canal.*

697. *Low angle* MCU: *Quinlan on his back, as in 691.*
VARGAS (*off*): Schwartz! (*Sound of running feet.*)
698. LS *of bridge: Menzies sprawled on right; Vargas races across, right to left.*
VARGAS (*shouting*): Is she there? Did you bring my wife?
SCHWARTZ (*running in from left, meeting him halfway*): She's in the car.
VARGAS: That's Menzies. (*Indicating him.*) He's dead. Quinlan's been shot, too. He's lying by the recorder. Down there. I've got it all on tape.
SCHWARTZ (*stooping by Menzies*): You sure you've got enough?
VARGAS: More than enough. Go play it back, you'll see.
Schwartz goes off right; then camera pans left to follow Vargas as he races ahead to cross the bridge.
699. LS: *Schwartz runs toward camera, through rubbish, splashing in shallow water, framed by structure of bridge in foreground.*
700. MS: *Susan in car; Vargas gets in beside her from right foreground.*
VARGAS: Susie!
They embrace.
SUSAN: Oh, Mike!
701. *High angle* LS: *Schwartz, back to camera, runs down rubbish-strewn incline, framework in foreground. He kneels by the recorder.*
702. CU: *the recorder. As Schwartz starts it, the camera pulls back and pans over to the speaker.*
MENZIES (*on tape*): All these years you've been playing me for a sucker.
703. *Low angle* CU: *Quinlan, on his back, eyes barely open, listens to tape. Like 691, but closer so only his head is visible.*
MENZIES (*on tape*): Faking evidence.
QUINLAN (*on tape*): Aiding justice, partner.
704. MLS: *Tanya runs toward us from left background. The camera follows as she crosses in front of Vargas's car (we see her only in silhouette) and out the right foreground.*
TANYA: Hank!
705. MS: *Susan and Vargas in the car, as in 700.*
VARGAS: Susie.
SUSAN: Yes, Mike.

VARGAS: It's all over, Susie. I'm taking you home. Home.
He starts the car, which begins to back out of frame to right.
706. *Low angle* LS: *the bridge. Tanya is a tiny figure crossing it, left to right. Quinlan's inert face, propped upright, is in extreme right foreground,* MCU.
MENZIES (*on tape*): How many did you frame?
QUINLAN (*on tape*): Nobody that wasn't . . .
707. *Extreme* CU: *Quinlan, eyes open, tear-stained, into camera.*
QUINLAN (*on tape*): . . . guilty . . . guilty . . . guilty.
708. *Low angle* LS: *Tanya on the bridge, Quinlan in right foreground, as in 706.*
TANYA: Hank! (*Crossing the bridge, she leaves frame at right.*)
MENZIES (*on tape*): No, I ain't working for Vargas.
Quinlan leans forward, rising laboriously. As the back of his shoulder moves into center frame, we briefly glimpse Menzies sprawled on the bridge behind him on the right.
QUINLAN (*on tape*): Vargas! Vargas!

709. *Very low angle* MS: *Quinlan begins to move left down incline.*
    MENZIES (*on tape*): I'm working for the department, Hank.
710. CU *of recorder in Schwartz's hand.*
    MENZIES (*on tape*): Now you better give me that gun, Hank.
    Camera pans over to speaker.
    QUINLAN (*on tape*): Okay, here it is!
    Camera zooms in on speaker.[18]
    MENZIES (*on tape*): Give it to me.
    QUINLAN (*on tape*): Vargas! (*Sound of shot.*)
*711. *Low angle* MS: *Menzies slumped over bridge.*
712. *Very high angle* MLS: *Menzies slumped over edge of bridge in left foreground; Quinlan looks up from below. Rubbish all around.*
    QUINLAN: Pete . . .
713. *High angle* CU: *Quinlan, looking up, face in harsh chiaroscuro.*
    QUINLAN: . . . that's the second bullet I stopped for you.
714. CU: *Quinlan's hand in upper right of frame. A drop of blood falls on it from above.*
715. *High angle* CU: *Quinlan, as in 713, looking up.*
716. *Tilted low angle* MLS: *Menzies' arm over edge of bridge in upper right of frame, dripping blood.*
717. *High angle* CU: *Quinlan, as in 713. He staggers back.*
718. *High angle* LS: *Tanya hurries off bridge, left to right.*
719. MS: *Quinlan, face toward camera, arms extended at his sides, staggers backwards toward the water.*
720. LS: *Tanya approaches top of incline, facing camera on right.*
721. *High angle* LS: *Quinlan, arms outstretched, falls backwards into the water.*
*722. CU: *Schwartz's hands turn off the recorder and snap it shut.*
*723. MS: *crouching, Schwartz emerges from under bridge.*
*724. CU: *Tanya, facing camera, looking off toward left, melancholy.*
*725. *High angle* LS: *Quinlan floats, arms outspread in water, surrounded by rubbish.*
726. MS: *Tanya facing camera. First the aerial of the recorder, then Schwartz enter from bottom of frame, in right foreground.*
    SCHWARTZ (*scrambling up*): His famous intuition was right after all.
    He framed that Mexican . . .

727. CU: *Tanya, as in 724.*
 SCHWARTZ (*off*): . . . kid, Sanchez. But he didn't even need to. The kid
 confessed about that bomb. So, it turns out . . .
728. *High angle* LS: *Quinlan's corpse, as in 725.*
 SCHWARTZ (*off*): . . . Quinlan was right after all.
729. CU: *Tanya, as in 724.*
 TANYA: Isn't somebody going to come and . . . take him away.
 SCHWARTZ (*off*): Yeah, in just a . . .
730. MCU: *Tanya in center, Schwartz in right foreground, both facing toward
 the left.*
 SCHWARTZ: . . . few minutes. (*Turning to her.*) You really liked him,
 didn't you?
731. CU: *Tanya, as in 724.*
 TANYA: The cop did. The one who killed him. He loved him.
732. MCU: *Tanya, Schwartz, as in 730.*
 SCHWARTZ: Well, Hank was a great detective all right.
 TANYA: And a lousy cop.
 SCHWARTZ (*smiling, turning toward her*): Is that all you have to say
 for him?
733. CU: *Tanya, as in 724. Pianola theme on soundtrack.*
 TANYA (*still staring impassively off left*): He was some kind of a man.
 (*After a long pause.*) What does it matter what you say about people?
 (*She turns toward right, hair blowing in wind, and leaves the frame.*)
734. *Low angle* MS: *Schwartz turns around toward camera to watch her go.*
735. LS: *Tanya, on left, walks along highway, away from camera. Derricks
 on right. Pianola theme still.*
 SCHWARTZ (*off*): Goodby, Tanya.
 TANYA (*turning back*): Adios.
 She turns and resumes her slow walk away.

Notes on the Continuity Script

1. Welles has said that four scenes not shot by him were included in the release version of his film, and this scene may well be one of them. The dialogue is quite different from the corresponding scene in the shooting script.
2. At this point in the release version is a shot omitted from the longer version:

   LS: *Lot with upended carts, as at conclusion of 92. Vargas slowly emerges from background as Menzies enters from left foreground.*
   MENZIES: Anything wrong, Vargas?
   VARGAS (*coming forward, discouraged*): I just couldn't catch him.
   He moves out of the frame in left foreground as Menzies follows, baffled.

3. In the release version the shot ends here, followed immediately by shot 99.
4. In the release version, Menzies does not interrupt this shot. It is followed by a MCU of Tanya looking after Quinlan that the longer version omits.
5. In the release version, the camera does not follow Susan and Vargas into the lobby. Instead, we cut directly to shot 183, where Vargas's line about his mother-in-law is concluded. Vargas's first line in the present 183 is omitted.
6. Welles's producer, Albert Zugsmith, reports that this scene (207–209) was shot by Harry Keller: see James Naremore, *The Magic World of Orson*

Welles (New York: Oxford University Press, 1978), 179. Oddly, the surviving copy of the shooting script includes this scene (identified as a process shot), though without most of Susan's sexual byplay.

7. In the release version, this episode (220–226) comes after the present shot 252.

8. In the release version, this episode (239–252) follows directly after the present shot 205, which dissolves into an establishing shot omitted from the longer version:

   Dissolve to low angle LS: *flat boxy motel cabins under bright, cloudy sky.*

   In the release version, we do not see the Night Man through the window in shot 239.

9. Quinlan's line and the sound of the punch are omitted in the release version.

10. The camera was mounted on the hood of the car. Contrast the obvious use of projected backgrounds in the scene (207–209) reportedly shot by Harry Keller.

11. In the release version, the voice says, "It will make you feel real good" instead of the present line.

12. In the release version, the shot begins here.

13. Ordinarily, night scenes were shot "day for night" (i.e. in daylight, using a special filter). Welles shot "night for night," so that anything to be seen had to be individually illuminated. This accounts for the odd luminous glow of objects like the tree at the motel or the derrick in the final sequence.

14. In the release version, we cut directly from this shot to the middle of 541.

15. In the release version, the shot begins here.

16. In the release version, the shot ends here.

17. Apparently a mismatch: 609 showed the approach to the bridge. Evidently, in fact, three different bridges are conflated: one with a wooden railing (here and in 619), one with a stone balustrade (620 ff.), and an earlier one of stone without a balustrade (612 ff.).

18. In the release version, the shot begins here, and the first two lines are heard over shot 709.

The Shooting
Script(s)

Until John Stubbs, a film scholar at the University of Illinois, found a copy of Welles's shooting script in a private collection, it was generally supposed to have been lost. Stubbs's ground-breaking discovery provides an important basis for understanding the evolution of *Touch of Evil*. In the essay reprinted here in slightly abridged form, Stubbs compares the four versions: the novel, *Badge of Evil*, by "Whit Masterson" (Robert Wade and William Miller, 1956); the first screenplay, written for Universal Studios by Paul Monash and dated July 24, 1956; Welles's screenplay, dated February 5, 1957; and the completed film. Monash's script is in the Special Collection Division of the University of Wyoming Library. A copy of Welles's script is in the collection of Norman Gambill of South Dakota State University.

The Evolution of Orson Welles's
Touch of Evil from Novel to Film

John Stubbs

The Novel

Badge of Evil by Wade and Miller is, like the movie, the story of an investigation of a murder which leads to a more far-reaching investigation into the corruption of the police captain assigned to the murder case. The book is a competent, but not remarkable example of a crime detection thriller. It did, however, provide both Monash and Welles with a great deal of raw material to draw on and a series of problems to try to solve.

The opening of the novel is similar to the opening of the movie in that the novel begins with the death of Rudy Linneker (see footnote 6) in a violent explosion. In the novel version, Linneker is a wealthy lumberyard owner in a Southern California city. On the evening of his murder, he is in his beach cabana, awaiting his daughter whom he has invited for a late swim. We are told: "He heard no one come down the cliff stairway or walk across the sand to the cabana. But at eight o'clock, a hand reached through the window and dropped a package inside." [1] The dynamite explosion follows immediately. Different as this scene is from Welles's famous opening three-minute take, it does provide a basic strategy that was to survive to the movie version. The strategy involves the use of a point of view which is larger than Linneker's, but stops short of omniscience. Certainly, if there is to be suspense in the first scene, we must be told of, or shown, the threat to Linneker's well-being before the threat manifests itself to him. Yet, at the same time, the identity of the dynamiter must also be kept a mystery, since it provides an important puzzle for the narrative to solve. Wade and Miller's strategy, which is, of course, relatively standard in crime novels, will be continued at each later stage, but the time between the audience's recognition of the threat and the explosion will be expanded and the action taking place in this time span will be complicated in ways that will make the scene a dazzling piece of suspense.

From *Cinema Journal* 24, no. 2 (Winter 1985): 19–39. Stubbs's footnotes have been renumbered and several have been omitted.

1. Robert Wade and William Miller, *Badge of Evil* (New York: Dodd, Mead, 1956): 1.

Mitch Holt, the hero of the novel, is introduced immediately following the death of Linneker. This hero differs strikingly from the hero of Welles's movie, Mike Vargas. The hero of the novel is not a Mexican official on his honeymoon with an American wife, after having closed a drug investigation of the Grandi family; he is a white, Anglo-Saxon, assistant district attorney who has successfully prosecuted the Buccio family in a bar licensing case involving kickbacks. But Mitch's marriage, like the one in the movie, is interracial. His wife of nine years, Connie, is Mexican. American prejudice against Mexicans, crucial in the movie, is not a major issue in the novel. Yet a suggestion for Welles's extended treatment of social antagonism does exist here. Connie's Mexicanness is kept before us in that she and Mitch continually plan and postpone a vacation trip to her father's ranch in Ensenada. Furthermore, toward the end of the novel when Connie has been caught in a frame-up involving drugs, Mitch storms at the district attorney: "On top of everything else, she's of Mexican descent. You can make a lot out of that because, as every American jury knows, it's the foreign-born that cause all our crime and vice" (p. 184).

The police detectives of the novel also differ in certain ways from their counterparts in the movie. The superior officer is Captain Loren McCoy. He is the smaller of the pair, "lean and leathery, with a shock of white hair like bleached fleece." Considered a "legend" in detective work for thirty years, McCoy has been called out of retirement because of the importance of the Linneker case. His partner, Sergeant Hank Quinlan, is a large, burly man. Wounded in a gun battle several years earlier, taking a bullet intended for McCoy, Quinlan walks with a limp and uses a cane. His temper is explosive. Holt describes the pair to himself: "McCoy was obviously the thinker, Quinlan the doer." As such, McCoy and Quinlan, the little man and the big one, are visual stereotypes. In the later stages, both Monash and Welles will exchange the roles and the physical attributes of the pair to make them less stereotypical and, in Welles's case, to make the captain's role physically right for Welles.

The victim of McCoy's frame-up in the novel is Delmont Shayon, a young shoe clerk engaged to Linneker's daughter Tara, against the wishes of the father. Shayon is not a Mexican as his counterpart in the movie, Manolo Sanchez, is. However, Shayon is equally defensive about his social position. Many of Shayon's lines will be carried over into the movie directly from the novel. (The lines do not appear in the Monash screenplay.) For example, when the young man meets Holt for the first time to discuss the case, he says, "Now then, where shall we begin, Holt? Do you want to make a direct accusation or shall we play around with some nasty questions first?" When Mitch asks if Shayon is always so unpleasant, the shoe clerk responds, "Was I being unpleasant? Terribly sorry, old man. . . . I've been told I have a very winning personality. The best shoe clerk the store ever had and sales to prove it. That's the way I met Tara, you know, and I've been at her feet ever since" (pp. 35–36). With only slight alteration, these lines will be spoken by Sanchez in the interrogation scene in his apartment in the movie.

The novel tends to advance along a single narrative line. It raises an issue, offers a solution, and then moves to another issue. First, McCoy tries to arrest Shayon on bonafide grounds, and when this fails, motivated by a kind of hunter's pride, McCoy plants and "discovers" incriminating dynamite in Shayon's storage closet. Unlike the situation in the movie, though, Mitch clears Shayon of all charges shortly after his arrest and gets a confession from the real murderer. Then he turns his attention to the issue of the planted dynamite. As this investigation progresses, McCoy's psychological state deteriorates in clearly defined stages, ending with the ploy of luring Connie to a skid row hotel and attempting to frame her in a staged drug party.[2] This simple, linear progression of events will be rearranged and complicated later by Welles, as we shall see, to make the work thicker and richer.

After the opening when Linneker is killed, the novel, although written in the third person, follows mainly the narrative point of view of Mitch Holt. The emphasis of the novel is on reader identification with Holt. We look over his shoulder, learn only what he learns, and try to solve the various mysteries along with him. We tend also to share his emotional responses when he is threatened. This close identification is often one of the givens of the crime detection thriller. The difficulty with this approach here is that two of the most interesting pieces of action must take place "offstage." These are the psychological deterioration of McCoy and the abduction of Connie. Concerning the deterioration of McCoy, we encounter the signs of it as Mitch comes to them—a shotgun blast meant to frighten Holt off the case, a briefcase of notes slashed in rage, a rifle shot intended to kill Mitch, and the sight of the arrested Connie in her jail cell—but McCoy himself is out of view. Similarly, we do not see Connie's fearful situation during her abduction. Rather we wait with Mitch by the telephone for word of her.

The ending of the novel provides Welles with still more material. The device of

---

2. As in the movie, Mitch suggests to the police surgeon that Connie may have been given Demerol or sodium pentothal to simulate a drugged condition. Welles, like Wade and Miller, stops short of "contaminating" his heroine with marijuana or hard drugs.

portable shortwave recording equipment is a major element in all versions. Mitch, in the novel, convinces Quinlan to wear a "bug" to McCoy's ranch and to put direct questions to McCoy concerning the planting of evidence. Point of view remains with Holt. Crouched in his car, he listens to the conversation inside the ranch. Patches of the dialogue survive in the film in altered form.[3] McCoy confesses, and then, as Quinlan tries to arrest him, McCoy shoots his partner. Mitch flees with his recorded evidence and learns later that McCoy took his own life.

Rich as this conclusion is with material Welles will mine, there are certain problems that demand solution. Again, interesting action takes place "offstage." We do not see at first hand either the ending of the friendship between McCoy and Quinlan or the death of McCoy. Even more serious, though, is the problem of Quinlan's character motivation for interrogating his partner. Wade and Miller ask us to believe that Quinlan accepts Holt's plan out of a kind of sympathy for what had been done to Connie. This premise is at best a shaky one. It is another of the problems that will require Welles's eventual attention.

The Monash Screenplay

The screenplay by Paul Monash constitutes an interesting second stage of composition. Primarily, Monash attempted to transfer material from the novel into a series of dramatic scenes that could be filmed. The screenplay is too prolix, and it contains problems with character motivation and plot. . . . But Monash did make some changes and additions in the material from the novel which are quite striking. These were changes and additions Welles chose to keep.

In order to break down the novel's too clear-cut, melodramatic distinction between hero and villain, Monash set out to call attention to a parallel obsessiveness in the two. He changes the corrupt police captain at this stage to the big, heavy-set figure, now called Thomas Quinlan.[4] He is in his fifties and is not called out of retirement. (His partner becomes Sergeant Jack Miller, "a patient

3. An interesting example is McCoy's charge that Quinlan is wearing a "halo." At the stage of the "Revised Final Screenplay," Welles makes the charge into a question and creates a moment of suspense which he retains in the movie.
4. It is interesting that this switch of the bigger Quinlan to the more important role took place before Welles became involved with the project. The change, then, was not made initially to suit Welles as an actor in the part, but apparently to break away from the visual stereotypes of the novel.

plodding man," who limps, as his counterpart in the novel did, from a bullet wound sustained for his friend.) In the "Character List" at the beginning of the screenplay, Monash describes Quinlan as an officer who is "fanatic in his dedication," and in the screenplay itself, Monash emphasizes the relentlessness of Quinlan's pursuit of Shayon. A similar obsessiveness, Monash insists we recognize, exists in Mitch Holt. In the "Character List," Monash describes his hero: "He has a very clear sense of right and wrong, and becomes outraged when it is violated," and then Monash adds, "Between Holt and Quinlan there is a certain parallel." Mitch is as obsessed in this version with proving Quinlan guilty of planting the dynamite as Quinlan is with proving Shayon guilty of killing Linneker. He attempts to force an identification of Quinlan from a tenant at Shayon's apartment house, who had seen a heavy-set man from the back carrying an oily package up the stairs. When the tenant quite properly refuses to identify Quinlan as the man, Mitch flies into a rage and tries to shake the identification out of him. Here Mitch is at a point just short of planting evidence to "nail" his man. In the movie, Welles, too, will balance hero against villain, but not by having his hero nearly force evidence, rather by setting Vargas's rage over the kidnapping of his wife against Quinlan's mania to avenge his murdered wife.

One of Monash's most striking changes is that he makes Shayon guilty of killing Linneker. We are kept in doubt on this issue until the very end of the screenplay when Chief Gould, District Attorney Adair, and Holt gather in headquarters to hear the tape that will convict Quinlan. Gould receives a telephone call and reports: "Shayon just confessed. Linneker's daughter—it was her idea. Shayon's signing a statement" (p. 128). With this change, Monash extends suspense over the identity of the murderer and, more importantly, deepens our view of Quinlan whose intuition about Shayon proves correct. This change Welles will keep in his film, presumably for the same reasons, but he will cast a doubt on the confession by letting us see and hear the intensity of the grilling Shayon undergoes.

Another major change Monash makes is to extend the role of the gangster family. The Buccios of the novel become the Grandi family in Monash's version. (The family is still Italian.) In the novel, the Buccios provided a false alternative to McCoy as the source of Mitch's harassment. Here, the Grandis are a real source of menace. Mitch has prosecuted the father, Vincent Grandi, and is waiting for a verdict. As Holt comes home late at night after Linneker's death, three of the Grandi sons appear suddenly in front of him. Monash describes them: "The three men display a striking similarity in dress and appearance, all being in their twenties, with tight bodies in dark suits. We get from them a sense of potential violence, as explosive as dynamite" (p. 9). They threaten Mitch and then disappear. Later, however, after a guilty verdict has been returned against their father and while Holt is in a Grandi bar to get information, the sons beat him savagely and professionally. The menace of the Grandis will be, of course, extended even further by Welles. Moreover, Welles will make the menace of the Grandi family disturbingly sexual, as we shall see, by directing the menace more against Vargas's wife than against Vargas himself. It may be that the "germ" for the idea of sexual menace was given Welles by Monash's description of the "tight bodies" of the Grandi sons.

In his treatment of the opening scene, Monash uses the basic situation and strategy of the novel, but adds some elements of his own. With Linneker in the cabana now is an exotic dancer, Gail Harte. As was the case in the novel, Monash gives us a point of view that approaches, but does not quite reach, omniscience. He cross-cuts between the killer, whose face we don't see, and the activities of Linneker and Gail Harte. Monash's first shot reveals the killer's car speeding along a cliff road. The car stops above the cabana; the killer takes dynamite from the trunk; and he descends toward the beach house. Cha-cha music can be heard coming from the cabana. Inside, Linneker watches Gail dance, joins her in the dance, and then leads her to a couch. When the dynamite is thrown into the cabana, Linneker has to struggle almost comically to free himself from the uncomprehending woman's grasp to lunge for the dynamite. The woman's scream as she sees the dynamite coincides with the explosion. Several of the elements added by Monash will be carried over by Welles into his three-minute take. The exotic dancer, the use of a car (Linneker's, rather than the murderer's), and the cha-cha music are such elements. Furthermore, the irony Monash gets from playing off the lovers' entanglement against the bomb may have suggested to Welles the possibility of playing off the kiss of the Vargases against the explosion of Linneker's car.

For his screenplay, Monash constructs five scenes, not in the novel, which will survive in somewhat altered form in Welles's movie. Three are worth our consideration here if we are to have a sense of the evolution of the movie.[5] One such scene takes place when Mitch and the police gather at the site of the explosion. A

5. The two scenes not discussed here are one involving Ernest Farnum, Mitch's prime suspect, at a blasting site and one showing an argument between Holt and Jack Miller in the Hall of Records late at night.

detective bending over the corpse comments: "An hour ago Linneker had this town in his pocket. Now you can strain him through a sieve" (p. 3). These lines carry over into the movie, divided between District Attorney Adair and the police surgeon. (The lines don't appear in the novel.) Then comes a mildly antagonistic exchange between Holt and Quinlan. Mitch states that the district attorney asked him to see if he could be "useful." Quinlan tries to brush him off gently, "Look, Mr. Holt, leave us a clear field now. We don't have time to answer questions or make explanations" (p. 6). The scene ends when the daughter, now called Marcia, identifies her father. The Monash scene, relatively bland as it is, provided Welles with a basic situation that he would make one of the most dramatically intense in the movie. Welles will add a flaming fountain in the background and darting figures in the foreground who pass between the camera and the main characters. He will give Quinlan a dramatic entrance. And he will make the confrontation between Quinlan and Vargas bristle with racial hostility.

Another scene Monash adds and Welles keeps is one where Mitch gives his accusations to the district attorney and the police chief in the presence of Quinlan and Miller at headquarters. (In the novel, McCoy was not present when Mitch stated his case.) Mitch's charges are rejected when he fails in his attempt to have his witness identify Quinlan as the heavy-set figure with the oily package. Quinlan, then, asserts himself as a maligned servant of the public. He throws down his badge and tells Adair and Chief Gould: "After thirty years, walking beats, riding cars—thirty years of dirt and crummy pay. . . . Thirty years I gave my life to the department—and you let this lousy publicity hound accuse me, right in your office. . . ." (p. 83). This speech and almost two pages of additional dialogue (which didn't appear in the novel) will be used in the movie as Welles also gives Quinlan a moment of victory and of sham outraged innocence prior to his fall.

A final scene in the category under discussion involves a fight in the Grandi night club. The scene is not the fight scene mentioned earlier; it is an additional, later one. Monash has Holt burst in on the Grandis after he has seen his wife in jail, knock a Grandi son to the floor, and try to strangle him. The scene seems intended to provide us with a sense of rough justice. The Grandi son can be said to "deserve" the punishment in that he arranged the earlier beating of Mitch. The scene, however, ends in frustration for Mitch. The Grandis convince him that they were not behind the frame-up of his wife. In Welles's movie version of this scene, Vargas will be frustrated at first when he cannot identify his adversaries, and then he will administer his own "rough justice" after he does find some of them. In the main, though, Welles will use the scene to demonstrate Vargas's rage, which, as we noted earlier, Welles will parallel with Quinlan's sustained compulsion to avenge the murder of his wife.

In his handling of narrative point of view after the initial scene, Monash follows the model of Wade and Miller for the most part. This is to say that Monash restricts us mainly to scenes where Mitch Holt is present as observer or participant and restricts us mainly to knowing and seeing only what Mitch knows and sees. There are, however, some important instances where Monash does try to break out from the restraint inherited from the novel and to open up his handling of narrative point of view. The most obvious example is a brief scene between Quinlan and Miller at which Holt is not present. In this scene, an angry Quinlan orders a protective "stake-out" around Mitch's home to be removed, and a worried Sergeant Miller questions the wisdom of his partner's decision. Here, we receive privileged information that Holt does not, and we see a rift, however slight, between the officers which we hope Mitch will somehow be able to exploit. More than this, we also see Quinlan in a situation where he doesn't have to mask his emotions for Holt, and we get to know him a bit more fully.

Another instance is the confession sequence near the end where Miller questions his partner inside Quinlan's ranch, as Mitch records the conversation outside in his car. Here, Monash elects to cross-cut between the two locations. We are able to see Holt's reactions as he gets the evidence he needs, and we also witness directly the painful moments of Miller's discovery of how his partner had used him. In a very tentative way, then, Monash does begin to open up the narrative point of view of the work. He begins a process that Welles will carry much further.

For the ending of his screenplay, Monash supplies a sense of formal conclusion by having Police Chief Gould deliver an epitaph for the dead Quinlan. Responding to the news that Quinlan was right in his suspicion of Shayon, Gould states: "Yes, he was a good detective . . . (pause). But he was a bad cop" (p. 128). The epitaph seems a fair summation of Quinlan, pointing out the blend of skill and immorality in the man and putting final emphasis where it belongs. Welles will retain the epitaph, but will try to push it one step further to a generalization about the mixture in all men. In the movie, the detective Schwartz says to the prostitute Tanya, "Well, Hank was a great detective all right," and she reponds, "And a lousy cop." Then she adds, however, "He was some kind of man. . . . What does it matter what you say about people?" . . .

The Welles Screenplay

For his screenplay, Welles made numerous changes in the material he inherited. Many were small ones, designed to tighten the work. But two of his changes were rather large, and they were crucial ones in terms of making the work over into a *film noir* classic. They are Welles's introduction of the theme of American racism and his decision to open up narrative point of view.

The setting for the action is shifted by Welles from the Southern California city of the earlier versions to the town of Los Robles on the border between the United States and Mexico. The shift gives Welles a terrain where the issue of racism is traditionally at its most intense.

The possibility of treating American racist attitudes against Mexicans was probably suggested to Welles, as we mentioned earlier, by the relatively underdeveloped situation of the interracial marriage in the novel. Of course, abhorrence of any form of bigotry had long been a part of Welles's social and political liberalism. He rarely missed an opportunity to strike out at it. Moreover, in *Man in the Shadow*, the Zugsmith film prior to *Touch of Evil*, Welles rewrote and acted the part of a bigoted rancher who arranges the death of a Mexican ranch hand. The decision by Welles to treat racism in *Touch of Evil* adds a new dimension to it. The treatment, however, does not so much "ennoble" the work with a social purpose as it does put it on a more visceral level of social-sexual antagonisms.

Welles changes his hero at this stage from the American Mitch Holt to the Mexican Ramon Miguel "Mike" Vargas, special investigator attached to the minister of justice, and changes the hero's wife from the Mexican-born Connie to Susan, a young newlywed from Philadelphia. According to the odd double standard of Anglo-Saxon racism, the venturing forth of the Anglo-Saxon male into the more "primitive" or "libidinous" Latin race may be seen as a sexual proving, but the encroachment by the male of the "primitive" race into the Anglo-Saxon world for a partner is usually taken as a move threatening to Anglo-Saxon virility. In this sense, Vargas is a challenging figure despite the "social acceptableness" of his government position.

Susan, the American wife, is guilty of a good deal of unconscious racism in this version. Not the least of it is that she Americanizes her husband's name to "Mike." (Interestingly, the one time she does call her husband "Miguel" is when she is in bed at the motel listening to him on the telephone. At this point, she is more than willing to stereotype her husband as the "Latin lover.") She calls the Grandi boy "Pancho," and she attempts to dismiss a Grandi messenger with the words, "I don't want any postcards." When threatened in her Mexican hotel, Susan's impulse is to flee to an American motel. "You'll know I'm safe there," she tells her husband and then, on reflection, adds, "Oh, Mike—Did I say the wrong thing again?" (p. 31).

If Susan is an unconscious racist, Welles's villain, now called Captain Hank Quinlan, is a quite knowing, American bigot. In this version, Welles makes Quinlan the limping figure, instead of his partner, thus effecting a complete exchange of name, size, and characteristics with the sergeant of the original novel. Presumably, this was done to give a visual emphasis to Quinlan's moral twistedness, as Hawthorne did with Roger Chillingworth and Shakespeare with Richard III, but we might also note in passing that the final change gave Welles a nice piece of stage business to use with his character. Certainly, a major part of Quinlan's moral twistedness is his intense racism. (A fine ironic touch at this stage is Welles's change of the devoted partner's name to one with a Mexican flavor—Pete Menzies.) Quinlan uses every chance he gets to insult or deprecate Mexicans. Arriving at the explosion site, Quinlan remarks to Adair, "Pete says you even invited some kind of Mexican." Welles explains in his stage directions: "This causes embarrassment, since Quinlan, perhaps without realizing it, has just come to a stop next to Mike" (p. 12). To Vargas's polite response, Quinlan answers, "Well you don't talk like one, I'll say that for you. Mexican, I mean." While investigating on the Mexican side of the border, Quinlan refers to the Mexican police, in Vargas's hearing, as "Keystone Cops." Then finishing the investigation on the Mexican side, he tells his group, "Let's get back to civilization." In questioning Sanchez, the suspect in this version, Quinlan addresses him as "boy" six times. Later, Quinlan is horrified to learn that Vargas "invaded" his ranch to search for dynamite, and he attacks his superiors for listening to a "lousy foreigner" when Vargas brings charges against him. The conflict between Quinlan and Vargas, then, is not just a battle over how the law should be enforced; it becomes also a racial grudge match.

Welles makes three more changes in his raw material which add to the racial friction. First, he changes Marcia Linneker's lover to the Mexican Manolo Sanchez. While Sanchez speaks many of the same defiant lines as his predecessor in the novel, the lines take on more bravado, for Sanchez knows he will encounter racial antagonism from the American police. Moreover, Rudy Linnekar (Welles changes the spelling of the name in the screenplay)[6] becomes not

6. Moreover, he continues the new spelling in the movie. The words "Linnekar Construction Company" appear on the screen on the side of a detonator.

just a snob in rejecting a shoe clerk as a suitor for his daughter, but a racist in objecting to a "Mexican shoe clerk son-in-law." Second, Welles makes the Grandi family predominantly Mexican in order to fill out the pattern.[7] Welles even seems to milk some comedy from Uncle Joe Grandi, the family head, as the stereotype of the bumbling foreigner. Welles inserts into the screenplay the business of Uncle Joe's toupee falling off as he tries to assert control of the family, and he depicts Uncle Joe's difficulty in following Susan's English when she insults him. Third, perhaps most importantly, Welles adds a statement from Quinlan toward the end of the screenplay that his wife was strangled by a "half-breed." This disclosure will be discussed more fully later. For the moment, though, we should notice that it is a part of a pattern of changes which keeps the work crackling with racial antagonisms.

In his handling of narrative point of view in the opening sequence, Welles follows the model of his predecessors. Again, our point of view approaches, but does not quite reach omniscience. And Welles retains a vestige of Monash's use of cross-cutting. He changes the setting from Linnekar's cabana to the border town, and he introduces the Vargases so that their importance is established from the first. Welles's conception of the sequence here is a significant step nearer to the final movie version. The opening shot is one of the time bomb. Then we see a shadowy figure put the bomb into the trunk of a convertible and go to a window of the night club "Grandi's Rancho Grande." Brassy, bump-and-grind music is heard. Following the point of view of the shadowy figure, Welles cuts to the interior of the night club. Rudy Linnekar is persuading a blond dancer, now called Zita, to leave with him. On the wall above them is the gyrating shadow of a stripper. Outside again, the shadowy figure scuttles to the car to make an adjustment on the bomb and then dashes away as Linnekar and Zita leave the night club.[8] Welles tells us then that "the camera follows the car as it moves through

7. It is interesting that Welles keeps the name "Grandi" for his gangster family when the "i" ending indicates the name is Italian, not Mexican. In the movie version, he has Uncle Joe call attention to this fact by stating, "The name ain't Mexican." Perhaps Welles intends by this statement to emphasize Uncle Joe's mixed heritage and link him more closely with the "half-breed" who murdered Quinlan's wife.

8. At this point in the screenplay, Welles indicates that the titles should begin to roll over the action which follows. Welles's direction is worth noting since most critics have blamed editors at Universal Studios for superimposing credits on Welles's masterful sequence shot. It now seems that they were only carrying out his original intention. Of course, it may be that Welles changed his intention after shooting the long take and preferred putting the titles at the end of the movie where most critics feel they belong.

the gaudy streets of the border town on its way to the frontier." Mike and Susan appear, and they stroll to the check point ahead of Linnekar's convertible. The rest of the sequence in the screenplay is designated as a single take. Contrapuntal conversations between the Vargases in their dealings with the customs officials and Linnekar and Zita in their dealings are almost exactly those of the movie. When Vargas kisses his bride, Linnekar's car explodes to end the sequence.

After the initial sequence, however, Welles radically changes his handling of narrative point of view. He opens up the narrative point of view of his predecessors, which restricted us mainly to scenes where Mitch Holt was present as a performer/observer. Now, in the Welles screenplay, we follow events in which Susan Vargas and Hank Quinlan are the important figures with whom we identify and to whom we look for reactions—events where Mike Vargas is not present. The expansion is an excellent idea, for it enables Welles to put on screen two of the most interesting aspects of the work: the terrorizing of Susan Vargas and the psychological deterioration of Hank Quinlan. The texture of the work deepens also in the sense that Welles has two or sometimes three narrative lines moving in parallel at any given time, as opposed to the single, linear plot progression of the earlier versions. Our identification with Mike Vargas is, of course, decreased in the Welles version, and we are less engaged in the mental process of problem solving with Mike. But clearly we are engaged, on the other hand, in the more emotionally charged experience of measuring his progress against the maneuvers of his antagonists.

The subplot in which Susan is the central figure involves three encounters with the Grandis, each increasingly menacing and each increasingly sexual. The first two encounters were invented by Welles, and the last was his reworking of "offstage" elements in the earlier treatments.

The first menace occurs when "Pancho" lures Susan to a Grandi hotel and engineers an apparently compromising photograph. Inside the hotel, Uncle Joe delivers a threat. Although Susan insults Grandi and gives him a threat of her own, we cannot fail to notice that the Grandis have brought her into their control with a minimum of effort.

The second menace comes when a Grandi boy, probably "Pancho," shines his flashlight on Susan through her window when she is packing in her hotel room. The act is, of course, voyeuristic. (She will take off her sweater in the movie version.) In addition, the act has racial undercurrents, for the male invading the privacy of the Anglo-Saxon woman is Mexican.

The third assault is more elaborate. Susan flees from her hotel in Mexico to a motel on the American side of the border. The motel, however, is owned by the Grandis, and after Susan prepares for bed she suffers an escalating series of menaces. She pounds on the wall to quiet a party group next door. She then finds that the lights and the telephone no longer function. There is a rattling at the door. A girl's voice through the wall speaks to her about drugs and tells her that the males of the party have gone to get a master key. Susan raises the shade on her window to discover a bulky figure in a leather coat staring at her. The Grandi boys then enter through the door which they have unlocked. The sequence, as presented at this stage, is terrifying. All sources of aid or reassurance fail Susan. She is vulnerable to intrusion through virtually all sources—the door, the window, and even, it seems, the wall. Welles will alter the elements of the sequence only slightly for his movie, but he will break it down into a series of discrete scenes and intersperse these scenes with the forward movement of the plot concerning Mike's efforts to expose Quinlan's guilt. The menacing of Susan, thus, becomes a continuing referral base against which we measure Mike's progress.

In the screenplay, Welles enlarges the depiction of Hank Quinlan. We have already seen that Welles now makes Quinlan the limping figure and imbues him with a deeply racist outlook. We should add that Welles makes him a reformed alcoholic who "falls off the wagon." In keeping with this enlarged depiction, Welles writes several scenes outside the point of view of Vargas where we get to know Quinlan more intimately. Two such scenes are worth our attention.

One scene takes place in a bar with Quinlan and Uncle Joe present. Quinlan is frightened by Vargas's challenge that Quinlan planted the dynamite in Sanchez's apartment and preoccupied with Grandi's proposal that they frame Susan in a drug party. Unthinkingly, Quinlan downs his first glass of bourbon in twelve years. On an unconscious level, Quinlan hastens his self-destruction. His act of drinking is surely one of self-loathing. Furthermore, since it is a source of pride with Quinlan that he frames only people his intuition tells him are guilty, we must note how far he is sinking, even by his own standards, when he enters into collusion with Grandi to frame a woman he knows is innocent. In the movie version, Welles will conclude the scene with a crane shot that moves up and away from Quinlan, as Welles moved up and away from Susan Alexander Kane in the bar in *Citizen Kane*. The camera movement in *Touch of Evil* is almost gentle. The implication is that we must pity Quinlan at this crucial movement in his decline.

The other scene involves Quinlan's murder of Grandi in the hotel room where

Uncle Joe has brought the unconscious Susan. In the stage directions, Welles states that a bright sign outside the window flashes on and off. The result should be a tension as we wish for cessation or at least variation of the light's regular pulsation. Welles tells us further than Quinlan moves and talks "almost like a sleepwalker." He has been drinking heavily. In this scene, Quinlan strangles Grandi and sinks to the level of murderer. As he does so, he whispers in Grandi's ear, "I'm a man with important work to do. You'd interfere with that work. . . . Who do you think's more important to the world—a dirty blackmailer like you— or me?" (p. 96). This is a megalomania which existed in the earlier versions. Welles, however, adds the detail that Quinlan's eyes go to Susan on the bed as he garrotes Uncle Joe with Susan's stocking. For an explanation of Quinlan's sexual association of the woman on the bed with the strangling of Grandi, we must wait for Welles's later piece of information about how Quinlan's wife was murdered. However, even without this information before us, we must feel that Quinlan's character deepens here in an interesting way. He is a man obsessed, as Macbeth and Othello were obsessed, and in this scene, Welles puts Quinlan, lost in obsession, directly in front of us.

A small, but effective addition Welles makes at this stage involves the use of Quinlan's cane as "ocular proof" which helps move Pete Menzies over to Vargas's side. The cane is discovered by Menzies after Quinlan leaves it behind in the hotel room where he strangled Uncle Joe. Welles sets up Pete's discovery in advance by having Quinlan forget the cane once earlier. (He will forget it twice earlier in the movie.) We may see Quinlan's act of forgetting his cane at the murder scene as another example of habitual forgetfulness or as a Freudian slip by a man who wishes finally to be caught. However, on a more basic level of storytelling, Pete's discovery of his partner's cane at last provides a believable motive for Pete to join forces with Vargas and wear the microphone when he interrogates Quinlan. The discovery of the cane, then, solves a serious problem in character motivation which existed in the original novel.

In an apparent move to create a mood of instability, Welles follows a strategy, at this stage, of cutting away "homes" or what we might call "safe bases." Gone is Rudy Linnekar's cabana as the site of the opening explosion. Gone, too, is the home of the hero and his wife. Reference is made to the ranch of Hank Quinlan, but the ranch is not shown. Instead of "homes," Welles gives us a succession of hotel and motel rooms, each alarmingly transient and each vulnerable to intrusion and attack.

A possible exception to this strategy, however, is a new location which Welles creates for the screenplay. This new location is Mother Lupe's brothel, where Quinlan goes to continue his drinking spree after the murder of Uncle Joe. The brothel is the closest thing to a "safe base" left in the work. In addition, Mother Lupe's place is a setting of exhaustion. Welles calls the woman herself a "venerable figure" and describes the interior of her brothel as follows: "a tatty little 'parlor' with dusty painted velvet hangings on the walls, rickety wicker-work furniture and a profusion of tattered silk-covered lamp shades" (p. 103). A player piano grinds out "Avalon" and then stops. " 'It's getting tired,' " Mother Lupe mutters. " 'It's old. Like us.' "

The brothel is the place where Pete Menzies, wired for sound, finds his partner. Pete leads him through the streets and questions him, while Vargas trails the pair with his recording apparatus. As Monash did, Welles cross-cuts between Vargas and the detectives, but with the action now outside, Welles can also describe deep-focus shots with Vargas in the foreground and the detectives in the background. As now conceived, the sequence has the potential to be visually rich, whereas in the novel, the episode was physically static and almost completely given over the dialogue. Moreover, Welles ends the sequence with the fatally wounded Menzies shooting Quinlan. Not only does Welles get Quinlan's death on screen, but in assigning the shooting to Menzies, he adds a final statement about the friendship or love between the two men. Realizing what his partner has become, Menzies feels he must put a stop to the deterioration. His act is as much an act of love as it is one of duty.

A last addition is information we receive about the murder of Quinlan's wife which comes out in Quinlan's confession to Menzies. According to Quinlan, his wife was strangled when Quinlan was a young man, and the guilty party was a "half-breed." Quinlan could not get enough evidence for an arrest. The murderer died eventually in "some mudhole in Belgium" in World War I. "He was," Quinlan tells Pete, "the last killer ever got out of my hands." With the addition of this revenge motive, Welles adds a possible explanation for Quinlan's racism as well as his mania to punish murderers. Certainly this information creates more sympathy for Quinlan than was the case in earlier versions. The information, furthermore, could enrich Welles's portrayal. Quinlan's motive for bringing killers to justice is now more complicated than mere hunter's pride. But coming as it does at the end, the information also runs the risk of reducing Quinlan to a puzzle with a single solution. Since Welles's distrust of "Rosebud" as sole explanation of Kane's character is well known, we might expect Welles to try to under-cut the importance of this revelation about Quinlan's past in the final version of *Touch of Evil*, the film itself.

The Film

In making the film, Welles followed his screenplay fairly closely, but he did use this stage as an opportunity for "fine tuning" the work. As we might expect, the largest area of change was that of visual presentation—make-up, costuming, set design, laying out of action, and cinematography. These matters were treated only briefly in the screenplay. While such a large area of change cannot be dis-cussed at length here, a few representative examples may be considered.

Welles's brilliant visual presentation of Quinlan, the character he himself plays, is one such example. Welles builds up his own, already bulky figure with padding and then wears a rumpled, tent-like overcoat while others wear only suits. Welles's heavy limp makes his movements seem painful. Yet because he manages to move quickly despite the limp, we get a sense of Quinlan's strong will. Welles uses a stubble of beard, and he gives Quinlan a scar beneath his left eye. Further, Welles adds at this stage the business of Quinlan's oral fixation. He eats candy bars, drinks coffee, and chews on huge cigars. (Lines referring to this oral fixation are added for the movie version: the prostitute Tanya's "You should lay off those candy bars," and Quinlan's "Didn't you bring me any doughnuts or sweetrolls?") And Welles has Quinlan trailed with pieces of trash as he walks the street toward Tanya's parlor early in the film. In short, the details of Welles's visual presentation of his "twisted" villain are worked out in so elaborate and skillful a manner that the figure becomes a striking grotesque. . . .

Perhaps the most interesting cinematic additions are Welles's long takes or sequence shots. Of course, at this point in his career, the long take had become almost a trademark of Welles films. Yet, even for audience members expecting Wellesian long takes, the examples in *Touch of Evil* can be breathtaking in their impact and effectiveness. Two such shots occur during the scenes of interroga-tion of Sanchez. The first shot runs five minutes and twenty-three seconds, and the second, five minutes and thirty-three seconds. The mood produced in both cases is one of claustrophobia. The fact that the scenes don't have the sense of release which comes from cutting is important. Furthermore, we are confined to three rooms in the first shot (the livingroom, the bedroom, and the bathroom) and one room in the second (the livingroom). Into this confined space, Welles brings as many as nine characters. Lighting comes from below eye-level and throws shadows on the far wall, in effect, doubling the number of figures in the room.[9] Through the use of an extreme wide-angle lens (18.5 mm), Welles is able to hold a number of figures within the frame at one time, even when the camera is in close to his characters, and, of course, given the distorting quality of the lens, the characters seem to "loom" at us when they approach the camera. Ceilings give us a further sense of confined space. Frequently while we watch main characters in the foreground, there is slightly disturbing movement from minor characters in the background. Occasionally, a figure will pass between the camera and the main characters whom we want to watch, causing another visual disturbance. All these elements combine to create a strong mood of tension.

The most successful use of the long take, however, comes in the opening sequence of the film, the sequence whose evolution we have been tracing from the original novel. Welles's shrewd stroke in adapting the sequence from his screenplay to the film was to eliminate the shot of Linnekar and Zita inside the Grandi night club. With this shot removed, Welles is able to film the entire sequence as a single shot running three minutes and eighteen seconds. André Bazin has praised Welles's sequence shots in general for the emphasis they place on character's relation to the *decor*.[10] But here in particular, the choice of a single take increases tremendously the tension of the movie's beginning. Welles makes us wait out every second of the brief time span we see marked on the bomb's dial. Meanwhile, he adds elements that increase our anxiety and make us wish for a speeding up of time. The music used for this sequence has a cha-cha rhythm section set against a jazz/swing melodic structure.[11] The choice of the cha-cha beat seems a return to Monash's idea. It begins the kind of pulsating effect that will be continued visually throughout the film by such things as the flaming fountain, the light outside the hotel window, and the pumping oil derricks. In the initial sequence, though, the music provides mainly a repetitive beat whose eventual interruption we anticipate. Welles changes the dancer's shadow of the

9. Julius Rascheff, *Touch of Evil: Color Microfiche Study Guide*, unpublished monograph (1975): 40.
10. André Bazin, *Orson Welles: A Critical View*, trans. Jonathan Rosenbaum (New York: Harper, 1978): 67–73.
11. Welles did control the choice of music in the film. Henry Mancini, music director on the film, has stated: "He [Welles] wrote to Joe Gershenson and outlined in detail what he thought the music should be. Joe sent the letter over to me, and it was like we had both been thinking of the same thing at the same time." Quoted in Joseph Curley, "Nobody Does It Better," *Millimeter*, 7 (June 1979): 30.

screenplay into a gigantic, expressionistic shadow of the dynamiter. Linnekar's convertible moves out of sight momentarily behind a building and then moves in and out of pockets of shadows during its progress to the check point. The car falls behind and catches up to the moving camera on a Chapmain crane. Pedestrians, other cars, and even two pushcarts come between us and our view of the convertible. These various elements unsettle us and play nicely *against* Welles's refusal to speed up time.

In the film version, Welles adds three pieces of action not in the screenplay. All three serve to open up further narrative point of view in the work. Two involve expanding parts for "stars" Dennis Weaver and Marlene Dietrich whom Welles was able to enlist for his film. Here commercial concerns and artistic ones seem to have overlapped perfectly, for Welles was able to use the abilities of these "stars" (in the case of Dietrich, we might say the "mystique") to add effective new elements to the movie.

For Dennis Weaver, Welles expanded the role of the night watchman. This character existed in the screenplay, but he appeared only briefly in the scene when Vargas came to the motel searching for his wife. For the movie, Welles places the night watchman also in the scene of Susan's arrival and in the action with the Grandi boys and makes him oddly introverted and sexually repressed. . . .

For Marlene Dietrich, Welles creates the part of the prostitute Tanya and expands her role over that of Mother Lupe in the screenplay. He adds a scene in Tanya's parlor early in the movie when Quinlan hears the tinkling of a player piano and follows it to Tanya's place. This scene sets up Quinlan's return to the parlor later, and it establishes Tanya's right to deliver Quinlan's epitaph. It also offers more information about Quinlan. . . .

A final action Welles adds is a short barroom scene near the middle of the movie. In this scene, Quinlan tells Menzies about the murder of his wife. The details are the same as those of the screenplay. The shift of this information, though, from the end to the middle is quite effective. It reduces the emphasis on the revelation. Now the revelation has importance still as information about Quinlan, but it is not offered as the single solution to a lengthily-developed puzzle. Furthermore, this scene is another where Quinlan is the object of our attention outside the point of view of Vargas. The scene is part of Welles's strategy of putting on the screen elements concerning Quinlan's psychological deterioration.

From this account of the evolution of the film, it should now be clear that *Touch of Evil* developed in stages of gradual change and refinement with several hands involved. Welles's debts to his predecessors are extensive. They are deeper than most viewers and critics have recognized. Wade and Miller provided much of the raw material: the opening explosion, the planting of evidence by the police captain, the gangster family, the framing of the hero's wife, and the final, recorded interrogation of the police captain by his partner. Monash complicated the depiction of the police captain and put him and the hero on more nearly equal footing. He expanded the role of the gangster family to one of menace and added the ironic twist of having the framed lover be guilty. And he wrote five new scenes which Welles used.

However, it should also be clear by now that Welles changed the versions of his predecessors in ways that made the work richer and more resonant. He did not try to "transcend" the detection thriller aspect of the work. Rather he worked within the boundaries of that genre to make *Touch of Evil* as intriguing and as viscerally disturbing as he could. In Welles's hands, the work became an extended piece against American racism, but the racism functions completely within the warp and woof of the *film noir* genre: it adds to the intensity of the antagonisms in the work. Importantly, Welles opened up narrative point of view and put on the screen the terrorizing of Susan and the mental deterioration of Hank Quinlan, two of the strongest pieces of psychological study inherent in the material. He smoothed away some of the narrative problems, added the engaging characters of the watchman and Tanya, and handled brilliantly matters of costuming, location, and laying out action. However, perhaps the best paradigm of the kind of change Welles made is to be found in the opening sequence shot. The novel and the Monash screenplay provided competent handlings of the explosion scene, but Welles, in his classic long take, made the tension of the scene almost unbearable. This ability to intensify the material he inherited is perhaps above all what entitles Welles finally to be considered the "author" of *Touch of Evil*.

Interviews, Reviews, and Commentaries

Interviews

The appearance of *Touch of Evil* at the 1958 Brussels World's Fair was the occasion of a long and wide-ranging interview with Welles published in two parts in *Cahiers du Cinéma*. It was conducted by one of Welles's most distinguished critics, André Bazin, together with Charles Bitsch and Jean Domarchi. James Delson's interview with Charlton Heston, originally published in the Canadian film journal, *Take One*, is perhaps the best account of the filming of *Touch of Evil*.

Interview with
Orson Welles

The Director and his Medium

Cahiers: It's been said that it was partly by accident you made *Touch of Evil*. Was someone else supposed to have made it?
Welles: No. But there are scenes in the film I neither wrote nor directed, about which I know absolutely nothing. In *Ambersons*, there are three scenes I neither wrote nor directed.
Cahiers: You made *Touch of Evil* because no other opportunities presented themselves?
Welles: My eighth film! You know, I've been working since I was seventeen, I've directed eight films, and I've been able to edit only three of them myself.
Cahiers: *Citizen Kane* . . .
Welles: *Othello* and *Don Quixote*—in seventeen years!
Cahiers: And *The Lady from Shanghai*?
Welles: No, not the final cut. You can still see my style of editing, but the final version of the film is not mine at all. They always tear the film out of my hands— violently.
Cahiers: Do you think there are great differences between your version of *Touch of Evil* and the studio's?
Welles: For me, almost everything that's called "directing" is a great bluff. In the cinema, there are very few men who are real directors, and of these, very few who have much opportunity to direct. The only "direction" of any importance is exercised in the process of editing. Yes, I edited *Ambersons*, in spite of the fact there are scenes in it of which I was not the author. But they changed my editing. The basic montage is mine, and where a scene holds together it's because I edited it. In other words, it all happens as if a man painted a picture: he finishes it and someone comes along to retouch it, but he is obviously not able to fiddle with the whole surface of the canvas. I'd been working for months and months on *Amber-*

From "Entretien avec Orson Welles," *Cahiers du Cinéma*, no. 84 (June 1958): 1–13; "Nouvel Entretien avec Orson Welles," *Cahiers du Cinéma*, no. 87 (September 1958): 2–26. Both parts have been translated, abridged, and slightly rearranged by the editor, who has also added subtitles.

sons before they took it away from me, so all that work is there, on the screen. But for my style, for my vision of the cinema, editing is not simply one aspect: it's *the* aspect. The notion of "directing" a film is the invention of critics like you. It isn't an art, or at best it's an art only one minute a day. That minute is terribly crucial, but it occurs very rarely. The only time one is able to exercise control over the film is in the editing. Well, in the editing room I work very slowly, which has the effect of arousing the ire of the producers, who then take the film out of my hands. I don't know why it takes me so much time: I could work forever on the editing of a film. So far as I'm concerned, a strip of film is performed like a musical score, and that performance is determined by the editing—just as one conductor will perform a piece of music with a great deal of rubato, another will play it dryly and academically, a third will be very romantic, and so on. The images themselves are not sufficient. They're very important, but they're only images. What's essential is the duration of each image and that which follows each image: the whole eloquence of cinema is that it's achieved in the editing room.

Cahiers: Montage does seem essential in your most recent films, but in *Citizen Kane*, *Ambersons*, and *Macbeth* and so on, you used a great many sequence shots.

Welles: Mark Robson was my editor for *Citizen Kane*. With Robson and Robert Wise, our assistant, we worked nearly a year on editing. So it's false to believe that there was nothing to edit just because I used many long takes. We could still be working at the editing today! You can see that in the course of these last years, I've deliberately used short takes in my films, because I had less money and a short-take style is cheaper. For a long take, an enormous amount of money is required in order to be able to control all the elements in front of the camera. . . . In *Touch of Evil*, for example, I did a shot that moved through three rooms, with fourteen actors, in which the frame varied between closeups and long shots and so on, and which lasted nearly a whole reel. Well! this was by far the most costly thing in the film. So if you notice that I don't use long takes, it's not because I don't like them, but because they don't give me the means to produce them. It's certainly cheaper to create this image and then that image and then still another image and seek to order them later, in the editing room. I prefer, obviously, to control the elements in front of the camera as it rolls, but that requires money and the confidence of your backers.

Cahiers: The idea of montage appears to be linked to that of short takes. If one refers to the experience of Soviet film, it appears that one can carry montage to its limits only with short takes. Isn't there a contradiction between the importance you accord montage and the fact that you like shots of long duration?

Welles: I don't believe that the whole business of montage is a function of the brevity of shots. It's an error to suppose that the Russians worked so much with montage because they shot their films in short takes. One can spend a lot of time editing a film in long takes if one is not content just to paste together one scene after another.

Cahiers: What's your goal in using the 18.5 [wide angle] lens so systematically and in pushing your techniques of editing so far?

Welles: I work, and have worked, with the 18.5 solely because other cineastes have not availed themselves of it. Cinema is like a colony: there are few colonists. When America was wide open, when the Spanish were on the frontier of Mexico, the French in Canada, the Dutch in New York, you can be sure that the English made their way to places that were still unoccupied. I don't prefer the 18.5: I'm simply the only one to have explored its possibilities. I don't prefer to improvise: it's just that no one had done it for a long time. It's not a question of preference. I occupy positions that are not occupied because, in this relatively new medium, it's a necessity. The first thing to be remembered about the cinema is its youth. And the essential job of every responsible artist is to cultivate what lies fallow. If everyone worked with a wide angle lens, I'd shoot all my films in 75mm [i.e., a narrow angle lens], because I take its possibilities very seriously. If there were other artists with an extremely baroque style, I'd be the most classical filmmaker you've ever seen. I don't act this way out of a spirit of contradiction. I don't want to oppose what has been made but to occupy an uninhabited terrain and work there.

Cahiers: Since you've utilized the 18.5 for a long while, you ought already to have explored a good part of this terrain; and yet you persist. Isn't there some affinity between you and this lens?

Welles: No. I continue to work with this lens because nobody besides me does it. If I constantly had to look at shots filmed with a wide angle lens, my eye would become weary. I always try in my films to make images of which I will not become weary or sated. If everyone used and abused the 18.5, I'd never touch it. I'd abandon this characteristic distortion and seek some other language to express myself. But I don't see enough of these images to become weary of them: so I'm able to look at this distortion with a fresh eye. It's not at all a question of some affinity between the 18.5 and me, but solely of freshness of vision. I'd love to make a film in 100mm in which one never left the faces of the actors: there would be millions of things to do. But the 18.5 is a capital new invention. It's scarcely been five years that we've found good 18.5s, and how many people have used them? Every time I give one to the head camera man, he's terrified; by the end of the film, it's his favorite lens. Maybe I'm near the point now of having done with the wide angle lens. It occurs to me that *Don Quixote* will mark the end of the 18.5. Or maybe not!

Cahiers: Do you in the same way accord so great a significance to montage because it's a bit neglected these days, or is it because it really is for you the very foundation of cinema?

Welles: I can't believe that montage isn't the essential thing for the director, the sole moment when he completely controls the form of his film. When I'm shooting, the sun determines some things against which I cannot contend, the actor introduces things to which I must adapt, and so does the story. I have to make do with dominating what I can. The only place I exercise absolute control is in the editing room. Consequently, it's then that the director is, all on his own, a true artist. For I believe a film is good only to the degree that the director has achieved control over his different materials, and is not content simply to bring about some safe resolution.

Cahiers: Your montage fragments are long because you try out different solutions for . . .

Welles: I seek the exact rhythm between one frame and the next. It's a question of the ear. Montage is the moment when film engages with the sense of hearing.

Cahiers: So it's not problems of narration or of dramatic tension that detain you?

Welles: No. Problems of form, like a conductor interpreting a piece of music with rubato or without. It's a question of rhythm, and for me, that's the essential—the heartbeat. . . .

[Welles is asked a number of questions about his work for TV.]

Welles: I'm always looking for synthesis. It's work that deeply engages me, for I ought to be true to what I am, and I'm nothing but an experimenter. My only value in my own eyes is that I don't enunciate laws but am an experimenter. To experiment is the only thing that arouses my enthusiasm. I'm not interested in works of art, you know, in posterity, in renown—only in the pleasure of experimentation itself. This is the only domain where I feel myself truly honest and sincere. I have no commitment to what I've made: it's really without value in my eyes. I'm profoundly cynical about my own work and about most of the works I see in the world. But I am not cynical about the act of working with a medium. It's difficult to explain. We who make a profession of experiment have inherited a long tradition. Some of us have been among the greatest artists, but we've never made the muses our mistresses. For example, Leonardo considered himself a scientist who painted and not a painter who might have been a scientist. I don't want to make you think I'm comparing myself to Leonardo. I just want to explain that there's a long line of people who judge their work according to a different hierarchy of values—almost of moral values. I'm not ecstatic about art. I *am* ecstatic about the human function, which implies everything we make with our hands, our senses, and so on. Once our work is finished, it doesn't have as much value in my eyes as it does in those of most of our aesthetes. It's the act that interests me, not the result; and I'm taken by the result only when it gives forth the odor of human sweat, or of a human thought.

Cahiers: Have you in mind any specific projects to direct?

Welles: No. I don't know. I'm seriously considering putting a complete stop to all cinematic or theatrical activity, to end it once and for all, because I've had too many disillusions. I've devoted too much work, too much effort, for what has been given me in return. I don't mean to say in money, but in satisfaction. So I contemplate abandoning film and theater because in effect they have already abandoned me. I have some films to complete: I'll finish *Don Quixote*, but I'm no longer eager to throw myself into new enterprises. This makes five years now that I've dreamt of quitting cinema, for I've spent ninety percent of my existence, and of my energy, without being able to function as an artist; and while a little youth is still left to me, I ought to try to find another area in which I'd be able to work, to stop wasting my life trying to express myself through cinema. Eight films in 17 years: it's not much. Perhaps I *will* make more films; sometimes the best way to do something one loves is to get away from it and then return. It's like a romantic story. You can wait before a girl's door for her to let you in, but she'll never open it for you. Better to leave: she'll write you! No, this is nothing dramatic, you know. It's not as if I were bitter or anything like that. But I want to work. Now I write and paint. I'm looking for some way to release my energy, because I've spent the greatest part of these past fifteen years looking for financial backing, and if I had been a writer or, especially, a painter, I wouldn't have had to do this. I also have a serious problem with my personality as an actor. I project a certain aura of success, which encourages critics all over the world to think it's time to discourage me a little, you know—"what would do him the most good would be to tell him that in the long run he's not so great as all that." But it's been twenty-five years now they've been saying this to me! No, I've really spent too many months, too many years, looking for work. And I have only one life. So for the moment, I write and I paint. I throw away everything I do, but perhaps I'll eventually do something good enough to keep: it has to happen. I can't spend my whole existence at festivals or in restaurants begging for money. I'm sure I can make good films only if I write the scripts. I could make thrillers, obviously, but I don't have any desire to. The only film I've ever written from the first word to the last and was able to bring to a proper conclusion was *Citizen Kane*. Well, too many years have gone by since I was given that opportunity. Can I wait another fifteen years for someone willing to place absolute trust in me again? No, I need to find another, cheaper means of expression—like this tape recorder! . . .

Quinlan and the Morality of Acting

Cahiers: We'd like to extricate a certain ideal character who runs through all your films, from *Citizen Kane* to *Touch of Evil*. Is he the man of whom Truffaut spoke, in *Arts*, à propos of *Touch of Evil*; that is to say, the man of genius who isn't able to restrain himself from doing evil? Or is it necessary to see a certain ambiguity in him?

Welles: It's a mistake to think that Quinlan finds any favor in my eyes. To me, he's hateful. There's no ambiguity in his character. He's not a genius: he's a master of his field, a provincial master, but a detestable man. The most personal thing I've put in this film is my hatred of the abuse of police power. And it's obvious: it's more interesting to speak of the abuse of police power in connection with a man of a certain size—not only physical but also with regard to his personality—than with an ordinary little cop. So Quinlan is better than an ordinary cop, which doesn't prevent him from being hateful. There's no ambiguity there. But it's always possible to feel sympathy for a son of a bitch. Sympathy is a human thing, after all. Hence my soft spot for men for whom I in no way hide my repugnance. And this sentiment does not come from the fact they're more gifted but from the fact they're human beings. Quinlan is sympathetic because of his humanity, not because of his ideas. There's not the least particle of genius in him: if he seems to have any such quality, I've made a mistake. Quinlan is a good technician, he knows his job: he's an "authority." But because he's a man of a certain breadth, a man of courage, you can't prevent yourself from feeling sympathy for him. In spite of everything, he's a human being. I believe that Kane is a destestable man, but I have a great deal of sympathy for him so far as he's a human being.

Cahiers: And Macbeth?

Welles: A similar case. More or less voluntarily, you know, I've played a lot of unsavory types. I detest Harry Lime, that little black market hustler, all these horrible men I've interpreted. But these aren't small men, because I'm an actor for characters on a grand scale. You know, in the old classic French theater, there were always some actors who played kings and others who did not. I'm one of those who play kings. I have to be, because of my personality. So naturally, I always play the role of leaders, men of some unusual breadth: I always need to be bigger than life. It's a fault of my nature. So it's not necessary to believe there's anything ambiguous about my interpretation. It's my personality that's responsible, not my intentions. It's very serious for an artist, a creator, to be at the same time an actor. He runs a grave risk of being misunderstood. Because my own personality intrudes between what I say and what you hear; and a great part of the mystery, of the confusion, of the interest, in all you can find in the characters I play comes from my own personality and not from what I say. I'd be very happy never to act in a film. I do act because often that permits me to work as a director. If there's any ambiguity, it's because I've acted too often in my films. Certainly Quinlan is a "moral" character, but I detest his morality.

Cahiers: Isn't this feeling of ambiguity reinforced by the fact that at the end of the film Quinlan has been right in spite of everything, since the young Mexican is guilty?

Welles: Despite everything, he's wrong. It's only an accident. Who cares about knowing whether he was mistaken or not?

Cahiers: Isn't it important?

Welles: That depends on your point of view. Personally, I believe in everything that's said by the character played by Heston. I'd be able to say everything Vargas says. He speaks as a man of dignity, according to the tradition of classical humanism, which is absolutely my tradition as well. So this is the angle from which you have to understand the film: whatever Vargas says, he says as my mouthpiece. It's better to see a murderer go free than for a policeman to abuse his power. If you have a choice between the abuse of police power and letting a crime go unpunished, you have to choose the unpunished crime. That's my point of view. So, let's accept the fact that the young Mexican is really guilty. What exactly is his guilt? That does not really concern us. The subject of the film is elsewhere. This man is just a name in a newspaper: no one gives a damn about knowing whether he's guilty or not. It's a purely incidental feature of the script. So they've trapped the guilty party. But it's a purely anecdotal event, it's not central to the theme. *The truly guilty one is Quinlan*. And when André Bazin writes that

Quinlan is a great man, etc., it's because Menzies, Quinlan's friend, says he's a great man. No one besides him says so. And Menzies says it because he sincerely believes it: this defines Menzies' character, not Quinlan's. Quinlan is Menzies' god. And since Menzies adores him, the real theme of the scenario is betrayal, the terrible necessity by which Menzies betrays his friend. And there, there *is* an ambiguity, because I don't know whether he should have betrayed him or not. No, I really don't know. And I forced Menzies into the betrayal, but the decision didn't come from him; and frankly, in his place, I wouldn't have betrayed my friend. . . .

Cahiers: Your sympathy for Quinlan is only human, then, it's not moral.

Welles: Absolutely. My sympathy goes to Menzies and especially to Vargas. But in his case it's not a human sympathy. Vargas is not so human as that. How could he be? He's the hero of a melodrama. And in melodrama, one's sympathy is drawn forcibly to the villain. I want to be clear about my intentions. What I said in the film is this: I firmly believe that in the modern world we need to choose between the morality of the law and the morality of simple justice; which is to say, between lynching someone or letting him go free. I'd rather have a murderer be free than have the police arrest him by mistake. Quinlan does not want to submit the guilty ones to justice so much as to assassinate them in the name of the law, using the police for his own purposes; and this is a fascist scenario, a totalitarian scenario, contrary to traditional law and human justice as I understand them. Thus, for me, Quinlan is the incarnation of everything I struggle against, politically and morally speaking. I'm against Quinlan because he wishes to arrogate the right to judge; and that's what I detest above all, men who wish to judge by their own authority. I believe that one has a right to judge only on the basis of a religion, or a law, or both together. If you decide on your own that someone is guilty, good or evil, it's the law of the jungle; you open the door to men who lynch their own kind, to little gangsters who roam the streets. But I have to like Quinlan because of something quite different I've given him: the fact that he's been able to love Marlene Dietrich, that he's taken a bullet intended for his friend, the fact that he has a heart. But what he believes is detestable. The possible ambiguity is not in the character of Quinlan, it's in the betrayal of Quinlan by Menzies. Kane too is a man who abuses the power of the popular press and sets himself up against the law, against the whole tradition of liberal civilization. He too holds cheap what I consider the very basis of civilization and tries to become the king of his universe, a little like Quinlan in his border town. It's at this level these men come together. And they also come together with Harry Lime, with his contempt for everything, who tries to make himself king of a world without law. All these men are similar, and each in his own fashion stands for the things I most detest. But I like and I comprehend—I have a human sympathy for—these different characters I've created. Morally I find them detestable—morally, not humanly. . . .

Cahiers: If as you've been saying, your characters are not humanly detestable, it must be that this "human" dimension represents for you, if not a moral norm, then at least a value.

Welles: The value lies in the fact that this is the best argument I can invent in favor of my enemies. Besides, when I get under the skin of a character, at once as actor and as author, and I become this character, I summon up the best of myself to fill out the role, so that the character I play is enriched by the best of my own nature.

Cahiers: You become the devil's advocate.

Welles: More than the devil's advocate. More. Because in becoming these characters, I transfigure them by giving them the best I have. But I detest what they are.

Cahiers: What do you think of Robert Browning, who said he had a conscience so elastic that he could adopt the point of view of his enemies?

Welles: He was an actor. I believe that all the great writers, and even merely competent ones, are actors. They have the actor's capacity to get under the skin of their main character and transform him—whether he be a murderer or no matter what else—with what they're able to give of themselves. An actor does just the same. And this quality often leads to a situation in which the protagonists of the story seem to speak for the author, even though they express only his talent, not his opinions. In other words, when Arkadin talks about cowards, he makes use of my sense of humor, but for all this I am not Arkadin and I don't want to have anything to do with all the Arkadins of the world.

Cahiers: You won't have us believe that such consistency in the choice of "detestable" characters doesn't imply more than just sympathy on your part. You're against them, yet you serve them better than an advocate! You'll have a hard time convincing us that at the same time you condemn them, you do not feel an admiration that is, in spite of everything, a way of bailing them out and giving them a chance for salvation. You give the devil a chance for salvation. That's important, after all!

Welles: All the characters I've played, and of whom we've been speaking, are versions of Faust, and I'm against every Faust, because I believe it's impossible for a man to be great without admitting that there is something greater than himself. This might be the Law, or God, or Art—it doesn't matter what the concept, but it ought to be greater than man. I have interpreted a long line of egotists, and I detest egotism—that of the Renaissance, that of Faust, every egotism. But obviously an actor is in love with the role he plays. He's like a man who embraces a woman, he gives her something of himself. An actor is not a devil's advocate, he's a lover, a lover of someone of the opposite sex. And for me Faust is like the opposite sex. It seems to me that there are two great human types in the world, and one of them is Faust. I belong to the other camp, but in playing Faust I want to be true and faithful to him, to give him the best of myself, and the best arguments I can find, for we live in a world that has been made by Faust. *Our world is Faustian.*

Cahiers: There are some actors who create any sort of character whatever. Now, we propose that in all your films, whatever the given pretext, even if the scenarios have nothing in common, your characters in their deepest natures turn out to be similar. So one could conclude that, whatever you may say, you may perhaps actually intend to condemn these characters, but it is a condemnation that . . .

Welles: I don't necessarily condemn them in the cinema, I condemn them only in life. In other words—it's very important to make this distinction—I condemn them in the sense that they're against what I'm for; but I do not condemn them in my heart, only in my mind. The condemnation is cerebral. And this is complicated by the fact that I play the role of those I condemn. Now you'll tell me an actor only plays the part he's been assigned: when one plays a character, one begins by getting rid of anything that doesn't correspond to the role. But one can never put anything into the character that doesn't exist. No actor plays something other than himself. And so, certainly, Orson Welles makes his way every time into all my characters. I can't do anything about it: it's he who plays them, not just physically, but the whole man, *Orson Welles*. Thus, I put aside part of my political and moral beliefs, I put on a false nose, I do all that: but it remains Orson Welles. There's no use fighting it. Since I believe very strongly in the quality of chivalry, when I play the role of someone I detest, I put great value on being chivalrous in my interpretation.

Cahiers: Certainly there's a great deal of generosity in all your films.

Welles: For me, that's the essential virtue. I hate all opinions that deprive humanity of the least of its privileges. If any belief demands the renunciation of anything human, I detest it. So I'm against every form of fanaticism, I hate political and religious slogans. I detest what supresses a single note on the human scale: one ought to be able at every moment to sound all possible harmonies. . . .

Cahiers: To return to your work, it seems to me that one sees in it a profound unity derived from a Nietzschean conception of existence. Is that accurate?

Welles: I don't know what it derives from, but I hope there's some unity in my work, because if what you've done doesn't belong to you as much as your flesh and blood, it's of no interest. I believe that any work whatever, and I'm sure you'd go along with me on this, is good to the degree that it expresses the man who made it. I always feel morally involved with my scripts. They don't interest me *as* scripts: for me, only the moral aspect is important. I hate rhetoric in any piece, I hate talk about morality, but the moral center of the piece is in my eyes essential.

Cahiers: Your morality is not the everyday one: it's a higher morality.

Welles: Ah well, I must say I take more interest in character than in virtue. You could call that a Nietzschean morality, just as I could call it aristocratic as opposed to bourgeois. Sentimental bourgeois morality disgusts me: I value courage above all other virtues.

Cahiers: That's what we meant to imply when we spoke of a different, superior morality.

Welles: I don't think it's so different. It's only different from the morality of the 19th or 20th century. . . .

Cahiers: We are struck by the theme of character in your work, from *The Lady from Shanghai* to *Mr. Arkadin*, and perhaps a little less explicitly in *Touch of Evil*. "It's my character"—isn't that what the scorpion said?* Is that an excuse the scorpion offers the frog? We'd like to know what the connection is between your own views and the story of the scorpion, because basically our whole conversation has been raising the question of the relation between the frog and the scorpion, don't you think?

Welles: Oh well, there's a lot to say about that. First: the frog is an ass!

Cahiers: You're not in favor of the frog's stupidity?

Welles: Oh no!

---

* "And now I'm going to tell you about a scorpion. A scorpion wanted to cross a river, so he asked a frog to carry him. 'No,' said the frog. 'No thank you. If I let you on my back you may sting me, and the sting of the scorpion means death.' 'Now where,' asked the scorpion, 'is the logic of that? No scorpion could be judged illogical! If I sting you, you will die—I will drown.' The frog was convinced and allowed the scorpion on his back, but just in the middle of the river he felt a terrible pain and realized that after all the scorpion *had* stung him. 'Logic!' cried the dying frog, as he started under, bearing the scorpion down with him. 'There is no logic in this!' 'I know,' said the scorpion, 'but I can't help it—it's my character.' Let's drink to character!" From *Mr. Arkadin*.

Cahiers: And you consider the scorpion a bastard?

Welles: Yes. Both of them! But let's speak seriously. I insist on the fact that I'm very serious in saying this: I give my enemies not only the best arguments but also the most eloquent means of defending their points of view. Nonetheless, I don't believe one can justify one's acts by invoking one's character, although I admit that it's very tempting to do so. Nothing in the world is more charming than a real son of a bitch admitting he's a son of a bitch. I always like a man to own up to being a bastard, a murderer, or whatever you want, to say to me, "I've killed three people." He's immediately my brother, because he's candid. I think this candour does not excuse the crime, but it renders it very alluring, it gives it a certain charm. This is not at all a question of morality. It's a question of charm.

Cahiers: That's a feminine conception of life.

Welles: The only good artists are feminine. I don't admit the existence of an artist whose dominant personality is masculine. This has nothing to do with homosexuality; but intellectually, an artist ought to be a man with feminine aptitudes. It's even more difficult for a woman, because she ought to have both masculine and feminine aptitudes and . . . that gets very complicated. For a man, it's quite simple.

Cahiers: So the scorpion is in part excused?

Welles: The moral of the story is that the man who declares to the world, "I am what I am, take it or leave it"—that this man has a kind of tragic dignity. It's a question of dignity, of size, of charm, of breadth—but that doesn't justify him. In other words, this story ought to be understood as serving a dramatic end, and not as justifying Arkadin or the assassination. And it is not through puritanism that I'm against crime. Don't forget, I'm also against police. It seems to me I'm very close to anarchist and aristocratic conceptions. Whatever judgment you may pass on my morality, you ought to try to see in it this essentially anarchist and aristocratic aspect.

Cahiers: You're against evil, but you think that character . . .

Welles: . . . is the essential thing! That's the traditionally aristocratic point of view.

Cahiers: Would you then go so far as to say that it's better to have character than to do good?

Welles: No, no. *Character* has two senses in English. If I speak of my character, that signifies that that's the way I am; it's the equivalent of the Italian, *sono fatto così*. But in the story of the frog, what's involved is the other sense of *character*. In English, "character" is not only the way you're made, it's also what you *decide* to be. It's especially the way you behave vis à vis death, because I believe you can judge men only on the basis of their behavior in the face of death. It's very important to make this distinction, because this sense of character can only be explained by anecdotes.

Cahiers: One might be able to translate it as "personality"?

Welles: No.

Cahiers: As "temperament"?

Welles: Not exactly. I'm afraid there isn't a perfect equivalent in French. It's not a conception of one's character but of "character" as such. Your character, my character—we understand them very well. But you can understand character as such only from an aristocratic perspective. I don't want to say that only the nobility with titles, land, and family names can grasp this sense. I don't want to seem like a snob. Character is an aristocratic conception, just as virtue is a bourgeois conception. Virtue—the hell with it! What is character? Here's an example. Colette, when the Germans came to look for her husband in order to deport him, this husband she loved so terribly, whom she adored—when they came one fine morning at six A.M. to arrest him, instead of a great dramatic farewell scene, with all the usual fuss, Colette simply whispered, giving him a little slap, "Go with them right away." Now that's character. Not Colette's character, not her in general, but this moment, this precise instant: it can last as long as a flash of lightning.

Two Notes on *Touch of Evil*

Cahiers: Don't you think the greatest influence one can demonstrate in your work is that of Shakespeare?

Welles: Oh yes, without a doubt.

Cahiers: For example, in *Touch of Evil*, the character of the Night Man.

Welles: A total Shakespearean Fool, and just like such fools, very much on the margin of the story. And you know, this role was improvised: no dialogue had been written for it. I hired the actor and constructed the character through improvisation. A famous American critic saw the film and hated it especially because of this character. He was astonished: why such a character? But why not? And furthermore: you don't meet anyone like this in real life! Okay, but there's someone like this in my film! This critic, like many other Americans, was really shocked by the Night Man. I'm very American myself. But my tastes aren't offended in the same way as those of the typical American, especially the American intellectual. This is very curious: it's not intentional, it's just the way things are. American intellectuals are complete strangers to me. I never succeed in communicating with them. I try, but when by chance they like one of my films, it's aways for the wrong reasons. I know they were offended by the Night Man because he's a true fool, a true Pierrot Lunaire. And it seems to me that such a lunar silhouette would inevitably be born from the climate that surrounds him. In other words, his dramatic justification is that the horror all around him is such that it could engender no other character, nothing other than (as you say) an Elizabethan figure. . . .

Cahiers: One odd thing in *Touch of Evil* is the staging of Heston listening to the confrontation between Quinlan and Menzies, so similar to that of Othello listening to the conversation between Iago and Desdemona.

Welles: I hadn't thought of it, but in fact, that's true!

Cahiers: While Quinlan and Menzies walk straight down the street, Heston is forced to make exhausting efforts to keep up along a rough, uneven route. Why does the character who listens have to follow such a path?

Welles: He has to walk through this terrible labyrinth, in the midst of the derricks, because he's the intruder. It's a scene in which there's no place for him. Two old friends are chatting. If they saw Heston, it would be all over. So I thought he ought to seem to be making an effort—to dig, as one digs for gold; to climb, the way one scales a mountainside. This job doesn't suit him and he hates it, as he says to Menzies. At this moment, Vargas loses his integrity. So he's thrust into a world to which he doesn't morally belong. He becomes the crude type who deliberately eavesdrops, and he doesn't know how to be such a person. So I tried to make it seem that the listening apparatus is guiding him, that he's the victim of that apparatus rather than simply of his curiosity. He doesn't know very well how to use his recording machine; he's able only to follow and obey it because this device doesn't really belong to him. He isn't a spy, he isn't even a cop.

Heston on Welles

James Delson

Int.: How did the *Touch of Evil* project come to be produced?

Heston: It was submitted to me in December of 1956 by Universal, for whom I had made a successful comedy called *The Private War of Major Benson*. Since its release I had finished *Ten Commandments*, done a play in New York, and I was loafing over the holiday when Universal sent the script.

"It's a good enough script," I said, "but police stories, like westerns and war stories, have been so overdone that it really depends on who's going to direct it." I told them I'd put it down and call them later.

They told me that although they didn't know who was going to direct it, Orson Welles was going to play the heavy. "You know, Orson Welles is a pretty good director," I said. "Did it ever occur to you to have him direct it?" At that time, Orson had not directed a picture in America since *Macbeth*. They were a bit nonplussed, but they got back to me in a couple of days and said "Yeah, well that's a very good idea. A startling idea."

Int.: At this time, was Welles considered a cult figure at all?

Heston: About *Citizen Kane* he was. There was a rich preoccupation with the idea of Welles as a rebel, I guess, but they brought him in on the picture. He totally rewrote the script in about seventeen days, which I knew he would, and didn't object to.

Int.: He got a solo writing credit for it.

Heston: Well he deserved it. He gives you your value. He has a reputation as being an extravagant director, but there are directors who have *wasted* more money on one film than Orson has spent on all the pictures he's directed in his career.

Nonetheless, people say "Oh, you can't hire Orson because he's extravagant." Mike Nichols went farther over budget on *Catch-22* than Orson has spent on all the films he has directed, put together. In my experience, in the one film I made for him, Orson is by no means an extravagant director. As I recall, we had

From *Take One*, vol. 3, no. 6 (July/August 1971): 7–10.

something like a forty- or forty-two-day shooting schedule and a budget of slightly under a million dollars, and we went a couple of days and about seventy-five thousand dollars over the budget. Now that really is not an outlandish, horrifying situation at all. The difference between that film *with* Welles and that film *without* Welles would be remarkable. His contribution as an actor, of course, was incredible. I would say the only major error that Orson made in the film was his conviction that he had to conceal something: the fact that his part was the best part in the film, as he had re-written the script. In fact, it was evident anyway—I knew it. *Touch of Evil* is about the decline and fall of Captain Quinlan. My part is a kind of witness to this. It would have . . .

Int.: I agree that he wrote the best part for himself, but you're one of the three or four actors who have worked with Welles without being dwarfed by him, physically in terms of screen persona, or dramatically in terms of just plain showmanship. In watching the film recently this is one of its aspects that I noted most carefully, knowing that this point would come up. I was looking to see how you would handle yourself when the famous Wellesian scene-stealing took place. In the scene where Joe Calleia "finds" the sticks of dynamite in the shoebox, Welles is playing it up, but you, through the opposite means, subduing every gesture and restraining yourself, manage to hold your own, which is a feat.

Heston: Well, I am happy to subscribe to the thesis that I can stand on equal ground with Orson in a scene, but that doesn't change the fact that Orson is party to that part, and that the film is *about* Captain Quinlan, really. But that's the way it should be. That's the story. I play a man who's looking for his wife, really.

Actually, I have Orson to thank for the fact that the part is as interesting as it was, because it was his idea to make it a Mexican detective. I said "I can't play a Mexican detective!" He said "Sure you can! We'll dye your hair black, and put on some dark makeup and draw a black moustache, sure you can! We'll get a Mexican tailor to cut you a good Mexican suit." And they did, and it's plausible enough I suppose. I play a plausible Mexican. As a matter of fact it doesn't contribute to the stereotype of the sombrero Mexican lazing around in the shade.

Int.: Did Universal agree to let Welles act in the film so long as he directed it?

Heston: They imposed on him, for budget reasons. They were willing to take a chance on him directing, but only on that budget.

Int.: Was casting begun immediately upon the signing of Welles?

Heston: No. The first thing was his reworking of the script. He wanted it to be set on the Mexican border, and they wouldn't go for location work at that time. You must remember that this was sixteen years ago. Welles found an entirely accept-able substitute in Venice, California.

Int.: It was more than acceptable. Remind me not to visit Venice, California. Welles achieved a new low in ramshackle buildings, locations, and degeneracy, as played most ably by US-for-Mexico shooting. In searching for locations, and other pre-production work, did you play an active part?

Heston: Not *nearly* the amount I do now. I was consulted about things, but did not really participate on a serious level. I helped in things like casting. I had approval.

Int.: Was there anybody cast who you were either exceedingly pleased or dis-pleased over?

Heston: I thought all of the casting was marvelous. There was some uncertainty over the casting of the girl, who was played by Janet Leigh.

Int.: I guess she was very big at that time.

Heston: The studio wanted to use her very much. This casting was, in fact, almost imposed, and . . . as a matter of fact, it turned out better than I thought it would. I thought she was quite good. I don't think Orson was terribly upset about it. All the other casting I had approval on and, as far as I know, Orson made all the other castings. There were some fine performances, especially Joe Calleia. I think it's one of the very best pieces of work he did in his whole career.

Int.: I thought the cameos were a nice touch.

Heston: Orson got his cronies to do them. Joe Cotten and Marlene Dietrich were fun, yeah.

Int.: Orson Welles as director. That's the dream of many fine actors. What is it that makes him special to work with?

Heston: He's exciting. He makes it fun.

Int.: Then why is it that he can't get the money to make films? He makes films that are literate, and as close as one can get to pure cinema, both in terms of artistic achievement and entertainment. I'm sorry. That was a rhetorical outburst. We were talking about how Welles works.

Heston: Film acting is not often very interesting. Even if you have a fascinating part with four or five major scenes, which is unusual, those scenes don't take up half the running time of the film, or the shooting time of the film, either. The bulk of your day is . . . well a good case in point is a scene from *Skyjacked*, where I came out of the flight deck and went into the john, where I saw the scrawled message saying that the plane was being skyjacked. I didn't say anything. I looked at Yvette (Mimieux), and in the course of that look, what they describe as a "charged look," I had to show "problems, what am I doing here, what are all these carryings on," and also "I'm involved in some kind of complicated relationship with this girl, and I'd really rather not be flying with her. All things considered, but on the other hand . . ." That's about all there is to the first shot. No lines . . . That was my first day's work on the picture. That's *all* there was to the first day. That's not all *they* did, but that's all *I* did. You understand the motivation, you've read the script, you know the importance of establishing the thing with the girl, but still it's really not the most marvelous day's work you've ever done. Orson has the capacity as a director to somehow persuade you that each time is *indeed* the most important day in the picture, and that's kind of marvelous, and I applaud it.

Int.: Is he this way with all the actors? Minor scenes as well, bit parts?

Heston: I think so, yes.

Int.: Can we talk about the first shot? The famous first shot?

Heston: This first shot in *Touch of Evil* is, as I said, technically one of the most brilliant shots I have ever seen in any film. Among film buffs it has become a classic shot.

Int.: It's in all of the books.

Heston: Is it? Is it in some books? Well, for the record, it begins on a close-up insert of a bundle of sticks of dynamite, and it pans up just enough to apprehend an unidentifiable figure dashing out of the frame. As the pan continues, you see in the middle distance a couple coming out of the door of a bar, and going even deeper into the background, and turning around the back of the building and disappearing. Led by the couple's exit, the camera pans down the alley in the direction in which the figure holding the dynamite has fled, on the near side of the building, going in the same direction. You see the figure (and of course now you can't possibly identify him) dart behind the building. Following with the camera, but still too far away to tell who he is, he lifts the trunk of a car and puts what is obviously a bomb into the car, slams the lid and disappears into the shadows just as the camera, now lifting above the car, picks up the couple coming around the other side of the building and getting in the car. You establish him as a fat political type and she a floozy blond type. And they carry on—there's enough awareness of their dialogue to establish a kind of drunken nonchalance.

The camera booms up on a Chapmain boom as the car drives out of the parking lot and out into the street. The boom sinks down, picks up the car, and picks up me and Janet Leigh walking along and talking. The camera then moves ahead of both us and the car, the car's progress being to some degree impeded by foot traffic, so as to keep us more or less in the same context. But first you pick up the car and then us walking, and in the course of our movement you establish that we are just married and honeymooning. All the time, on the sound track you hear the ticking of the bomb.

By this time we get to the border station and have a little dialogue that established me as a government official. We go through the Mexican station, and then through the U.S. station, and the car does too, and there's a little carrying-on that makes it clear that this fellow is a guy with some political clout.

Int.: And the girl says, "My watch is awfully loud, I think I hear something ticking."

Heston: No. "There's this ticking in my head" . . . she's drunk. The car zooms past us out of shot, we now being in the United States, and there's some dialogue to the effect that we've just been married and I haven't kissed her in an hour, and I pull her into my arms and kiss her and of course as our lips touch the car explodes off screen. That's quite a shot.

Int.: That is called Orson Welles.

Heston: It took *all* one night to shoot, as indeed it might. And the spooky thing about night-shooting, night exteriors, is that when the sun comes up that's all, you've got to quit. And we were shooting in Venice and we . . . Oh, I don't know, laying the shot was incredibly complicated. The boom work with the Chapmain boom was the major creative contribution. The men who ran the boom had a *terribly* difficult job, but they finally were getting so it was working well enough to do takes on it, and we did two or three or four takes, and in each take the customs man, who had just one line, would flub his line.

Int.: Oh Christ.

Heston: Cause he'd see this great complex of cars and lights and Chapmain booms bearing down on him from three blocks away, and they'd get closer and closer, and finally there they would all be, and he would blow his line. I will concede that Orson did not do a great deal to stimulate his . . . Orson said, "Look, I don't care what you say, just move your lips, we can dub it in later. Don't just put your face in your hands and say 'Oh my God, I'm sorry.'" And of course the fellow never did get the line. He finally managed to blow the line impassively. He just stood there moving his lips impotently.

Int.: At which point Welles gave him a medal and his walking papers. At this time, were you beginning to take a creative interest in the technical aspects of the films you were working on?

Heston: Well, you begin to, if you have any brains, the first time you work on a film. This was the first film on which I was quite as aware of the enormous creative composition of the camera, which is not surprising since Russ Metty was the cameraman. It was also the first film on which I spent any time in the cutting room. I sat and watched Orson fiddle with sequences with his cutter, and it was a very learningful experience.

Int.: That's the kind of experience that most of us would give our shirts for.

Heston: Yeah, it's valuable.

Int.: Is he a perfectionist?

Heston: No.

Int.: In terms of just putting things right?

Heston: I think that's the last thing Orson is. He probably has a larger measure of talent, whatever the hell that means, than anybody else I've ever met, but a perfectionist he is not. He can get an *incredible* idea about how to solve a scene, or a piece of casting, or a bit of writing, or an editing problem. But rather than polish it to perfection, he is likely to substitute still another idea that is nearly as good or maybe better. But, I would say, he is disinclined to sandpaper.

Int.: Does he get a lot of coverage? I know Sam Peckinpah sometimes uses eighteen or nineteen cover shots on one set-up.

Heston: No. Now mind you, at the time I made *Touch of Evil* I wasn't as sophisticated an observer of the mechanics of filmmaking as I am now. But, nonetheless, in my memory . . . well, the first shot is . . . what I've said to you. There is no cutting to that. They just got the slate off it and that's the first three minutes of the film.

Int.: The studio likes that kind of thing. (both laugh)

Was Welles doing any rewriting when the film was being made? Or was he working straight through?

Heston: Not once we started shooting. I think that's one of the reasons *Touch of Evil* could be said to have turned out better than *Major Dundee*. Sam had to attempt to undertake his rewrite while shooting the film. Orson undertook his and accomplished it before shooting.

Int.: How would you describe the working relationship you had with him during the film?

Heston: Enchanted. Orson *seduces* you in a marvelous way. You know he's one of the most charming men in the world, if it's important to him to be charming. He is, at *minimum*, interesting—but if it's important to him to enlist your support and cooperation, he is as charming a man as I have ever seen.

Int.: And was he so with the rest of the crew as well would you say?

Heston: Oh yes. See, that's an important thing. Orson elicits remarkable support from his companies, he asks a lot from them, his crews too, but he jokes with them and recognizes what they're doing, their contributions, and it works *marvelously*. They put out a great effort for him.

Int.: It shows in the fact that he got tiny performances, one-scene performances, that are memorable.

Heston: Yeah, that's it. Sam, on the other hand, *requires* your commitment, and that's not quite the same thing as *eliciting* your support. Because you can choose not to deliver your commitment. Personally, in my own style of work, I prefer working as an individual film actor, in a somewhat more detached manner. I think you tend to get into a hothouse atmosphere. You're living in each other's laps anyway, and it's long days, and I frankly prefer a little more detached and cool relationship. But you've got to do it the way the director wants. In both the case of Sam, who demanded it and required it, and Orson, who elicits it, that's the way you go. But some people won't make that kind of commitment to Sam.

Int.: On individual scenes, when you'd be working with Welles—would he say do this and this and this and this—in a way some directors will—or is he a director who will let you create and then say "Well, maybe this and maybe this?"

Heston: By and large, assuming the contribution of professional actors . . . in my experience on 40 films the complexities of the mechanics of filming and the creative problems they present tend to preoccupy a director to a large degree. A good actor is likely to have a fairly free hand in the shaping of his . . . certainly of his character, possibly of the scene as well. I'm not speaking of a Wyler or Stevens or Lean, but most directors, even directors like those I've mentioned, who work in *incredibly tiny detail* in altering facets of a performance, they often tend not to do so in acting terms, if you follow me. I think Wyler, for example, has an absolutely *infallible* taste for a performance. If he says it's right—it's *right*. There's just no question. But I don't think he's particularly emphatic with actors.

Orson probably taught me more about acting than any film director I've worked for. Which is not to say I necessarily did my best film performance for him, but he taught me a great deal about acting—the whole, acting generically. He's both specific in technical details, and in broad concepts about acting, and I found it an enormously stimulating experience.

Int.: The scenes you did with Welles—did you find those to be your most difficult scenes?

Heston: The most difficult?

Int.: The most difficult, or the most draining, I would say. It's really the word I would use. Draining would also mean that when you were finished with them you probably felt the most satisfied.

Heston: I recall performing in the whole picture, doing the whole picture, as being as satisfying creatively as anything I've ever done. I don't recall it as being—the part was not an enormously difficult part. There was never a scene that you look on as a major jump—you know, a barrier that somehow you have to clear. Like the dagger speech in *Macbeth*. Or Antony's suicide. They were scenes that you did with as much creative juice as you could call on at that time. Orson helps you quite a lot.

Int.: The sequence with the shoebox is a brilliant scene. It's also brilliantly directed and photographed, again because the camera is constantly moving in that scene.

Heston: That's about thirteen pages. That was the first day's work on the picture. And Orson deceived the studio, and he conned them, because the scene was scheduled for three days of shooting, which is about reasonable, which would be a little over four pages a day—which is a respectable day's work in an "A" picture. He, in fact, had rehearsed the scene in his home with the actors over a Sunday or two. He proceeded to lay out the scene in terms of *one* shot with a crab dolly, that encompassed all the eight or nine performers who had lines in the scene. The action ranged through two rooms, a closet and a bathroom, and, as I said, thirteen pages of dialogue. It was quite a complex shot, with doors having to be pulled, walls having to be pulled aside—very intricate markings, inserts on the shoebox, and things like that. All of which were in one shot.

When you're shooting, the production office is informed when the camera turns over the first time, when the first print is made, and so on. And of course we never turned a camera until way . . . Lunch went by, and uneasy little groups of executives began to huddle about in the shadows, not quite willing to approach Orson but increasingly convinced that they were on the brink of disaster, cause we hadn't turned a camera and it was, by now, three or four o'clock in the afternoon. Finally, at about 4:30, we turned. And of course it was tricky. We did several takes—seven or eight takes. Finally we got a print, just before six o'clock. And Orson said, "OK, that's a print. Wrap." He said, "We're two days ahead of schedule. We go to the other set tomorrow."

Int.: The executives must have been down on their knees.

Heston: Everybody thought it was marvelous. Of course he never did that again, you see, but they always thought he *might*.

Int.: It's a brilliant idea.

Heston: Just great. They never gave him any trouble again after that. They thought, "My God, he did three day's work in one shot!"

Int.: The little touches that he adds from scene to scene. Were they all in the script? The things like Akim Tamiroff's hairpiece which was a running gag throughout the whole film.

Heston: That was not in the script, no. And of course, I wasn't in those scenes, so I don't know how they were created, but I know they weren't—it wasn't in the script. The scenes are put together in a very loose atmosphere that makes for that kind of creativity.

Int.: Was there any ad libbing in terms of dialogue?

Heston: Orson has a marvelous ear for the way people talk. One of the many things I learned from him was the degree to which people in real life overlap one another when they're talking. In the middle of somebody's sentence you will, in fact, apprehend what he's talking about and you will often start to reply through his closing phrase. People do that all the time. Orson directs scenes that way—to a larger degree than most directors do.

There's a marvelously counterpointed scene in *Lady from Shanghai* in which the people sit in the dark—obviously he doesn't want a visual image to intrude— and you hear two conversations interwoven. He likes that, and I do too. I think it's very valuable, and I've tried to use it in scenes myself since. He not only changes dialogue, as . . . dialogue is changed all the time on film. It's some of the most creative work in putting a scene together.

Int.: All of Hawks.

Heston: Pardon?

Int.: All of Hawks had to be written on a daily basis.

Heston: It goes on all the time. Sure. Orson is, as I said, a very instinctive, intuitive creator, and he would restage whole scenes. I mean put them in different places. We were shooting in this crummy hotel in Venice, and at three o'clock in the morning—in the middle of night shooting—we were down in the basement of this old hotel, peeing in a drain in the corner of this old basement, and he said, "Gee, these pipes and this boiler. That's marvelous. You know this—we should do the scene with Joe Calleia here—where he shows you the cane."

He zipped up his fly and said to the first assistant, "Get Joe Calleia down here." They said, "Jesus, Orson, we were gonna do that scene on Friday, they've got it set up at the studio." He said, "That's terrible. That's no place. We're going to do it down here. We'll do it right now." And they said, "Well, we've got to finish this scene." He said, "I can finish this scene in one shot. It'll take you an hour to get Calleia out of bed. Get him down here and I'll have this scene finished by then." And he did.

Int.: That's beautiful.

Heston: And it is better there.

Int.: Cause that is the turning point of the film.

Heston: It's a great scene. And part of the reason it's good is he . . . Here's Joe Calleia getting up out of bed in the middle of the night, and staggering down to Venice. They take him down in this stinking basement and they give him the cane, and they say "Joe, now do it." And he says, "What—what—what???" "The scene." "Where?" You know, and it's marvelous.

Reviews

ariety's review typifies the response of the Hollywood establishment to a motion picture that falls, as the reviewer complains, into no readily marketable category. Universal tried to promote it as a modest sex-and-violence thriller, and it is significant that *The New York Times* assigned it to their second-string reviewer. Ironically, Howard Thompson, though he can see little real substance in the film, proved to be more sympathetic—if only out of deference to Welles's reputation—than the *Times'* chief reviewer, Bosley Crowther, is likely to have been. But critical recognition of Welles's achievement came only when *Touch of Evil* was shown to European audiences at the Brussels World's Fair in 1958. André Bazin and the other young critics and film makers associated with *Cahiers du Cinéma* were particularly lavish in their praise, seeing in Welles a natural ally of what became known as the "new wave" of French cinema. The year after François Truffaut reviewed *Touch of Evil*, his own *Les Quatre Cents Coups* ("The Four Hundred Blows") launched a long and notable directoral career.

Variety

Orson Welles scripts, directs, and stars with Janet Leigh and Charlton Heston. Confusing, somewhat "artsy" film. So so prospects.

Orson Welles is back at it, playing himself as writer–actor–director and turning out a picture, "Touch of Evil," that smacks of brilliance but ultimately flounders in it. The Universal release falls in no category—it's not a "big" picture nor is it in the exploitation class—and must depend solely on star names of Welles, Charlton Heston, and Janet Leigh for boxoffice lure. The added "guest" names of Marlene Dietrich and Zsa Zsa Gabor may help but overall prospects look rather slim.

Welles establishes his creative talent with pomp, but unfortunately the circumstances of the story suffer. There is insufficient orientation and far too little exposition, with the result that much of the action is confusing and difficult to relate to the plot. Taken scene by scene, there is much to be said for this filmization of Whit Masterson's novel, "Badge of Evil." Welles's script contains some hard hitting dialogue, his use of low key

lighting with Russell is effective and Russell Metty's photography is fluid and impressive, and Henry Mancini's music is poignant. But "Touch of Evil" proves it takes more than good scenes to make a good picture.

Within the framework of major action, Welles's direction moves with reasonable motivation, filling the picture with emotional touches that can be accepted. On the fringe, however, Welles has drawn a few eccentric characterizations that, although amusing, are disturbing to the flow of action.

In his role as actor, Welles portrays an American cop who has the keen reputation of always getting his man. Before you know it, he's hot on the trail of those scoundrels who blew to smithereens the wealthy "owner" of a small Mexican border town. Heston, a bigwig in the Mexican government, just happens to be around with his new American bride, Janet Leigh, and gets himself rather involved in the proceedings, feeling the dynamiting has something to do with a narcotics racket he's investigating. When Heston discovers Welles "always gets his man" because he plants evidence for someone else to find, he starts a good deal of trouble, which results, among other things, in Miss Leigh's being accused of a murder committed by Welles, the timely death of Welles himself, and a complete shakeup of the whole town.

Off his rocker since his wife was murdered years ago, Welles supposedly is deserving of a bit of sympathy. At least, there's a hint of it in dialogue, even though it isn't seen in his characterization. Aside from this, he turns in a unique and absorbing performance. Heston keeps his plight the point of major importance, combining a dynamic quality with a touch of Latin personality. Miss Leigh, sexy as all get-out, switches from charm to fright with facility in a capable portrayal. Two of the best performances come from Joseph Calleia and Akim

Tamiroff, with good work done by Joanna Moore, Ray Collins, Valetin de Vargas, and Mort Mills. Dennis Weaver, as the night man, is fine though exaggerated.

Spicing up the Albert Zugsmith production are a single close-up of Zsa Zsa Gabor as a non-stripped stripper, a word or two from Joseph Cotten who's slipped in without screen credit, and a provocative few minutes with gypsy-looking Marlene Dietrich. Miss Dietrich is rather sultry and fun to watch, even though it's somewhat incongruous to see her walk into the Mexican darkness at the picture's finish, turn to wave, then wail, "Adios."

Ron.

New York Times

Howard Thompson

Thanks to Orson Welles, nobody, and we mean nobody, will nap during "Touch of Evil," which opened yesterday at R.K.O. theatres. Just try.

The credits come on, for instance, to a sleepy, steady rumba rhythm as a convertible quietly plies the main street of a Mexican border town. The car is rigged with dynamite. And so, as a yarn-spinning director, is the extremely corpulent Mr. Welles, who co-stars with Charlton Heston and Janet Leigh in this Universal release.

Mr. Welles also adapted the novel by Whit Masterson called "Badge of Evil" (which would have been more like it), helping himself to a juicy role of a fanatical Texas cop who frames a Mexican youth for murder, and clashes with an indignant Mexican sleuth, Mr. Heston. In addition to battling Mr. Welles, a psychopath who runs the town, Mr. Heston has to fend off a vengeful narcotics gang menacing his young bride, Miss Leigh.

Any other competent director might have culled a pretty good, well-acted melodrama from such material, with

From *New York Times*, May 22, 1958.

the suspense dwindling as justice begins to triumph (as happens here). Mr. Welles's is an obvious but brilliant bag of tricks. Using a superlative camera (manned by Russell Metty) like a black-snake whip, he lashes the action right into the spectator's eye.

The careful groupings of the cast, the overlapping of the speeches, and other stylized trade-marks of the director's Mercury Players unit are here. But the tempo, at least in the first half, is plain mercurial, as befits a thriller.

Where Mr. Welles soundly succeeds is in generating enough sinister electricity for three such yarns and in generally staging it like a wild, murky nightmare. Miss Leigh has the most blood-curdling time of all in two sequences, one involving a strangulation in a hotel room. The other, her seige by some young punks in an isolated motel, should make any viewer leery of border accommodations for a long time to come.

However, while good versus evil remains the text, the lasting impression of this film is effect rather than substance, hence its real worth. The cunningly designed climax, for instance, barely alludes to the framed youth at the outset (in a fine, ironic twist, by the way). The entire unsavory supporting cast is excellent, including such people as Joseph Calleia, Akim Tamiroff, and Ray Collins. Marlene Dietrich, as an incidental "guest star," wisely advises Mr. Welles to "lay off the candy bars."

Two questions—the first to Mr. Welles, who obviously savors his dominant, colorful role. Why would a villainous cop, having hoodwinked the taxpayers for some thirty years, suddenly buckle when a tourist calls his bluff? And why, Mr. Heston, pick the toughest little town in North America for a honeymoon with a nice morsel like Miss Leigh?

Arts

François Truffaut

Y ou could remove Orson Welles's name from the credits and it wouldn't make any difference, because from the first shot, beginning with the credits themselves, it's obvious that Citizen Kane is behind the camera.

Touch of Evil opens on a shot of the clock of a time bomb as a man places it in the trunk of a white car. A couple have just gotten into the car and started off, and we follow them through the city. All this happens before the film starts. The camera perched on a motorized crane loses the car, finds it again as it passes behind some buildings, precedes it or catches up with it, right up to the moment when the explosion we have been waiting for happens.

The image is deliberately distorted by the use of a wide-angle lens that gives an unnatural clarity to the backgrounds and poeticizes reality as a man walking toward the camera appears to advance ten yards in five strides. We're in a fantasy world all

through this film, the characters appearing to walk with seven-league boots when they're not gliding on a moving rug.

There are movies made by incompetent cynics, like *The Bridge on the River Kwai* and *The Young Lions*, movies that are merely bluff, designed to flatter a public which is supposed to leave the movie house feeling better or thinking it has learned something. There are movies that are profound and lofty, made without compromise by a few sincere and intelligent artists who would rather disturb than reassure, rather wake an audience up than put it to sleep. When you come out of Alain Resnais' *Nuit et Brouillard*, you don't feel better, you feel worse. When you come out of *White Nights* or *Touch of Evil*, you feel less intelligent than before but gratified anyhow by the poetry and art. These are films that call cinema to order, and make us ashamed to have been so indulgent with cliché-ridden movies made by small talents.

Well, you might say, what a fuss over a simple little detective story that Welles wrote in eight days, over which he didn't even have the right to super-

From *Arts*, June 4, 1958; tr. by Leonard Mayhew in François Truffaut, *The Films in My Life* (New York: Simon and Schuster, 1978).

vise the final editing, and to which was later added a half-dozen explanatory shots he'd refused to make, a film he made "to order" and which he violently disavowed.

I'm well aware of all that, as well as that the slave who one night breaks his chains is worth more than the one who doesn't even know he's chained; and also that *Touch of Evil* is the most liberated film you can see. In *Barrage contre le Pacifique*, René Clément had complete control; he edited the film himself, chose the music, did the mixing, cut it up a hundred times. But Clément is a slave nonetheless, and Welles is a poet. I warmly recommend to you the films of poets.

Welles adapted for the screen a woefully poor little detective novel and simplified the criminal intrigue to the point where he could match it to his favorite canvas—the portrait of a paradoxical monster, which he plays himself—under cover of which he designed the simplest of moralities: that of the absolute and the purity of absolutists.

A capricious genius, Welles preaches to his parishioners and seems to be clearly telling us: I'm sorry I'm slovenly; it's not my fault if I'm a genius; I'm dying: love me.

As in *Citizen Kane*, *The Stranger*, *The Magnificent Ambersons*, and *Confidential Report*, two characters confront each other—the monster and the sympathetic young lead. It's a matter of making the monster more and more monstrous, and the young protagonist more and more likable, until we are brought somehow to shed real tears over the corpse of the magnificent monster. The world doesn't want anything to do with the exceptional, but the exception, if he is an unfortunate, is the ultimate refuge of purity. Fortunately, Welles's physique would seem to preclude his playing Hitler, but who's to say that one day he will not force us to weep over the fate of Hermann Goering?

Here Welles has given himself the role of a brutal and greedy policeman, an ace investigator, very well known. Since he works only by intuition, he uncovers murderers without bothering about proof. But the court system, which is made up of mediocre men, cannot condemn a man without evidence. Thus, Inspector Quinlan/Welles develops the habit of fabricating evidence and eliciting false testimony in order to win his case, to see that justice will triumph.

After the bomb explodes in the car, all that's necessary for everything to go awry is for an American policeman on his honeymoon (Charlton Heston) to meddle in Quinlan's investigation. There is a fierce battle between the two men. Heston *finds* proof against Welles while Welles *manufactures* evidence against him. After a frantic sequence in which Welles demonstrates that he could doubtless adapt de Sade's novels like nobody else, Heston's wife is found in a hotel, nude and drugged, and apparently responsible for the murder of Akim Tamiroff, who in reality has been killed by Quinlan—whom Tamiroff had naïvely helped set this demonic stage.

As in *Confidential Report*, the sympathetic character is led to commit an underhanded act in order to undo the monster: Heston records the few decisive sentences on a tape recorder, sufficient proof to destroy Welles. The film's idea is summed up neatly in this epilogue: Sneakiness and mediocrity have triumphed over intuition and absolute justice. The world is horrifyingly relative, everything is pretty much the same—dishonest in its morality, impure in its conception of fairness.

If I've used the word monster a number of times, it's merely to stress the fantastical spirit of this film and of all Welles's movies. All moviemakers who are not poets have recourse to psychology to put the spectator on the wrong scent, and the commercial success of psychological films might seem a good enough reason for them to do this. "All great art is abstract,"

Jean Renoir said, and one doesn't arrive at an abstraction through psychology—just the opposite. On the other hand, abstraction spills over sooner or later onto the moral, and onto the only morality that preoccupies us: the morality that is invented and reinvented by artists.

All this blends very well with Welles's supposition that mediocre men need facts, while others need only intuition. There lies the source of enormous misunderstanding. If the Cannes Festival Committee had had the wisdom to invite *Touch of Evil* to be shown rather than Martin Ritt's *The Long Hot Summer* (in which Welles is only an actor), would the jury have had the wisdom to see in it all the wisdom of the world?

Touch of Evil wakes us up and reminds us that among the pioneers of cinema there was Méliès and there was Feuillade. It's a magical film that makes us think of fairy tales: "Beauty and the Beast," "Tom Thumb," La Fontaine's fables. It's a film which humbles us a bit because it's by a man who thinks more swiftly than we do, and much better, and who throws another marvelous film at us when we're still reeling under the last one. Where does this quickness come from, this madness, this speed, this intoxication?

May we always have enough taste, sensitivity, and intuition to admit that this talent is large and beautiful. If the brotherhood of critics finds it expedient to look for arguments against this film, which is a witness and a testimony to art and nothing else, we will have to watch the grotesque spectacle of the Lilliputians attacking Gulliver.

—1958

Commentaries

The essays in this section have been chosen to represent critical approaches to *Touch of Evil* which complement the reading of the film in the Introduction. William Johnson's essay, somewhat shortened for this volume, stresses the thematic concerns manifest in the entire Welles *oeuvre*. Jean Collet's exploration of the implications of montage in *Touch of Evil* draws upon, and extends, the ideas of André Bazin. Stephen Heath's essay is only a small portion of a massive study employing more recent structuralist and semiotic techniques.

Orson Welles: Of Time and Loss

William Johnson

J udged by first—even second or third—impressions, Welles's films are a triumph of show over substance. His most memorable images seem like ele-
phantine labors to bring forth mouse-size ideas.

His films bulge with preposterously vast spaces: the echoing halls of Kane's
Xanadu; the rambling castles of Macbeth, Othello, and Arkadin; the vertiginous
offices of *The Trial*; the cathedral-like palace and tavern of *Falstaff*.

His camera moves with a swagger, craning down through the skylight of El
Rancho in *Kane* and up over the bomb-carrying car in *Touch of Evil*. When the
camera is still, the composition may cry out for attention with anything from
multiple reflections (the hall of mirrors in *Lady from Shanghai*) to a flurry of
silhouettes (the battle in *Falstaff*).

The action often runs along the edge of violence, and sometimes topples over
with a spectacular splash: Kane destroying Susan's room after she leaves him;
Mike's brawl in the judge's office in *Lady from Shanghai*; Macbeth overturning
the huge banquet table after Banquo's ghost appears; Vargas running amuck in the
bar in *Touch of Evil*. At other times Welles expresses his love of spectacle in a
show-within-a-show: the dancing girls at Kane's newspaper party and the opera
in which Susan stars; the magician's act in *Journey into Fear*;* the Chinese theater
in *Lady from Shanghai*; the flea circus in *Arkadin*; the slide show that begins and
ends *The Trial*.

What makes all these Barnum qualities really seem to stick on Welles the
director is the style and appearance of Welles the actor. With the sole exception
of *Magnificent Ambersons*, the bravura manner of Welles's films centers around
characters that he himself plays. It is Welles whose voice booms across the cav-
ernous drawing room of Xanadu, it is Welles who overturns the banquet table at
Glamis castle, it is Welles who conducts the slide show in *The Trial*. And the
Barnum image is reinforced by his roles in other people's films, from the tongue-

From *Film Quarterly* 21 (1967–1968): 13–24.
*Welles's hand in *Journey*, officially directed by Norman Foster, is uncertain, and I have avoided
citing any further examples from this film.

in-cheek sophistries of Harry Lime in *The Third Man* to the flamboyant magic of Le Chiffre in *Casino Royale*.

Of course, showmanship can be sublime, and even the harshest critics of Welles's films have some kind words for *Citizen Kane*. Judged simply by its style, the film must be accounted an impressive achievement for any director, let alone a twenty-five-year-old newcomer to the movie medium. Many of the stylistic effects that Welles used with such apparent ease in *Kane* have become common screen currency only during the last ten years—wide-angle perspective, unusually long takes, abrupt cuts, intricate leaps in time, terse vignettes, heightened natural sound, and so on. Though precedents can be found for each of these devices, Welles was the first director to develop them into a full-blown style. With the exception of some typical forties process shots, the whole of *Kane* looks and sounds almost as modern today as it did in 1941—a good deal more modern, in fact, than many films of 1967.

Moreover, Welles's protean style clearly reflects the character of Kane—himself a kind of Barnum who conceals his private self behind a dazzling set of public images. It's possible for a critic to see no deeper into *Kane* than this and still give the film high marks for matching style and content.

Judged by these standards, Welles's other films are inferior. Neither their stylistic inventiveness nor their matching of style and content stands out so obviously as *Kane*'s. After a brilliant start, Welles's directing career seems to decline into potboilers (*The Stranger*, *Lady from Shanghai*, *Touch of Evil*), distortions of literary originals (the Shakespeare films and *Trial*) and a rehash of *Kane*—*Arkadin*—which demonstrates only too clearly the coarsening of his showmanship.

The foregoing view of Welles is, I believe, utterly wrong, and yet it has plausibility because it rests on a few points of truth. *Arkadin*, for example, *is* an inferior rehash of *Kane*, with grotesques instead of characters and with episodes loosely strung together instead of interlocking. *Macbeth*, with or without due allowance for the conditions under which it was made, *is* often ludicrous. There are other examples which I will come to later.

But it's difficult to maintain a balanced view of Welles's strengths and weaknesses. While his detractors see little but empty showiness, anyone who likes most of his work runs the risk of slipping to the opposite extreme. With a filmmaker as vigorous and idiosyncratic as Welles, it's temptingly easy to find some justification for nearly everything he does. *Arkadin* is based on an exciting and fruitful idea; some of the sequences in the film are excellent; many others are exciting or fascinating—and so I could go on, justifying the film piece by piece to the conclusion that it is all good. But here I'd be falling into the same trap as those who deny the originality of *Kane* because (for example) Renoir had previously used deep focus. It's the total effect that counts, and just as the total effect of Welles's deep focus is quite different from Renoir's, and much more far-reaching, so the total effect of *Arkadin* falls far short of its piecemeal felicities.

Similarly, Welles's films *are* showy, but this is only one side of them. The other, quieter side gives a far better clue to what his films are all about.

One of the finest scenes in *Kane* features no craning or dollying, no dramatic chiaroscuro, no optical distortions, no unusual sound effects, no jump cuts or, for that matter, cuts of any kind whatsoever. The reporter visits Kane's former lawyer, Bernstein, to see if he can explain "Rosebud." Bernstein suggests that it may have referred to some very fleeting experience in Kane's past, and cites as an example his own memory of a girl dressed in white whom he glimpsed forty years earlier. "I only saw her for a second," says Bernstein, "and she didn't see me at all, but I bet a month hasn't gone by that I haven't thought about her." Throughout the scene the camera remains absolutely still: all one sees is the back of the reporter's head, Bernstein at his desk and rain falling outside the window. This unexpected plumbing of the depths of the cheery Bernstein is made all the more moving by the sudden stillness with which Welles films it.

One of Welles's films—*Magnificent Ambersons*—is nearly all stillness, or only the most leisurely of movements. Its tempo is set by the horse and buggy typical of the age that is ending when the film's action takes place. . . .

The elegiac mood of *Ambersons* sets it apart from the rest of Welles's films, but its theme recurs in all of them, sometimes burrowing deep beneath the surface, sometimes coming out into the open as in the Bernstein reminiscence. This theme can be summed up as loss of innocence.

Bernstein's regret for a bright moment of his youth is a minor variation of the theme. It is Kane himself who provides the first and most sustained example of lost innocence—though it is one that may easily be misunderstood. Because Freudian symbolism was just creeping into Hollywood films when *Kane* appeared, the sled named Rosebud was widely seized upon as a psychoanalytic key to Kane's character. It is a simpler and more lyrical symbol—of Kane's childhood innocence that cannot be recovered.

Welles does not, of course, thrust a symbol at us and leave it at that. He has designed the whole film so as to bring Kane's predicament to life before our eyes; and he does this largely by giving an almost tangible presence to the passing of time. This might be called a 3-D film, with time instead of spatial depth as the salient third dimension. Nearly everything in the film contributes to this effect: the juxtaposition of scenes showing the different ages not only of Kane but also of those who know him, notably Jed Leland alternating between handsome youth and garrulous senility, Susan between wispy naiveté and sufficient toughness to leave Kane; the use of a different quality of image and sound in the newsreel of Kane's life, adding distance to the events featured in it and, by contrast, adding immediacy to the events filmed straight; and even such normally gimmicky devices as the dissolves from a still photograph to its subject in motion. Above all it is the structure of the film that brings Welles's theme to life. Two strands are intertwined throughout. In the film's present tense, there is the reporter's vain search for the meaning of Rosebud, which mirrors the aged Kane's own yearning for his lost innocence. Concurrently, the flashbacks into Kane's past follow him step by step as he loses that innocence. These alternating images of past and present fuse together stereoscopically into a powerful, poignant vision of Kane's loss.

Welles's other films present variations of this basic theme. Whereas *Kane* states it comprehensively, spanning almost a lifetime of change, several of the other films focus on particular stages: on the initial innocence of Mike in *Lady from Shanghai* and of Joseph K in *The Trial*; on the moment of loss for Macbeth and Othello; on a time long after the loss for Arkadin and for Hank Quinlan in *Touch of Evil*. In the other three films the theme is not tied so closely to a single character: in *The Stranger*, Nazi-in-hiding Franz Kindler threatens the innocent coziness of a New England village; in *Falstaff*, as in *Ambersons*, the loss of innocence lies in the transition between two historical ages.

Far from clashing with this lyrical theme, Welles's bravura qualities enrich it. Kane's onslaught on Susan's room comes to a halt when he sees the snow-scene paperweight: the sudden stillness, the whiteness of the paperweight as he cradles it in his hand, his whisper of "Rosebud" are all the more moving because of the lengthy destruction that went before. Similarly, in *Touch of Evil*—the most agitated of all Welles's films—the calm of Tanya's place draws a charge of lyrical power from the surrounding frenzy. The odd parlor, where a TV set is perched on top of a player piano, is like a time machine that whisks Quinlan away to confront him with his distant, innocent past.

In all of his films Welles uses this contrast between movement and stillness to embody the fragility of life, to compress the change of a lifetime or even of an age into a few vivid moments. . . .

Falstaff is one gigantic contrast of this kind. Its opening and closing scenes form a reflective prologue and epilogue that stand apart from the main action. The epilogue is straightforward: it shows Falstaff's bulky coffin being trundled slowly off into the distance. The prologue is more unusual. To create it, Welles has sliced half a dozen lines out of the middle of the scene in which Shallow summons potential recruits for Falstaff (*Henry IV* Part II, Act III, scene ii). In these few lines Falstaff and Shallow reminisce about their youth. "We have heard the chimes at midnight, Master Shallow." "That we have, that we have. . . . Jesus, the days that we have seen!" Singled out in this way, the brief exchange carries a more powerful charge of nostalgia than in the scene as Shakespeare wrote it; and since the main action of the film is appended to the prologue like a huge flashback, this nostalgia affects everything that follows. Indeed, Welles has left the time and place of the prologue so vague that one may end up linking it with the epilogue, as if Falstaff and Shallow are viewing the past from some limbo outside time.

Seen in this context, such excesses of agitation as the battle scenes are only minor flaws. They do not in any way undermine the total effect of the film, of action embedded in reflection. . . .

Though nostalgia for lost innocence recurs in all the films, in none except *Arkadin* is there any sense of Welles repeating himself. Endless variations on his basic theme are possible, and Welles remains receptive to any or all of them. This is where his other Barnum characteristics—from swaggering camera to tongue-in-cheek humor—come into play. They are usually a sign of the unexpected. . . .

Welles's ability to bring out the unexpected in things usually taken for granted is at work throughout his best films. The most obvious example is found in the opposition between old and new in *Ambersons*. George, who stands for the innocent age that is dying, is the film's most objectionable character; Gene Morgan, who is helping create the age of noise and crowds and air pollution, is its most likable.

Characters like Kane and Quinlan gain depth from similar contradictions. Here, though, Welles avoids not only the obvious cliché of making them out-and-out monsters but the less obvious cliché of making them sympathetic monsters. They do not arouse any set pattern of responses.

One's feelings about Kane, for example, change continually from repulsion to pity, indignation to amusement. . . .

The cross-currents in *Touch of Evil* are even more complex, though at first sight they do not seem so: Vargas is likable and right, Quinlan is repulsive and wrong. But it so happens that Quinlan is right about Sanchez's guilt (as he was no doubt right about many he framed in the past), which means that the moral issue between him and Vargas is not at all neat and abstract—it pivots on the possibility that a callous murderer may not only get away with his crime but his victim's daughter and wealth, too. Moreover, despite Vargas's moral stand, he is teetering on the same brink that Quinlan stepped over decades before, when his wife's murderer escaped punishment for lack of evidence. As soon as Vargas learns that his own wife has been abducted he too takes the law into his own hands. "I'm not a police officer, I'm a husband!" he shouts in the bar where Grandi's gang hangs out, and when they refuse to tell him anything he tries to beat the information out of them. It is only a touch of evil indeed that separates his destiny from Quinlan's. *

Welles's gift for making a vivid point with some unexpected development is at work even in the minor characters of *Touch of Evil*. Two of these, in particular, are involved in the moral issue—or rather, represent the kind of bystanders who try to avoid getting involved. The night man at the motel where Susan Vargas is being held prisoner is a weak, neurotic creature, so outraged at the slightest infringement on what he considers to be his rights that he has no thought to spare for anyone else's rights. In most films he would merely be contemptible; Welles makes him hilarious and unforgettable. Then there is the blind woman in the store where Vargas phones his wife. As he talks, the woman stands utterly still beside a sign that reads: "If you are mean enough to steal from the blind, go ahead." The scene arouses no sympathy for the woman but a sense of unease. The impression is that she is trading on her helplessness, refusing to take the slightest responsibility for what other people may do.

Perhaps the most subtly unexpected relationships in any of Welles's films are found in *Falstaff*. As portrayed by Shakespeare, Falstaff is not only lazy, gluttonous, cowardly, lecherous, dishonest and the rest but also a great innocent. He is devoid of malice or calculation; no matter what is done to him, he remains open and trusting. He lives in a dream world where there are no politicians or policemen or pedagogues; and when Hal destroys that world by rejecting him, he does not adjust to reality but dies. . . .

Like Gene Morgan in *Ambersons*, Hal is changing the world for both better and worse. His political techniques, which Shakespeare depicts more fully in

---

* In the novel from which Welles adapted the film, *Badge of Evil* by Whit Masterson, the framed man is innocent and there is nothing to explain why the police officer ever started framing suspects. These touches are Welles's own.

Henry V, will lead to Maoism and McCarthyism, but they will also lead to honest and efficient government. While the mood of the film is in sympathy with Falstaff, Welles makes it clear that there can be no final choice between Falstaff's anarchic freedom and Hal's well-ordered conformity.

The struggle between tradition and progress, old and new, order and disorder is one of the most powerful forces behind Welles's work. It is reflected in his American background and his love of Europe, and in his film-making that embraces both Shakespeare and modern American thrillers.

This drive to reconcile the irreconcilable goes beyond the subjects and themes of his films. In his European-made films it is at work even in the casting, which almost seems to be done on the assumption that Europe is a single country. The entire shaping of each film from *Kane* through *Falstaff* shows a desire to burst out of commonly accepted limitations. Welles is not content with a single viewpoint—in *Kane* there are at least seven different ones (the reminiscences of the five people interviewed by the reporter, the newsreel, and the God's-eye-view opening and closing scenes), while in all his films he alternates between the detachment of stationary long shots and the involvement of wide-angle close-ups or of dolly shots that stalk the action like a hungry leopard. He is not content with the straightforward flow of time—four of his films (*Kane*, *Othello*, *Arkadin*, *Falstaff*) begin with the end of the action before leaping to the beginning, and *Kane* continues leaping throughout; *Ambersons* frequently skips across the years with the most laconic of vignettes. In *Touch of Evil* and *The Trial* the leaps are not so much in time as in space.

The same drive makes itself felt in almost every aspect of Welles's style. It is found not only in the contrast between successive scenes—from stillness to movement, as described earlier, or from silence to noise, darkness to light, and so on—but also within individual scenes, many of which contain visual extremes or discords that threaten to burst the frame. Welles is continually using a wide-angle lens to throw a gulf between foreground and background, making figures near the camera loom preternaturally large over those further away. There are more unusual optical devices: the paperweight that falls from Kane's dying hand, covering and distorting half of the image; the hall of mirrors in *Lady from Shanghai*, splintering the screen into a dozen images; the magnifying glass that enlarges the flea trainer's eye in *Arkadin*. In other scenes the splintering is done by highlight and shadow: the reporter gesturing in the projector beam in *Kane*; Macbeth's breastplate highlighted, the rest of him in deep shadow after his "Tomorrow, and tomorrow, and tomorrow" soliloquy; the silhouetted funeral procession in *Othello*; the zebra stripes of light and dark that fall on Joseph K as he runs out of Titorelli's studio.

Welles's persistent attempts to harness opposites and contradictions generate a tremendous potential energy in his films. Usually this energy is released little by little, like a controlled nuclear reaction, maintaining a steady urgency that compels attention. But even his most controlled films are often on the verge of exploding. The three Shakespeare films, for example, suffer in varying degrees from inconsistency of acting styles and accents. . . .

The two biggest casualties of Welles's explosive pressure are *Arkadin* and *The Trial*. *Arkadin* is like a grenade that flies apart chiefly along its groovings: each episode holds together fairly well, but fails to connect with the others. *The Trial* is more like the nuclear explosion with which it ends: nearly everything in it disintegrates.

All the centripetal elements of Welles are present in force in *The Trial*. The repeated use of an extreme wide-angle lens exaggerates the depth of each scene, which is further splintered by the application of chiaroscuro to complex settings (the halls and catwalks of the law offices; Hastler's candle-dotted apartment; the cathedral). There are abrupt leaps in space and time not only from episode to episode but frequently from scene to scene. Both the cast and the locations are multinational.

Even the style and mood of the film come in fragments. Much of the decor derives from German expressionism of the 1920s, as do the *Metropolis*-like scenes in the vast office where Joseph K works and the rows of bare-chested accused waiting outside the law courts. The opening scenes in Joesph K's room are more like Hitchcock of the *Rope* period. The scene with Leni and Block in Hastler's kitchen (filmed partly with a long-focus lens) have a quiet hallucinatory quality reminiscent of *Last Year at Marienbad*.

The idea of continually changing the settings and mood of the film sounds as if it might have created an apt sense of unease, keeping the audience in the same off-balance frame of mind as Joseph K. Occasionally it does work like that. There is one superb example when K first visits the law courts and walks from a deserted corridor into a jam-packed courtroom. Welles intensifies the transition by having everyone rise to their feet as K enters, and the noise of their movement bursts into the silence like a menacing roar. (This is Welles's own addition—in Kafka's book no one in the courtroom takes any notice of K.)

Most of the transitions, however, break the tension instead of heightening it.

The varied settings do not fuse together into an eerie world of their own but remain obstinately separate. Thus when K walks from the huge office into the storeroom where the policemen are being punished, the agoraphobic size of the former and the claustrophobic darkness of the latter tend not to reinforce but to neutralize each other. Time and time again in the film the nightmare is short-circuited.

To explain the failure of *The Trial* it's easy to fall back on the accusation of size and showiness. It's easy to argue that Welles's style is too florid for Kafka, who relied on restraint to convey the bizarre misadventures of Joseph K. But these criticisms are irrelevant because they can be leveled at Welles's other films which do not fall to pieces.

Consider *Othello*, which has just as many reasons as *The Trial* for disintegrating. Much of the film leaps from place to place with no regard for topographical continuity: any attempt to visualize the interior layout of Othello's castle is quite pointless. As with *The Trial*, Welles in adapting the original shifts some scenes and alters others (such as the extended bath-house scene where Iago kills Roderigo). He breaks up the rhythms of Shakespeare's play, sometimes accelerating, sometimes almost halting the action. The settings and the cast are multinational. Most disruptive of all, his work on the film continued on and off for a period of three years.

Yet the film translates Shakespeare into screen terms with a superb coherence. Welles sets the whole tragedy in perspective with an opening sequence that interweaves the funeral corteges of Othello and Desdemona and the dragging of Iago to his punishment. In contrast to the sweeping flow of these scenes, the beginning of the action has a staccato rhythm as Iago and Roderigo follow Othello and Desdemona to their wedding and then rouse Brabantio. Calm is restored when Othello comes to justify his marrying Desdemona. But from this point on the staccato rhythm associated with Iago gradually imposes itself on Othello's stately rhythm, and the increasing complexity of the film's movements suggests the increasing turmoil of doubt in Othello's mind. In the death scene, when Othello has finally decided there *is* no doubt of Desdemona's infidelity, the stately rhythm reasserts itself. Then there is a brief flurry of movement as Iago's duplicity is exposed and Othello kills himself, followed by a reprise of the grave calm of the opening scene. . . .

The binding force in *Othello* and in most of Welles's other films is his use of symbolism. Even the most explicit of Welles's symbols do not exist in isolation: they are rooted deep in the action of the film and share the same degree of reality.

Rosebud, for example, appears at first to be a pat and superficial symbol. As with all mysteries, its revelation is something of a letdown: the sled is "only" a symbol of Kane's childhood. But the symbolism is not confined to the object itself. In fact, the adult Kane is never seen looking at it—the word Rosebud is triggered by the sight of Susan's paperweight. But here again the symbolism goes beyond the object. The paperweight is not merely an artificial snow scene recalling a real one but a snow scene encapsulated and unattainable, like Kane's lost innocence. Moreover, when the paperweight appears in close-up Welles highlights it so that it takes on a glowing halation—very much like the glare of the stage lights when Susan makes her operatic debut. Kane drives Susan to her vocal disaster not just to show his power but because, his own desire being unattainable, he wants hers to come true. Susan fails—the ironic floodlight flickers out as her voice trails away—and she is able to come to terms with reality. But the glow of Kane's desire continues to the end: the paperweight falls and smashes only after his death.

There are further ramifications to this symbolism. When the paperweight is shaken, its artificial snow settles again with preternatural slowness, prolonging and intensifying the matter-of-fact snowfall that covers the sled after young Kane leaves home. This slow settling, which is paralleled in the lingering dissolves between the reporter's interviews and his interviewee's reminiscences, suggests not only the loss of Kane's childhood innocence but the loss of all things with the relentless flow of time. At the end of the film Welles brings out this wider implication still more powerfully by accelerating the time effect. The whole of Kane's life is compressed symbolically into a few seconds as the sled—his childhood reality and manhood dream—burns and dissolves into smoke.

I'm not implying that Welles consciously planned all these interrelationships. But I do believe that he chose the particular objects, incidents, and techniques in these scenes because they felt right to him—and they felt right because they connected with the underlying symbolism. Anyone who thinks my analysis is farfetched should try to explain why the burning of Rosebud is such a powerful scene—even more powerful than the book-burning scenes in *Fahrenheit 451*. After all, a sled lacks the ready-made associations that books have; and Rosebud is not even a new and handsome object like Dali's *Secret Life*, over whose destruction Truffaut lingers for the longest time. It is the interlinking of symbols beneath the surface of *Kane* that accumulates the power of the final scenes.

This symbolism underlying conspicuous symbols can be found in nearly all of Welles's films. Anyone who's seen *The Lady from Shanghai* will remember the squid that pulses up and down in the aquarium as Mike and Elsa kiss. In isolation this might be an overemphatic comment on Elsa's predatory nature, but it works because Welles has imbued the whole film with visual and verbal imagery of the sea. The Lady herself comes from one seaport and has settled in another (San Francisco), and many scenes take place on or by the water. The squid is one of several images involving dangers that lurk beneath the surface, just as they lurk behind Elsa's alluring exterior: there are shots of a water snake and an alligator, and Mike relates a parable about sharks that destroy one another. Even the hall of mirrors connects with the pelagic imagery: the multiple reflections are like waves receding row after row, and when the mirrors are smashed Mike can finally step out onto terra firma, ignoring Elsa's last siren call. It is this cumulative imagery that helps place *The Lady from Shanghai* above other superior thrillers, which owe their success either to a series of disparate effects (like *The Wages of Fear*) or to sheer verve (like *The Big Sleep*). . . .

In films with fewer centrifugal pressures than *Othello* or *Kane* the underlying symbolism plays a less important role. Indeed, it may merge indistinguishably into style: the leisurely movement of *Ambersons* and the vast spaces of *Falstaff* might be described as both medium and message.

Elsewhere the symbolism may be too rigid for the theme, or the theme too weak for the symbolism. *Macbeth* is conceived in terms of darkness, which is appropriate enough, but the darkness hardly varies: the film consists of one low-key scene after another. There is no vivid impression of Macbeth sinking from innocence into evil and despair as there is of Othello sinking from innocence into anguish. In *The Stranger* Welles does oppose darkness with light, as the film alternates between the shadowy belfry where Frank Kindler tinkers with the church clock and the whiteness of the New England colonial buildings. But here the situation is too static: the Nazi war criminal pretending to be a good small-town citizen is unchangingly evil all along.

Arkadin fails because its symbolism doesn't counteract but reinforces the centrifugal pressures. In order to suggest the multiple layers of Arkadin's personality, Welles locates the film in different elements—land, sea, air—and in different climates, from the sunny Mediterranean to wintry Germany. But the symbolism lacks a second layer of its own that would bind this geographic diversity together.

As to *The Trial*, it has no underlying symbolism whatsoever—all its symbolism is on the surface. The trouble is not so much that Welles departs from the book but that he does not depart far enough. . . .

It may be argued that *The Trial* is not meant to be coherent like Welles's other films for the simple reason that it is portraying an incoherent world—that by basing the style of this film on loose ends and nonsequiturs, Welles conveys the sharpest possible sense of the menacing absurdity of modern life. This is all very plausible and could lead to long and inconclusive discussion about the merits of portraying incoherence incoherently, boredom boringly and so on. Luckily Welles has provided his own standard of comparison in *Touch of Evil*, which portrays the incoherence of modern life with a remarkable coherence of style and symbolism.

This is a film of darkness. It begins and ends in the night, and there are many other nocturnal or twilit scenes in between. But it is not a monotonously dark film like *Macbeth*. The night is punctuated throughout with lights that make the darkness more menacing, from the glare of the exploding car to the pulsing of neon signs.

It is in this mechanical pulsing rather than in the light and darkness themselves that the underlying symbolism is to be found. *Touch of Evil* is geared to the automatic machinery of our time. The film opens with a close-up of the time bomb as it is set to tick its way to destruction. The film ends with Quinlan unwittingly confessing to a tape recorder. The two machines are uncannily similar in appearance—and also in effect, since the recorder in its own way destroys Quinlan as thoroughly as any bomb.

In between these two mechanical destroyers, other machines dominate the action. In the famous three-minute opening scene the camera follows the car but never allows a clear glimpse of the man and woman riding in it. When Susan Vargas stands on the hotel fire escape calling for help, the engine of Vargas's car drowns out her voice and he speeds unknowingly past her. Quinlan's car is his alter ego: it is big and fat (and Welles exaggerates its fatness with the wide-angle lens), and when it lurches across the quarrying site where the dynamite was stolen it translates Quinlan's lazy ruthlessness into action. In a way, Quinlan himself is a machine—he has lost nearly all of his human flexibility in order to become an efficient manufacturer of convicted criminals. In the final scene his voice is heard alternately from the radio pick-up and direct from his mouth, as if there were little difference between the two sources; while all around him the oil wells pump on and on in a monstrous parody of his obsession.

Though Quinlan is the only character who has succumbed to the temptation of being a machine, nearly everyone in the film is under pressure to do so. Action, dialogue, camera movement, and editing conspire to keep the film rolling onward with machine-like relentlessness. Characters are caught up in this tremendous momentum in much the same way that Joseph K is caught up in the legal labyrinth of *The Trial*: the important difference is that the momentum of *Touch of Evil* is not conveyed indirectly through fantasy but as a direct, tangible force.

A few of the characters avoid being caught up in the momentum—at a price. Tanya and the blind store woman choose to be bystanders in life. The night clerk at the motel is outraged to find himself in a situation that requires positive action. The scenes involving each of these three have an unexpected spaciousness that heightens the ruthless urgency of the rest of the film.

It is the character who accepts the greatest responsibility, Vargas, who runs the greatest risk of succumbing to the machines. The time bomb at the beginning of the film is in the hands of a murderer; the recorder at the end is in Vargas's hands. There is no doubt that Vargas is right to destroy Quinlan; but the film leaves the audience to wonder whether in so doing Vargas has begun to destroy himself.

I don't want to overpraise *Touch of Evil*. For all its richness it remains a thriller with a Hollywood hero.* But it does succeed superbly where *The Trial* fails—in revealing a nightmare world behind everyday reality.

Moreover, in *Touch of Evil* Welles is once again several years ahead of his time. It is only in the sixties that film-makers have really assimilated the effects of post-World War II technological development on everyday life. Before then technology was usually featured either as mere decor or (in its noisier and uglier manifestations) as the antithesis to a quiet upper-income semi-rural existence. Welles makes it an integral part of life, and though he also uses it to symbolize the temptation of evil he certainly does not present it as the cause. In this, *Touch of Evil* anticipates Truffaut's approach to gadgetry in *The Soft Skin* and, more indirectly, Godard's in *The Married Woman*. It's also worth noting that a 1967 film like Furie's *The Naked Runner*, which links modern gadgetry to the amoral expedients of espionage, says nothing that *Touch of Evil* didn't say far better and far less pretentiously ten years before.

It may seem a measure of Welles's limitations that his Hollywood-made *Touch of Evil* is better than his independently made *Trial*. But his work resists easy generalizations. Each of his really outstanding films—*Kane, Ambersons, Othello*, and *Touch of Evil*, with *Falstaff* as a close runner-up—was made under very different conditions. If his most independent film is a failure, it may well be because he seized the opportunity to take bigger risks.

---

* Even though Charlton Heston plays Vargas well, the mere fact that he is a star suggests that Vargas is unequivocally in the right.

In every one of his films Welles has taken some kind of risk. He has always been willing to pit his recurring theme of lost innocence and his elemental symbolism against the explosive diversity of his other resources. His films depend for their success on a fine balance of all kinds of opposites—sophistication and simplicity, realism and expressionism, introversion and extroversion, clarity and confusion. And yet, with each film, he has rejected the cautiousness and calculation that could assure him of balance at the expense of richness and resonance. He himself has never lost all of the innocence with which he first tackled *Kane*.

Touch of Evil, or Orson Welles and the Thirst for Transcendence

Jean Collet

The beauty of *Touch of Evil* is without doubt less obvious, less revolutionary, than that of *Citizen Kane*. We must seek it out in the depths, not only in the moral preoccupations of Orson Welles, but especially in the perfect adequation between those moral preoccupations and the mise en scène of the film. Unless we are able to decipher an ethics in style itself, we risk condemning one of Welles's most important works.

It would appear that the mise en scène of Orson Welles is habitually grounded in two quite distinct registers (and we must refer the reader, once again, to the magisterial analyses of André Bazin, particularly in "The Evolution of the Language of Cinema"[1]). First register: the use of the sequence shot, with its abundance of realism and ambiguity. Before the all too well known sequence shots of *Citizen Kane* and *The Magnificent Ambersons* the spectator retains his freedom. He can give the image the interpretation of his choice, from among all the possibilities it offers him. At the level of style, the sequence shot is the sign of a liberal auteur, perfectly respectful of the spectator to whom he addresses himself. (The sequence shot is also time recaptured: we shall return to this.)

Second register dear to Welles, and the opposite of the first: montage. A montage that is even excessively rapid, a condensation of action. If the sequence shot is "time recaptured" in its purity, its original ambiguity, then montage is obviously time shattered, foreshortened, reassembled in an artificial order by an arbitrary will. With regard to the spectator, montage ordinarily betrays an authoritarian attitude. Before a rapid montage, carried to its extreme, the spectator is no longer free: ambiguity disappears. According to the principle of montage,

Translated from Jean Collet, "*La Soif du mal* ou Welles et la soif d'une transcendance," *Études cinématographiques* 24–25 (1963): 108–119.
1. André Bazin, *What Is Cinema?*, trans. Hugh Gray (Berkeley: University of California Press, 1967): 23–40.

each shot, solidly bolted to the shot that precedes it and to the one that follows it, ought to bear a precise signification. It is not by chance that montage has been the weapon *par excellence* of all propaganda films. At the level of style, this is the traditional sign of tyrannical auteurs who brutalize the spectator, who impose their vision upon him. No doubt Kafka was thinking of the cinema of montage when he wrote in 1924, a little before his death: "The quickness of the movements, the rapidity of the succession of images . . . these appropriate our gaze. They inundate consciousness. Cinema implies that the eye, which hitherto has been naked, should assume a uniform." [2] He could not know that this observation would one day be turned against the cinematic auteur of *The Trial*.

Orson Welles, the director: is he then a tyrant or a liberal? This is the whole question, since one cannot be both at once. It seems to me that the principal interest of *Touch of Evil* is to pose this question—and to respond to it. At first glance, the response seems easy. *Touch of Evil*, coming after *Mr. Arkadin*, confirms a return by Orson Welles to the "cinema of montage." From the close-up of the bomb that opens the film to the night in whose depths Quinlan finally loses himself (his future, as Tanya says, having finally been "all used up"), our gaze is controlled. Those moments when the camera ceases to guide our attention are rare. Only the great central confrontation that brings Quinlan, Vargas, and Menzies together around Sanchez (the presumed murderer) and the shady Grandi, only this sequence is treated with a certain degree of continuity. Even so, it is broken into by a parallel montage of scenes at the motel where Susan's distress is mounting.

For Welles, moreover, the difference between sequence shots and short takes is not essential. The choice between them is often justified on economic grounds, and montage retains the same importance in his eyes whether it joins short takes or long ones. [3] What may we conclude? Is there no difference for him between a montage of tiny fragments and a succession of sequence shots? We should note, at least, that he always reserves the power to *control* the image, sooner or later, thanks to the editing process—in other words, to choose the best point of view. This is very far from the unvarnished realism of Rossellini, Rouch, or Godard. These men, in opting for location shooting as a sort of fruitful constraint, make us feel that the camera is here rather than there because over there a wall is in the way. Their point of view is contingent. It is that of a reporter who tries to catch

2. Cited in Gustav Janouch, *Kafka m'a dit* (Paris: Calmann-Levy, 1952).
3. Interview, *Cahiers du Cinéma*, this volume.

sight of an accident over the shoulders of the first witness. The realism of Welles has always been of a wholly different nature. This colossos does not accept obstacles as a salutory constraint: he pushes them about until they prove to be stronger than he is. If he sometimes restores the purity of passing time, it is never merely a slice of time snatched up accidentally by an observer who is just doing what he can. It is a gaze that knows what it wants, that controls, that—to the very limits of its human and technical possibilities—makes a choice. When Welles ceases to exercise his power of choice—when he ceases then to direct our gaze—it is because he has been obliged to let go, to let us go. This comes about not through any respect for some fundamental ambiguity in the nature of things, nor for the pleasure of abandoning oneself to a mystery, but with the high strung rage of a fist that suddenly unclenches, scattering the treasures on which it cannot retain its grasp.

The celebrated shot of the buggy in *The Magnificent Ambersons*, for example, does not in any way resemble the fixed shots of Renoir's *A Day in the Country*. In 1948, André Bazin was right to compare them; today, we need to distinguish them. For Welles, realism arrives, as it were, after the event. The final stroke of the scene [revealing how far apart the would-be lovers really are] is what authenticates it. But Welles's brand of realism also makes itself felt in the way the outside world keeps intruding into their abortive conversation. His realism is a kind of nostalgia for the very possibility of conversation. It is present in the whole setting, those "others" absurdly taking the place of a couple that has failed to reach accord. We scarcely need to underline the fact that for Renoir, in contrast, the world that reveals itself in the depth of field is not a menace to the lovers' absorption in one another: it is a supplement of being, a refuge. Under Renoir's gaze, the characters do not seek to isolate themselves from surroundings that weigh in upon them, but to plunge more deeply into a world they love. In Welles, on the contrary, all the dynamism of the mise en scène comes from the characters' struggle to tear themselves away from a hostile world. The sequence shot in *Touch of Evil* that sets police against suspects has sustained comparison to a chess game—as, indeed, might all Welles's sequence shots. This is not the site of recovered harmony but the terrain of a battle, an impossible dialogue of diverse subjectivities. In this connection, let us note a detail that seems to me of considerable importance. In this shot (as in that of the kitchen in *Ambersons*, for example), contrary to what Bazin thought, the camera is not rigorously fixed. The slight reframings that accompany the movements of the characters seem to translate the director's hesitancy to attach himself to one character rather than to another; in other words, to take the point of view of one rather than that of another. If this minimal hesitation gives the shot a maximum of dramatic efficacy, it is perhaps because it sums up, with the greatest possible density, Welles's characteristic attitude before his universe. His mise en scène is a confrontation of opposed points of view. "Welles": it is a gaze that wishes to be every gaze at once. Obviously, it is when this gaze flickers between several characters, ready to choose but suddenly paralyzed, that dramatic intensity reaches its pitch. No doubt Welles, had he been free to do so, would have applied this principle to many sequences in *Touch of Evil*. His world is a world pulled overly taut, always ready to shiver into fragments, to relapse into dust. All the energy of the director consists—from explosion to explosion—in desperately gathering together the shards, in combining anew the elements of the puzzle until the edifice thus rebuilt gives way again to an insupportable pressure: the impossible unity of different subjectivities.

This is what Françoise Prébois has analyzed very well in an excellent note on *Touch of Evil*. "The cinema of Welles becomes more and more subjective. But paradoxically, from the interior toward the exterior. In *Kane* and *Magnificent Ambersons* we find side by side projects of subjectivisation (different points of view in *Kane*: of Susan on the stage, of the young man in the loges) and of objectification thanks to fixed, wide angle shots encompassing, in a given setting, a group of characters prey to a crisis captured at its climactic moment (the kitchen scene in *Ambersons*, for example). In *Touch of Evil* subjective shots constitute most of the film." [4] This subjectivity is not that of an auteur who judges his characters, for Welles the director is still an actor, one who weds himself to the subjectivities of his characters. "An actor," he has said, "is in love with the role he plays. He is like a man who embraces a woman, he gives her something of himself. An actor is not a devil's advocate, he is a lover, a lover of someone of the opposite sex." [5]

This clash of subjectivities, in which one can recognize the driving force of Welles's films, leads us to a few further remarks. The montage of *Touch of Evil* is not a means of imposing upon the spectator the auteur's point of view. Welles's montage is not that of Eisenstein. Rather than each shot rendering precise the significance of the preceding or following shot, it destroys it, it contradicts it, it shatters it. The sequence in which the montage culminates is the murder of

4. *Image et son*, no. 139, March 1961.
5. Interview, *Cahiers du Cinéma*, this volume.

Grandi: this is the scene from which detractors of the film fetch their arguments. Quinlan has switched off the light. The scene will be illuminated only by the blinking of neon signs in the street. The extreme brevity of the shots, the extreme distortion introduced by the wide angle lens, the violence of the gestures: all may seem to be designed solely to shock the spectator with an outdated expressionism. The distant music, without melody, a mere rhythm with indistinct harmonies, seems to support this thesis.

Now in fact, the music and the lighting are perfectly realistic: this is what one would see and hear in this room, at this hour. As for the cutting, it corresponds to the successive points of view of Grandi, of Quinlan, and of Susan. That there is an intention in this accelerated "jumble" of points of view, in their hallucinatory succession, seems clear. It is to prevent the spectator from adhering to a single character; to force him, on the contrary, to be everywhere at once, to play all the contrary games: the *satisfaction* of Grandi when the prostitutes hand Susan over to him, the *machiavellianism* of Quinlan who annihilates this little hood Grandi by strangling him, and finally the *terror* of Susan when she awakens with the corpse over her head.

If Welles abuses his authority over the spectator, it is not, then, in order to limit for him the significance of what he shows but, on the contrary, to multiply the significance of one image by another. For the spectator, such montage is not essentially different from a sequence shot. Far from violating our liberty, Welles uses force only to extend that liberty, to augment the embarrassment of choices, to deepen the ambiguity of reality. One cannot insist too often on the moral import of this style. Just as Vargas uses a police device (the tape recorder) to assemble evidence against the policeman Quinlan and so to defeat the police system, so Welles avails himself of an authoritarian montage for no other purpose than to augment the spectator's perplexities. He violates him only in order to render him more free. And just as Welles deplores the necessity, for Vargas, of resorting to police methods in order to overthrow Quinlan, he deplores, for himself, the necessity of abusing montage in order to overthrow ready-made opinions—opinions too subjective, too sure of themselves. At this point in our analysis, it would be naive to suppose that the end justifies the means—that is to say: at the level of the plot, that Vargas, a spy in spite of himself, remains a knight of liberal values; at the level of mise en scène, that Welles manipulates the spectator with impunity in order to make him play all roles at once.

As for Vargas, it is clear. André Bazin has pertinently compared the final sequence where Heston records the conversation of Quinlan and Menzies to the scene in which Othello eavesdrops on the conversation of Iago and Bianca. But one may not simply transpose by analogy the behavior of a character into the attitude of the director and his camera. Would a great cinéaste like Welles suddenly become the victim of his apparatus, prisoner of a camera that carries him away? No great work of art is made without bearing witness to a combat with the "object" of art. It is true that Welles's camera seems fascinated by certain objects, drawn in by them: the bomb (in the very first shot), the tape recorder at the end, the acid thrown at Vargas's face, the loudspeaker in Susan's room, Quinlan's cane, and so on. Objects of terror or of manipulation, all bear witness to that "touch of evil" which possesses the camera itself, that atrociously contagious will to power which diffuses itself through every level of the Wellesian universe.

But if Vargas does not resist the temptation to manipulation, if he obeys his tape recorder, Welles resists his camera. During the last sequence, when everything would justify our espousing Vargas's point of view, after having for so long listened to Quinlan's, Welles still resists. He fragments his narrative more than ever: his text and his cutting make us leap from one character to another. High angle shot of Vargas, low angle shot of Quinlan and Menzies. We take time, furthermore, to justify Quinlan and attack Menzies. "Vargas'll turn you into one of these here starry-eyed *idealists* . . . the ones making all the real trouble in the world." "Pete, that's the second bullet I stopped for you." Until the end, until Tanya's final judgement, "He was some kind of a man," Welles sets in opposition the witnesses to this absurd trial. To follow Vargas, to condemn Quinlan, this would be a final solution of a facility that would satisfy many spectators. This would be the camera purring around the hero/avenger, a complaisant camera, slackly committed to immediate appetite, to whims—like Antonioni's camera. For Welles, this would be to surrender to his own "touch of evil": to make short work of the mystery of beings, to justify one in order to cast down another.

From this angle, moreover, the extreme fragmentation of the film reveals its admirable morality. Welles does not "control" his universe for the pleasure of dominating it but, on the contrary, in order to escape from what is stronger than he is. The force of this montage does not apply itself to crushing the spectator but to breaking a charm that Welles himself is the first to feel deeply: the charm of Quinlan, the charm of Vargas, the solipsistic charm of all those who consider themselves in the right. In this ascesis resides the paradox of montage for Welles. The weapon of dictatorship becomes the weapon of detachment; the privileged language of the partisan becomes an instrument of lucidity. Subjectivity turns against itself in order to strive toward objectivity. It scarcely needs to be emphasized that this is the whole subject of *Touch of Evil*. A psychological or dramatic or ethical analysis of the film would lead us to the same conclusions. It seemed to us more interesting, however, to come upon them in the course of a survey of the mise en scène alone. Too great a separation has usually been made between the noble liberal purpose of *Touch of Evil* and its "gaudy" style.

Welles's montage demands one further observation. Like all his other films— *The Trial*, in particular—*Touch of Evil* is a film about time. In Antonioni or Rossellini, the use of a long take, preferably a lateral tracking shot, corresponds to an evocation of duration. Real time is essential for them: it explains, it motivates, the actions of their characters. This is why there are in general in their films neither flashbacks nor foreshortenings of any importance. In time as in space, their point of view is contingent. Welles, in contrast, deforms space and time together, dilates them and shrinks them in turn. He dominates the situation or plunges into it. This has often been said about most of his films, and it is particularly obvious in *Kane* and *Ambersons*. It is no less true of *Touch of Evil*. Here, as he always does, Welles develops a snapshot. He corners a character in the privileged moment when his actions are about to come to the surface. His camera, therefore, never simply moves along with the course of time. It turns time around, it shatters the present through contact with a suddenly restricted future. The past invades consciousness; memory—like the memory of Kane's sled—unfurls itself, rendering illusory the real world. The protagonist dies vanquished by the past. (This might easily be applied to *The Trial*: it has been noted that time in *The Trial*, time impregnated with nightmare, is not foreign to that of *Marienbad*.)

In *Touch of Evil*, Welles has emphasized with a thousand details this sudden congealing of time, this forced march towards death, this nausea of memory that will swallow Quinlan. The nocturnal decor of the first sequence is an anticipatory replica of the final decor. Is it necessary to point out that Quinlan's first appearance takes place in a landscape of derricks, a landscape that he will see again only when it destroys him? Is it necessary to say again that the indecisive chases of the film's beginning—the boobytrapped car, the pursuit of Sanchez, Susan, and Grandi—prefigure in their mise en scène the *only* decisive chase of the film: Quinlan tracked down by his own actions, vanquished (like Joseph K.) by his own culpability? And that, after all, Quinlan will judge himself, will condemn himself (like Joseph K.), since the tape recorder will suffice to confound him: his own voice will dictate his verdict.

The trial of Quinlan, like those of Kane, of Amberson, of Mike O'Hara, of

Arkadin, of Joseph K., requires a suspension of duration: the future needs to be put in parentheses. All at once, the past surges up into consciousness like a malefactor; consciousness everywhere begins to leak, drowned little by little, submerged by the "flaw" of which every unfamiliar face becomes an insupportable mirror. To say this is already to describe all the settings of the film: no longer settings, therefore, but the projection into space of a moral obsession. Quinlan could not have died otherwise than in the murky water in which, little by little, he is engulfed, while Menzies and Vargas, among the derricks and the antennae, give themselves (as Quinlan says) the haloes of angels. The symbolism, for there is symbolism involved, is not plastered on by a facile intelligence. The moment of Quinlan's death is impregnated by the shuddering contraction of a whole aesthetic universe, the agony of all Wellesian heroes, cast down, every time, irretrievably. In this manhunt, Welles explicitly emphasizes that "inversion of time" which will precipitate Quinlan into his torment and which is the characteristic of every "inquest." This is the substance of all those scenes at Tanya's, whose dialogue is of a tragic eloquence. "Have you forgotten your old friend?" "That pianola sure brings back memories." Tanya's pianola, the only pure rhythm in this syncopated film, like the heart that still beats though the organism is in the throes of death: it is the last spasm of life, an unbearable tenderness under the very gaze of death. Like Albinoni's adagio in *The Trial*, it is the apparition of a lost happiness that only music is capable of painting on the threshold of hell.

And this is why Menzies whispers to his accomplice, "I'll get him out. Away from that music," at the very moment Tanya has responded to Quinlan, "Your future's all used up." Quinlan has known it ever since he met Vargas. And doubtless for much longer, ever since the death of his wife precipitated him into the fatal mesh of resentment. Since, as he confesses to Menzies, he "thinks about it all the time," time itself has congealed for him around a morbid image. Quinlan has entered a landscape from which one can never again escape, just as Joseph K. entered the labyrinth of the Court. The only time the world seems real to him, the only moments when he can delay the fatal issue, are those moments when he turns against others the criminal mechanism of which he is himself the prisoner. Fleeing his own death, he can do no more than to fling it away, for a little while, in the pursuit of others: to strangle Grandi, to seek to corner Vargas, to confound Sanchez. The sequence shot (already cited) with Sanchez, Grandi, and Vargas is one of the rare moments in which Quinlan can hope to escape from his "trial," to justify himself—in which one can observe the hero's efficacious struggle to plunge back into the stream of normal life. Time then ceases to flow toward death: we recover a sense of real duration. This dialectic of duration and "inquest" (which is to say, time re-wound) is one of Welles's most decisive stylistic conquests. If *Touch of Evil* seems crudely linear (the film's action covers something less than 48 hours), the auteur is only that much more deft in weaving into the interior of this conventional frame the extraordinary skein of a race against death.

Here we can offer still another after-the-fact justification—though no longer on a moral level this time—of the fragmentariness of the film. *Touch of Evil* seems to base its dramatic interest on a banal use of parallel montage. Usually, parallel montage consists in developing in time what you cannot represent in space. It is a simultaneity that becomes a succession (the novelistic "meanwhile": for example, Vargas, Menzies, and Quinlan confront one another about shady cops who take bribes and *meanwhile* the Grandi boys seize Susan in order to inject her with drugs).

This procedure, banal enough on the dramatic level, takes on in Welles a particular significance. Not only are the two parallel actions linked causally (Susan is maltreated because a bribe has in fact been exchanged between Grandi and Quinlan) but they also maintain a rapport with an infinitely more profound necessity. In using, throughout his film, an excess of parallel montage, in obliging the spectator to leap ceaselessly from one place to another, Welles attempts to give density to "the present." The confrontation of subjectivities no longer has only a psychological and a moral function, but an ontological one as well: the same instant refracted through diverse minds. (A project one will not go wrong in comparing to that of Resnais in all his work and especially in *Hiroshima Mon Amour*.) Welles gives us here additional proof that his subject is not, is never, merely the analysis of character, but the rapport between a character (or several characters) and History. What is history if not the sum of the (subjective) testimonies of all who have lived? (A question analogous to that of Resnais leaving the Bibliothèque Nationale at the end of *Toute la mémoire du monde*.) What is knowledge?

This passage from the personal to the collective, from the particular to the general, is a theme that *indisputably* links Resnais and Welles. Resnais explores it by flashback, Welles by parallel montage (*Touch of Evil*) or flashback (*Citizen Kane*). It is without doubt one of the most modern themes of the cinema, the most timely, the most urgent. It leads directly to the universe of the concentration camp, and it is not by accident that these two auteurs converge again in *Night and Shadow* and *The Trial*. Perhaps it has not been sufficiently remarked that the motel to which Janet Leigh resorts (in *Touch of Evil*) sprawls on a desolate field of bungalows like those of an internment camp. Jean Domarchi correctly emphasizes that Welles calls the motel the Mirador,[6] and that people are treated there with the most refined developments of the methods of the police themselves. It is obvious that *Touch of Evil* is a meditation on the abuses of the police state, a meditation that would logically find its sequel in *The Trial*.

But what one can easily note on the thematic level is, once again, rooted in a coherent aesthetic universe. The rapport of subjectivities, expressed by parallel montage, is at the same time both an endeavor to attain that objectivity without which there are only monsters preying upon one another without mercy, and also the very condition of the possibility of justice, as it is of liberty. It is, finally, a quest for transcendence. The collision of points of view dear to Welles is a way of escaping from himself, from his deliriums, from his own duration, in order to attain the time of history, the world of community. Without this effort, the world would be governed by the delirium of monsters, History would be a hecatomb, a concentration camp, the forced march of slaves. "All the characters I've played," says Welles, "are versions of Faust, and I'm against every Faust, because I believe it's impossible for a man to be great without admitting that there is something greater than himself. This might be the Law, or God, or Art—it doesn't matter what the concept, but it ought to be greater than man."[7] Is there a better definition of transcendence?

"Before the gate of the Law, stands a guard. A man comes from far away, who desires access to the Law." Welles, the director, is he not this pioneer of knowledge before the gate of truth? In front of the door closed to the camera, he turns around and it is the Babel of our subjectivities that he contemplates. *Touch of Evil* is the trial of all these modern Fausts, beginning with this seductive Faust called the cinema.

6. Jean Domarchi, "Welles à n'en plus finir," *Cahiers du Cinéma*, no. 85, July 1958. ["Mirador" = observation post.]
7. Interview, *Cahiers du Cinéma*, this volume.

Film and System:
Terms of Analysis

Stephen Heath

In the first part of his essay, Heath divides the action of the film into segments, and diagrams the first three segments in such a way as to reveal the alternation of different lines of the narrative:

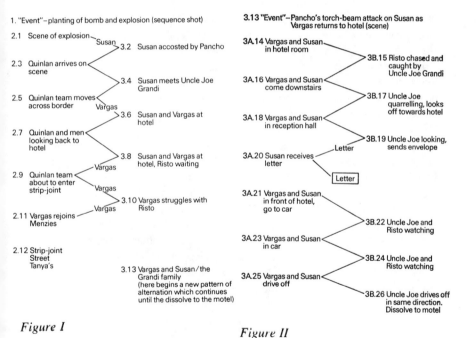

Figure I

Figure II

From *Screen* vol. 16, no. 1 (Spring 1975): 35–48.

For each segment, Heath then analyzes the different "codes" by which the film's meanings are conveyed. Some of these codes are familiar: narrative, character, camera work, light, music. Others may require a word of explanation. Heath discovers that *Names*, or the absence of names, may be significant. Under the heading *Author* he calls attention to those elements through which the director imposes his own personality or point of view, his particular stylistic signature. *Partition*: it is often found that elements of a segment fall into patterns of binary opposition—Mexico/America, etc. *Exchange*: but it is then discovered that apparently opposed elements relate or correspond to one another. *Repercussions*, finally, refers to the way in which elements of a segment may refer back or forward to other segments with which they have no obvious narrative connection.

It will be observed that not every code is treated in every segment. Heath's assumption is simply that the film communicates through a complex variety of levels of which we would remain unaware were we to confine our attention to the surfaces of the story. The analysis reprinted here is in Heath's whole essay only a preliminary step in an elaborate reconstruction of the film's "system," its structure of intricately interrelated parts.

1. *Description*: An unbroken shot, lasting for some two and a half minutes, which moves from a close-up of a man holding a bomb, his hand regulating the dial mechanism, to the planting of the bomb in the boot of a car, and from there to a long track backing in front of the car as it drives through the crowded streets of a town (title and credits are shown over during the car's progress), coming to a stop at a customs post; here the camera holds a conversation between the two occupants of the car, a couple on foot and a customs official, keeping the couple in frame when the car leaves over the border (Figure III). *Narrative*: The planting of the bomb followed by the suspense of the car's journey until the explosion heard off at the end of the segment, the suspense being created by a variety of means across the range of matters of expression—length of shot, tracking ahead of car, rhythmic insistence of the music, dialogue (woman passenger: "Hey! I've got this ticking noise in my head"), etc. This effectively enclosed action also poses clearly the term of its potential development, the enigma of the identity of the killer and thus of his motive (who? why?). The close-up on which the shot opens shows only the trunk and arms of the man with the bomb and when the whole of his body is seen it is impossible to fix his face (this remains true even

when the individual frames are examined on a viewing-machine). *Character*:
The conversation at the customs post permits the introduction of four important
characters (two are important by their immediate death, which is the premise of
the narrative and the coefficient of the filmic operation—its movement and displacement; two are protagonists in the narrative and factors in that operation):
the two passengers, first seen as they leave a night-club and walk to the car while
the bomb is being planted, are Rudy Linnekar, middle-aged, apparently pros-
perous (car, manner), and an unnamed woman, blonde, youngish, visibly not his
wife (speech, manner, dress, genre conventions); the couple on foot, first seen
during the car's drive through the town, are Vargas, treated as a celebrity for just
having smashed a drugs racket, and Susan, his wife. An atmosphere of gaiety is
stressed—the carnival air of the crowded streets, the joking at the customs post,
Vargas and Susan out for a stroll on their honeymoon, Vargas "hot on the trail of
a chocolate soda for my wife." The relationship man-wife is heavily underlined
and marked with surprise: Vargas ". . . my wife"/Official "Your what!?"/Susan
"Yeah, you're right, Officer!" (note, indeed, the ambiguity of Susan's response);
the end of the segment, moreover, is the interruption of the seal of union: (V and
S in medium close-up about to embrace) S "Mike, do you realize this is the very
first time we've been together in my country?"/V "Do you realize I haven't
kissed you for over an hour?"/Explosion. *Partitions*: The segment situates the
locus of the action as a border town, both on image—the customs post—and
sound—the dialogue concerning customs formalities—tracks. In addition, emphasis is placed on nationality: Linnekar and Susan are American, Vargas and the
blonde are Mexican. *Exchange*: The elements of partition at once become terms
of exchange: Mexican/American : : Mexican/American or Vargas/Susan : :
Blonde/Linnekar: Vargas is to Susan as Linnekar to the blonde, therefore if Linnekar is torn to bits in the explosion, Vargas must be torn from Susan by the force
of contagion; Susan is to Vargas as the girl to Linnekar, the other—the foreigner—to the man, therefore if the girl is an explosive sexuality that kills Linnekar (by metonymy—the very motion of desire), Susan is an uncontrollable
demand from which Vargas must separate himself in order to maintain his position (narratively, the split between Vargas as husband and Vargas as official with
the Mexican government). This process of exchange is given as the organization
of the segment: the tracking—for the most part in high angle—lays out the town
(spatial definition of the constant motif of "crossing the border") and, in so
doing, picks up Susan and Vargas as they walk through the streets to create a
choreography of alternation—overtaking/being overtaken—between them and

the car, forced to go slowly because of the crowd. Thus the partitions, nationality and border, are brought together filmically into a composite figure that plays across the action. *Repercussions*: The segment depends on an extreme mobility of the camera, not simply in distance covered (the long track) but also in variation of shot angle: at the moment of the bomb plant, the camera pulls up into a high angle shot that looks down on the car, the angle then being reduced to the horizontal towards the end of the car's progress. This is the setting off of a series of modulations which form a number of systems at different levels of the film; here, for instance, deciding the extreme mobility (up and down) of the final segment, the "answer" to this one and thereby the binding of the discourse in a circle of accomplishment and resolution. "Repercussions" is merely a heading for the notation of such structural elements however manifested, elements which repercute over the film, *scoring* it, pushing with and against the narrative, according and fluctuating the discourse. It is the interlocking of these elements with the figures of exchange (which they help define) to hold the levels together in a sliding, since over-determined, coherence that produces the pleasure of the film, and its system. *Light*: Night-time; oscillation of light and dark during segment according to the stages of the car's journey through the town. *Music*: Brass and saxophone theme, ominously deep-toned, with an insistent bongoish rhythm vaguely "Mexican." "*Author*": The opening of *Touch of Evil* with its "extraordinary" tracking shot has become a famous point of reference in "film culture" and the "breathtaking achievement" it represents is one element among many others which can be systematized in reading as the signature "Orson Welles," the style of the author. (Welles, of course, entered Hollywood exactly as "the author"; that is the meaning of the terms of the contract with RKO in 1939.) The sole interest here is in the author as an effect of the text and only in so far as the effect is significant in the production of the filmic system, is a textual effect. The present heading was introduced to allow this to be made clear from the outset of the commentary.

2.1 *Description*: Cut from Susan and Vargas about to embrace at the end of 1. to a shot of the car exploding, then back to their reaction; they begin to run in toward the explosion with the camera tracking back and there follows an "account" of the confusion of the scene handled in a small number of shots (6, joined by cuts). *Narrative*: Vargas sends Susan back to their hotel and involves himself in the scene of the explosion. *Character*: Introduction of Schwartz who describes himself as an official in the District Attorney's service; Vargas's impor-

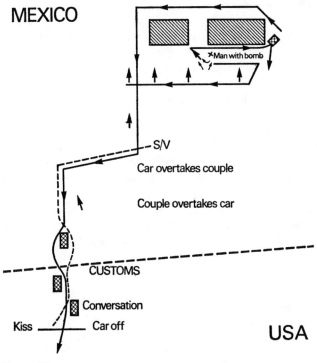

Figure III

tance and responsibility are shown—in short, his "position." *Partitions*: Vargas's
nationality is marked (he speaks in Spanish) and the figure traced by the movement of 1. is recapitulated in a dialogue that also stresses the enigma of the
explosion: Detective "That bomb came from the Mexican side of the border"/
Vargas "The car did." *Exchange*. The kiss is interrupted, the honeymoon post-
poned ("We'll have to postpone that chocolate soda, I'm afraid"); involved in the
explosion, Vargas sends Susan away, back over the border: V "This could be very
bad for us"/S "For us?"/V "For Mexico, I mean." The ambiguity of the involvement is evident: official, Vargas, is caught up in the explosion; husband, he is
touched by its contagion. *Repercussions*: The sound off at the close of 1. carries
over into this segment, links kiss and explosion, as too does movement in frame:

from Vargas bending down toward Susan's lips to the car flying up in the air. The shot of the explosion is brutal: seen in long shot with the camera static, the car goes up, bursting into flames, and comes down, at which point the camera zooms in on the blazing wreckage (in the space of two or three seconds); this giving a kind of accentuated cadence of violence—car up/camera static/ /car static/ camera in. Emphasis on the violence is continued in the film (in this section: 2.3 DA "An hour ago Rudy Linnekar had this town in his pocket"/Doctor "Now you can strain him through a sieve"; and beyond: II e Quinlan "An old lady on Main Street last night picked up a shoe—the shoe had a foot in it"), but, more crucially, violence is also the overbalance of the narrative: the answer to the explosion is the discovery not of its perpetrator but of its detonator, of the "fault"— the blonde (or) Susan. *Light*: Night-time; flames and headlights. *Music*: None.

3.2 *Description*: Cut to Susan making her way back through the streets and accosted by Pancho with a note ("Follow this boy at once—he has something very important for Mr. Vargas"); handled in three shots. *Narrative*: The segment begins with the Grandi aggressions against Susan (and Vargas); closing on Susan's decision to follow Pancho, it dispatches the narrative sharply forward (what will happen?). *Character*: Introduction of Pancho, marked with "Mexican-ness" and a certain foreboding of sensuality (pose, manner, expression, leather jacket, insouciance, Susan's reaction); Susan manifests a kind of exasperated determination and a sense of repartee. *Partitions*: Pancho is Mexican to Susan as American (Pancho speaks Spanish and bystanders interpret between the two); Susan has crossed back into Mexico, Pancho will lead her over the border again into America (S "Across the border again?!"). *Exchange*: Pancho is to Susan as Vargas is to Susan, Mexican to American; the walk through the town and over the border taken by Vargas and Susan in 1., is now to be taken by Pancho and Susan. If Pancho is a "boy" ("Pancho," indeed, is a slighting nickname given by Susan), Susan "nevertheless" takes the encounter as sexual (once away from Vargas, all Susan's encounters are sexual incidents); whence a layer of divisions: to follow Pancho is to follow Vargas ("something very important for Vargas") but to follow Pancho is to lose—or to abandon—Vargas by the fact of the substitution, putting Pancho in the place of desire (S "What have I got to lose? Don't answer that!"); thus, on the one hand Susan goes with Pancho, on the other she invokes the image of Vargas as husband-official (the official position of her sexuality)—but this is precisely what separates her, narratively and symbolically, from Vargas: Bystander "Lady, he says you don't understand what he wants"/S "I understand very well what he wants. . . . Tell him I'm a married woman and my husband is a great big official in the government ready and willing to knock out all those pretty front teeth of his." *Names*: Pancho, a main character, has no name throughout the film other than the nickname of his relation with Susan (unnameable, he is a *mixture*—Vargas, in 3.8, "This . . . this 'kid' [word spoken with difficulty], what did he want?"). In the novel *Badge of Evil*, Vargas is called Holt and there is no equivalent to Pancho (apart from the basic elements of the conflict between official and crooked policeman, novel and film have little in common). Where does the name "Vargas" come from? From Pancho, as though to confirm the exchange: the actor Valentin de Vargas. *Repercussions*: The series of scenes that play out the Susan-Pancho encounter, terminating in the half-rape in the motel; the return of the narrative and the position of Vargas: in IV c he does knock out Pancho's teeth. *Light*: Night-time; brightly lit streets. *Music*: "Mexican" theme (different to 1.), insistent bongoish rhythm.

2.3 *Description*: Cut to the scene of the explosion; in some eleven shots (fixed and moving, near and general) the confusion is described as first the DA then Marcia Linnekar arrive; the twelfth shot marks the entry of Quinlan and what follows is dominated by the tension of his dialogue with Vargas, mostly in shot/reverse shot. *Narrative*: The start of the investigation into the explosion and thus of the conflict between Quinlan and Vargas. *Character*: Introduction of the DA (Adair), Marcia Linnekar, Sergeant Pete Menzies (shown as Quinlan's right-hand man), Chief Gould and, most notably, Hank Quinlan. The segment is centered on Quinlan's arrival, which constitutes an event both for the narrative (the investigation) and, so to speak, for itself—Quinlan's "character" is an event. Everything works towards this centering: the wait for Quinlan (he is the last on the scene), the terms of the anticipation of his arrival (DA "Well here comes Hank at last. Vargas, you've heard of Hank Quinlan, our local police celebrity?"/V "I'd like to meet him"/Doctor "That's what you think"), the presentation of the final entry (after the eleven shots of confusion, there is a sudden moment of stillness as, framed alone in low angle, Quinlan throws open his car door, pauses and climbs out). Quinlan's appearance is shabby and slovenly (his dress contrasts with Vargas's suit and the DA's dinner jacket—Quinlan "Well, what do you know! the DA in a monkey suit!"); the shot of him getting out of the car emphasizes his cigar and his cane; he moves with difficulty because of his immense bulk (his *flesh* is constantly stressed in close shots, here and in the rest of the film) and walks with a limp (his "game leg"; explained to Vargas as the source of his "intuition"—its twinges "talk" to him). *Partitions*: Quinlan is American, Vargas Mexican: this is Quinlan's opposition—"I hear you even in-

vited some kind of a Mexican"; "You don't talk like one—a Mexican, I mean"—
and the response is to clarify Vargas' status—DA "I don't think Mr. Vargas
claims any kind of jurisdiction"; V "I'm merely what the United Nations would
call an observer." At one point, however, Vargas is framed alone against a poster
reading "Welcome Stranger! to picturesque Los Robles the Paris of the Border"
and the end of the segment is straight conflict between Vargas and Quinlan, each
singled out in turn in near close up/close up as in the last two shots: V "Captain,
you won't have any trouble with me"/Q "You bet your sweet life I won't." *Repercussions*: Having identified her father's body, Marcia refuses to look at the woman
who was with him—"I'm not acquainted with my father's girlfriends." The response and disdain (but what is Marcia's position?) confirm the sexuality (Quinlan in this same segment talks of "some jane, some strip-teaser"), mark the bad
object, and that object is erased from the screen, in and from the diegetic space:
the characters facing the camera in near close shot look down but the bodies are
never seen; unless it be to place us in the reflection of violence: a low angle shot
shows the Doctor crouching and bending forward ("now you can strain him
through a sieve") with a group of onlookers behind—we are in the impossible
position, the object is the loss of position, of point of view, our death./The initial
low angle shot of Quinlan inaugurates a series that combines shot angle and
narrative meaning in an easy evidence: dominating, Quinlan is not seen in high
angle until the turning point of the deal with Grandi and then at the beginning of
the end, the exit from Tanya's to the final showdown. This system, be it noted, is
a partial system: it forms a whole but does not circumscribe all the low angle
effects in the text (which could be systematized, for example, with regard to the
signature "Welles"). *Light*: Night-time; light from headlights, etc. *Music*: None.
"*Author*": Quinlan's arrival exceeds the diegetic space; it is prepared as "a great
moment of cinema," a star turn—the colossal entry of Quinlan-Welles. Doubled
with effects of style (shot angles, distortions, framing), by the signature, it marks
a circulation and a division: actor-director; of interest if it signifies in the system
as a problem of position.

   3.4 *Description*: Cut to Susan arriving at a hotel with Pancho; inside, the
meeting with Grandi: variations on shot/reverse shot. *Narrative*: Begun in 3.2,
the first of the Grandi aggressions crystallizes in the behaviour towards Susan
and the vague menaces ("advice") transmitted through her to Vargas. *Character*:
Introduction of Uncle Joe Grandi, brother of the Grandi whose drug racket has
been smashed by Vargas. *Partitions*: Grandi speaks Spanish with Pancho, has
difficulty in following Susan's rapid delivery, is endowed with "Mexican-ness" in

his appearance; at the same time, he is an American citizen and declares that his name "ain't Mexican." Like Pancho, he is a mixture, and the idea of the Grandi "family" stresses this ("some of us in Mexico, some of us on this side"). *Exchange*: As Susan and Pancho arrive at the hotel, camera tracking with them in close medium-shot, Susan is called from off ("Hey lady!"); while she turns, there is a cut to a fixed shot of a Mexican woman holding up a baby; cut back to a medium shot of Susan standing in the hotel entrance with Pancho and smiling towards the woman off (towards the camera)—suddenly they are illuminated by the light from a flash-bulb. In this brief incident Susan is thus tricked into having her photo taken and the narrative expectation is clearly that some form of blackmail is in preparation. The expectation, however, is not to be fulfilled, the incident comes to nothing; what remains of it—what determined it?—is precisely this image, the photograph: Pancho for Vargas, here is Susan's honeymoon snap (outside the hotel), with the baby as mediation. *Names*: The segment indicates that "Pancho" is a nickname, and an insult: Grandi "Why you call him Pancho?"/Susan "For laughs, I guess." Against the nickname, Susan places heavy emphasis on "Mike," "my husband," "Mr. Vargas."/It should also be noted that the name "Grandi" is sometimes spelt "Grande" by Welles critics; the film provides no clear way of deciding and all that is important is its "foreign-ness," its (ironical) semantic possibility of "bigness," its translation into such "jokes" as "Grandi's Rancho Grande" (the name of Uncle Joe's night-club cum strip-joint), its "mixedness" ("the name ain't Mexican"). *Repercussions*: The scene in the hotel is crucial over the whole of the film: the composition within the frame, for instance, turning Susan and Grandi in patterns of domination with Pancho as a kind of "floater," is the beginning of a series of systems and partial systems which themselves become supports in various chains of substitution and exchange. Central in this respect, mentioned now simply for later reference, is the shot of Grandi in medium shot on the left-hand side of the frame cocking his gun across Susan standing back from him facing the camera, with Pancho off in the position of the camera (in our position), almost mirrored in frame in a mirror behind Susan. An early shot of Grandi shows him knotting his tie in that same mirror with Susan coming up behind him; the last shot of Grandi has him hanging over Susan in mirror image, strangled with her stocking./The menace with the gun is also the menace with the large cigar Grandi smokes (close-ups show Grandi and Susan together with the cigar a kind of trait pointed at her); the cigar joins Grandi and Quinlan and both aggress Susan, but Grandi is small, as much dominated by Susan as dominating her; by being Quinlan, he can have Susan, but

in this way he is Susan to Quinlan: once again, a mixture./There are no children
in the film; the baby held up to Susan posing with Pancho in Vargas's place has its
answer, however, in [a later shot]: crossing the street to phone Susan, held by
Pancho in the motel, Vargas's path intersects that of a woman pushing a pram;
image twice over of his displacement, Vargas sees nothing (at the moment of the
intersection he puts on dark glasses) and he enters the blind woman's shop to
reject the image—the film-photo—of Susan's desire./During the conversation
with Grandi Susan comments: "You know what's wrong with you, Mr Grandi?
you've been seeing too many gangster movies." In one sense, the classic analysis
applies: the reference to film in the film draws attention to the film at the same
time as it confirms its illusion (one might equally consider in this context perhaps
the reverse deep focus/flattening effects of the shots into the mirror in the
segment); in another, that analysis misses the point: the reference misfits the
attention-confirmation mould because of its literal truth—this is *not* a gangster
movie, which is its problem, the running down of the narrative from here until
the halt in the scene that contains the only other vocally declared reference to the
movies: the scene in Tanya's, the other side of the illusion. *Light*: Night-time;
illumination of the flash-bulb, inside the hotel the constant effect of a neon sign
outside flicking on and off. *Music*: Din of music in the street, as though from
nearby bar; heard more or less distantly throughout the conversion inside.

2.5 *Description*: Cut from Susan leaving the hotel to Quinlan leading a group
of men through the town streets; one shot with tracking movement. *Narrative*:
The investigation gets underway. *Partitions*: Quinlan has crossed over into Mexico—DA "Quinlan, we just can't cross over into Mexico like this!"; "This is
Mexican territory, what can we do?"—and is repeating in reverse the car's passage in 1. The jurisdiction—Quinlan or Vargas—thus changes; at the end of the
segment Menzies turns to ask Vargas whether there is any objection to them
asking a few questions. *Exchange*: As Menzies turns, he finds that Vargas is
missing; Vargas has left the group (though he is never actually seen in it) to rejoin
Susan, inaugurating thereby that mediation between the alternating narrative
strands previously discussed. *Repercussions*: Quinlan is on his way to the strip-
joint for information concerning the woman killed with Linnekar; seen as the
men go up the main street, a hoarding can be distinguished above the entrance
reading "20 sizzling strippers"; the words operate a condensation over different
matters of expression: Rudy Linnekar goes up in flames with a sizzling stripper
(sexuality explodes) and the rhythm of the shot of the explosion comes back as
the dance of the accentuation of the body, the zoom in of the fascinated gaze, and

the horrified effacement—burning, the stripper herself must be burnt, wiped out, placed outside, the position of death./Emphasis on Quinlan's cane as he is seen walking along. *Light*: Night-time; the crowds have gone, open streets, a few signs and doorways lit up. *Music*: None.

    3.6 *Description*: Cut to Vargas opening the door into the hotel lobby to greet Susan; one shot, slight movement following Vargas inside. *Narrative*: Vargas joins Susan who starts to relate her adventure. *Light*: Night-time; interior lighting. *Music*: None.

    2.7 *Description*: Cut to Menzies and the others in the street, still looking off towards Vargas and Susan (the hotel is glass-fronted); Quinlan, who has been some way ahead of the group, also comes back to look; one shot. *Narrative*: The narrative content has already been given in the description; the segment functions as an element of the alternation (in future when description and narrative fold together without need for further commentary, the heading "narrative" will simply be omitted). *Partitions*: Told that the woman is Vargas's wife, Quinlan adds: "Well what do you know! She don't look Mexican either." *Exchange*: If Susan does not look Mexican, what does she look like? For Quinlan, there is no doubt: she is a "jane," no different than the stripper (2.3); so she too will have to be wiped out. *Light* and *Music*: As 2.5.

    3.8 *Description*: Cut to Vargas and Susan in the hotel lobby; their conversation is followed until a cut to show them from outside through the glass fronting and to take in the entry of a youth who waits out of their sight; as Vargas leaves and begins to cross the street into camera, there is a tracking movement backwards to hold Vargas and the youth coming after him. *Narrative*: Susan has been telling Vargas of her encounter with Pancho and Grandi and is arguing with him about whether or not they should stay in Los Robles. The start of the second Grandi aggression. *Character*: Tension between Vargas and Susan. In fact, this tension plays across and into the terms of partition and exchange: divided from his American wife by the explosion, Vargas, the Mexican official, split between his official position and his position as husband, now uses both positions to maintain the division: V "I can't just walk away from all this. . . ."/S "Of course! Even on his honeymoon, the Chairman of the Pan-American Narcotics Commission has a sacred duty to perform!"/V "Suzy, you know it's more than just a high-sounding title, now they're pushing my *wife* around!"/S "Can't we forget about that?" The position must be safeguarded—restored—at all costs, both Vargas's *and Susan's*. *Light*: Night-time; lit interior, street with lighting from hotel. *Music*: None.

2.9   *Description*: Cut to Quinlan and his men seen from behind in near shot
3.10   about to enter the strip-joint from the back way; cut to Vargas turning
2.11   along a wall to catch them up; as he does so, a voice off calls him and
there follows a confrontation with the youth in a brief shot/reverse shot alternation ending in a struggle which itself ends with the youth breaking away and
Vargas returning, rejoining Menzies and exiting as though to catch up Quinlan
again. *Narrative*: The three segments are taken together because of their rapidity
of succession and their homogeneity; Vargas, as it were, quickly crosses from
one strand to the other and then back; the investigation continues its first stage
and the second Grandi aggression is completed. *Character*: Introduction of
Risto, the youth (named only in 3B.15); a younger version of Pancho, but more
nervous and less overtly sensual. *Repercussions*: In 3.4 Susan is called by a voice
off and has her photo taken with Pancho; here Vargas is called by a voice off and
has vitriol thrown at him by another Pancho (from the same "family"). The
terms of the repercussion are those of part of a spiral of exchange./In the
struggle, the vitriol misses Vargas and splashes over a poster advertising the main
attraction in the strip-joint, Zita; as segment 2.12 makes clear, Zita is the woman
with Linnekar in the explosion: thus, for a second time, the sizzling stripper is
herself destroyed, burnt by the vitriol which sizzles on the soundtrack while the
image of Zita is held blackened and smoking in near shot. The spiral of exchange
comes round again: Susan is always potentially interchangeable with Zita, a mirror image (S to Z; for Vargas, she is always SuZy), and the problem then is to
destroy that image, her image—narratively, by framing her for murder; symbolically, but this is more difficult and the difficulty is the systematic movement
of the film, by wiping her out, like Zita./Entering the back way, Quinlan comments: "The key to this whole thing's the dynamite; the killer didn't just want
Linnekar dead, he wanted him destroyed, annihilated." The comment is narratively proleptic—the whole "thing" of the action of the framing of Sanchez
hinges on two sticks of dynamite—but at the same time paralipsistic—attention
is fixed on the annihilation; the motive of the killer is a feint, as the narrative
recognizes by providing no answer to the comment in those terms. *Light*: Nighttime; modulations of dark—street—and light—back entrance. *Music*: "Modernish"—colorless—vibraphone theme coming from inside strip-joint.

2.12 *Description*: Cut to inside strip-joint, sequence-shot of Quinlan's progress through the place and his brief questioning of the "Madame"; cut to Quinlan
and his men coming out into the street; as they come across, a pianola is heard
and, after an insert shot of the pianola playing, Quinlan makes his way towards

the source of the sound; cut to him opening the door; there then follows the scene between him and Tanya. *Narrative*: The first stage of the investigation is completed (Quinlan learns nothing) and the narrative then seems to run down. *Character*: Introduction of the "Madame" (the sole and brief appearance of Zsa Zsa Gabor) and of Tanya.

3.13 *Description*: Cut to a high angle shot of Vargas crossing the street in the direction of his hotel; the camera moves rapidly upwards and to the left, briefly glimpsing an open window through which a torch [flashlight] is being shone, until a cut fixes the window opposite and Susan, changing clothes in her hotel room, caught in the beam; the confrontation that follows is treated in variations of shot/reverse shot across the axis of the torch beam. *Narrative*: The man with the torch is Pancho and this is thus the third Grandi aggression. *Exchange*: Interposed between Vargas and Susan, Pancho fixes her as the stripper; framed in the spotlight on the window-stage, Susan exits and the light continues to play tantalizingly over the empty space, awaiting her reentry which comes with a provocative acceptance of the role—"See any better this way?" (Susan putting herself in the beam); as she finishes dressing, she comments: "You can turn it off now, buster, you're wasting your battery!" *Repercussions*: (*Light*) The filmic system depends constantly on light as a material for the realization of significance, for the realization of a number of systems and partial systems. This segment witnesses, so to speak, the materialization of that dependence and mobilizes those systems, pulls them into activity. Susan is here attacked by light as earlier (3.4) she had been held by Pancho and Uncle Joe in the alternating rhythm of the neon sign: the first attack is gentle (the rhythm is not insistent, the effect of the alternation is muted), the second is direct, the illumination of Susan from the distance of the look, gaze and object defined by the rod of light; Zita/Susan—the body imaged and "looked" (nothing happens to Susan in the narrative finally except that Pancho *looks*). Zita, however, is herself alight, "sizzling": between the two attacks on Susan, her image is destroyed, blackened; in the rod of light, Susan plays Zita's part and turns it round in the assumption of its desire, breaks the distance—unscrewing the light bulb in her room, Susan hurls it across at Pancho—and plunges everything into darkness. In short, from explosion to darkness, a confusion produces a range of figures of light, and for that confusion, the position of Susan (object? subject?), the system knows only two solutions, illumination or extinction; otherwise, there is only an empty margin—the blackness edging the circle of light; the moment of the hand on the light bulb. *Music*: Dramatic scoring: ominous motif on initial shot of Vargas, bongo rhythm takes over with loud insistence—orchestra (saxophone meandering) behind from time to time—and comes to a climax as the light bulb crashes on the floor of Pancho's room.

3A.14 *Description*: Cut as the crash is heard to Vargas opening the door into Susan's room; then four shots for their conversation, ending with their exit. *Narrative*: Tension between Vargas and Susan. *Repercussions*: (*Light*) The whole of the brief exchange between the two centers on the question of the light. Vargas enters the darkness and light floods in from the hall corridor: V "Suzy, What are you doing here in the dark?"/S "There isn't any shade on the window"/V "Well, can we turn the light on now?"/S "No, we can't"/V "Why not?"/S (exasperated) "Because there isn't any bulb any more"/V "Suzy . . ."; she cuts across him and he follows her out, the door slamming black. Tightly constructed, the scene turns round from the previous segment; the bulb flung at Pancho hits Vargas too (the sound of the crash merges onto the cut) and the shot/reverse shot alternation along the rod of the torch beam is repeated in four shots on the line of the dialogue about the light; the closing darkness of the one becomes the beginning of the other which itself ends in darkness again; Pancho establishes Susan as Zita, Vargas wants her as Suzy (he uses the name as an argument—as, precisely, a position). *Music*: None.

3B.15 *Description*: Cut to Pancho who, looking down from his window, catches Risto in the street below in his torch beam; Risto runs off and there is a chase through the empty streets until he is finally brought to a halt by Uncle Joe and helpers; eight shots with a variety of movements and angles. *Narrative*: Dissension in the Grandi family: Risto bolts because Uncle Joe is angry at the vitriol attack which had not received his authorization. This dissension, however, has no narrative consequences, being exhausted in this segment and its continuation in 3B.17. *Partitions*: The dissension serves to emphasize the fact of the Grandi family, its ramifications—Risto is Uncle Joe's nephew, the son of his brother (the Grandi arrested thanks to Vargas)—and, once more, its mixedness—is Risto Mexican or American? *Exchange*: Risto's sole action in the film is the throwing of the vitriol. Motive? Obviously (deducing from the premises of common sense psychology) revenge for the arrest of his father; but what Risto says (in 3B.17) is that he wanted to give Vargas and Susan something to think about on their honeymoon. As Pancho spotlights Susan, so Risto destroys Zitas's image—for Vargas? for Susan? *Repercussions*: During the scuffle with Risto, Uncle Joe loses his toupee (his "rug") and this is stressed again in 3B.17. The "comedy" of Uncle Joe's person is a focus on a mixed body, male and female, and this focus, and hence the loss of the hair-piece, is to be climaxed in the scene of his strangulation by Quinlan (IV a). *Light*: Night-time; streets, sky clearing at end. *Music*: None.

3A.16 *Description*: Cut to Susan and Vargas coming downstairs in the hotel; Vargas is called to the telephone in the lobby; three shots, of which the last is a close medium shot of Vargas taking the call. *Narrative*: Tension continues between Vargas and Susan. *Partitions*: V "This isn't the real Mexico, you know that; all border towns bring out the worst in a country, you know that." *Repercussions*: While on the phone, Vargas opens his briefcase and checks his gun; the visual stress on this action is a preparation for its answering correspondence, the scene at the motel when he will open his case and find the gun missing (III n). A more classic example of practicability—preparation, fulfilment, hence exhaustion—would be difficult to imagine; but the instance is more than this: metonymically, the checking of the gun is the verification of Susan (the gun is Vargas's position) and its loss is then, exactly, the loss of Susan; the gun becomes a factor in the circulating exchange./The telephone call has a narrative function (it concerns the investigation) and it fits, over this, into a series that, also, has its force in the movements of exchange (connection/disconnection). *Light*: Lit interior. *Music*: None.

3B.17 *Description*: Cut to the street where the quarrel between Uncle Joe and Risto is in full swing; Uncle Joe turns to look off. *Narrative*: The end of the Risto incident. (For the rest, see commentary at 3B.15.)

3A.18 *Description*: Cut, as Uncle Joe looks, to a very brief long shot of Susan and Vargas seen across the street just inside the hotel entrance. *Light*: Early morning, between night and day. *Music*: None.

3B.19 *Description*: Cut to Uncle Joe who sends a nephew over to Susan with an envelope; brief shot across to the hotel as the nephew leaves on his errand. *Narrative*: The dispatch of the letter. *Exchange*: As Quinlan in 2.7, so Grandi, in the same position, catches Susan in his look. *Light*: Early morning, between night and day. *Music*: None.

3A.20 *Description*: Cut to Susan in the hotel lobby; she comes out to receive the envelope and opens it; explanatory insert, the words "A souvenir with a million kisses—Pancho" on the back of the photo taken in 3.4. *Narrative*: The delivery of the letter and the "completion" of the action it involves, since narratively nothing comes of it. *Exchange*: The close-up of the photo developed confirms the framing of Susan and Pancho for us (in the position of the camera) in 3.4. *Repercussions*: In 3.2, Susan was given a letter concerning Pancho; here, she is given a photo-note from Pancho; the chain continues, and breaks: from Susan to image, another chain has begun—the flash-bulb, the torch-beam . . . *Light*: Lit interior; exterior dawn. *Music*: None.

3A.21   Cut to hotel entrance seen front on, Vargas coming out to rejoin
3B.22   Susan; cut to the hotel seen from across the street, Vargas and Susan
3A.23   cross to their car, movement in to them at the car; during the conver-
3B.24   sation that follows and ends with them driving off, two shots are
3A.25   inserted of Grandi watching, with Risto just behind him; after the car
3B.26   leaves, three shots of Grandi getting in his car and driving off in the

same direction—dissolve to establishing shot of the motel. *Narrative*: These six segments are taken in a group as a result of their coherence; they give the continuation of the tension between Vargas and Susan, with the decision that the latter should go to the motel, and of the Grandi aggressions, his exit after them. *Partitions*: Vargas wants Susan to go back to Mexico City, she wants to stay: S "I'll go to the motel"/V "What motel?"/S "Well there must be one somewhere on the American side of the border"/V "The American side of the border!"/ S "Well I'll be safer there and you won't have to worry about me. Did I say the wrong thing again?!"/V "No. I suppose it would be nice for a man in my place to be able to think he could look after his own wife in his own country"; in every sense, the tension is that of *place*. *Exchange*: How can Vargas keep Susan safe? He gives her to Menzies (to Quinlan) to take to the American motel owned by Grandi who owns the strip-joint which employed Zita who exploded—economy and logic begin to turn together. *Light*: Dawn. *Music*: None.

Filmography and Bibliography

Welles Filmography, 1941–1973

The list that follows cites the script writer and script source for those feature films of Welles that have actually been released. More complete filmographies, including unrealized projects, as well as radio, television and stage projects and Welles's performances as actor or narrator, may be found in Naremore and McBride (see Bibliography).

1941 *Citizen Kane*
Original screenplay by Welles and Herman J. Mankiewicz, with the assistance of John Houseman. A great deal of controversy about the authorship of the film was raised by Pauline Kael's *The Citizen Kane Book* (Boston: Little Brown, 1971). Welles's own response was printed in the London *Times*, November 17, 1971. For a balanced assessment, see Robert Carringer, "The Scripts of Citizen Kane," *Critical Inquiry* 5 (1978): 369–400.

1942 *The Magnificent Ambersons*
Screenplay by Welles, based on the novel by Booth Tarkington.

1943 *Journey Into Fear*
Screenplay by Welles and Joseph Cotten, based on the novel by Eric Ambler (New York: Knopf, 1940).

1946 *The Stranger*
Screenplay by Anthony Veiller, with the assistance of Welles and John Huston, based on a story by Victor Trivas and Decla Dunning.

1946 *The Lady from Shanghai*
Screenplay by Welles, from Sherwood King's novel, *If I Die Before I Wake* (New York: Simon & Shuster, 1938).

1948 *Macbeth*
Screenplay by Welles, adapted from the play by Shakespeare.

1952 *Othello*
Screenplay by Welles, adapted from the play by Shakespeare.

1955 *Mr. Arkadin* (British title: *Confidential Report*)
Screenplay by Welles, based on his own novel, *Mr. Arkadin* (Paris: Gallimard, 1954; London: W. H. Allen, 1956; New York: Crowell, 1959).

1958 *Touch of Evil*
Screenplay by Welles, adapted from an earlier script by Paul Monash, based on the novel *Badge of Evil* (New York: Dodd, Mead, 1956) by Whit Masterson (pseud., Robert A. Wade and H. Billy Miller).

1962 *The Trial*
Screenplay by Welles, based on the novel by Franz Kafka.

1966 *Chimes at Midnight* (later U.S. title: *Falstaff*)
Screenplay by Welles, adapted from Shakespeare's *Henry IV, Parts I and II*, with additional material from *Richard II*, *Henry V*, and *The Merry Wives of Windsor*. Narrative commentary from Raphael Holinshed's *Chronicles*, the 16th century (1577, 1587) source used by Shakespeare himself.

1968 *The Immortal Story*
Screenplay by Welles, based on a story by Isak Dinesen (pseud., Karen Blixen) in *Anecdotes of Destiny*.

1973 *F for Fake*
Screenplay by Welles, employing material from an earlier film by François Reichenbach.

Selected Bibliography

Only items in English have been included. For an excellent bibliography that includes the extensive French literature on Welles, as well as a number of important interviews, see Peter Cowie's book, cited below.

Bazin, André. "The Evolution of the Language of the Cinema." Trans. Hugh Gray. In *What Is Cinema?*, vol. I, pp. 23–40. Berkeley: University of California Press.
———. *Orson Welles*. Trans. Jonathan Rosenbaum. New York: Harper and Row, 1978.
Belton, John. "A New Map of the Labyrinth: The Unretouched *Touch of Evil*." *Movietone News* no. 47 (January 21, 1976): 1–9.
Bessy, Maurice. *Orson Welles*. Trans. Ciba Vaughan. New York: Crown, 1971.
Bogdanovich, Peter. *The Cinema of Orson Welles*. New York: The Museum of Modern Art Film Library, 1961.
Comito, Terry. "*Touch of Evil*." In *Focus on Orson Welles*. Ed. Ronald Gottesman. Englewood Cliffs, N.J.: Prentice Hall, 1976: 157–163.
Cowie, Peter. *The Cinema of Orson Welles*. New York, 1973; rpt. New York: Da Capo, 1983.
Goldfarb, Phyllis. "Orson Welles' Use of Sound." In *Focus on Orson Welles*. Ed. Ronald Gottesman. Englewood Cliffs, N.J.: Prentice Hall, 1976: 85–95.
Heath, Stephen. "Film and System: Terms of Analysis." *Screen*, vol. 16, no. 1 (Spring, 1975): 7–77; vol. 16, no. 2 (Summer, 1975): 91–113.
———. "Film, System, Narrative."

In *Questions of Cinema*. Bloomington: Indiana University Press, 1981: 131–144.

Higham, Charles. *The Films of Orson Welles*. Berkeley: University of California Press, 1970.

Houseman, John. *Run-Through: A Memoir*. New York: Simon and Schuster, 1972.

Jameson, Richard T. "An Infinity of Mirrors." In *Focus on Orson Welles*. Ed. Ronald Gottesman. Englewood Cliffs, N.J.: Prentice Hall, 1976: 66–84.

McBride, Joseph. *Orson Welles*. New York: Viking Press, 1972.

Naremore, James. *The Magic World of Orson Welles*. New York: Oxford University Press, 1978.

Noble, Peter. *The Fabulous Orson Welles*. London: Hutchinson, 1956.

Place, J. A., and L. S. Peterson. "Some Visual Motifs of Film Noir." *Film Comment* (January 1974): 30–34.

Schrader, Paul. "Notes on *Film Noir*." *Film Comment* (Spring, 1972): 8–13.